Tammie Matson is an Australian wildlife conservationist with a grand passion for Africa and all its wildlife, especially elephants. She worked for many years in southern Africa, before becoming the head of WWF Australia's species program in 2007, and a voice for threatened species worldwide. Having worked on human-elephant conflict in Namibia and India, she moved to Singapore in 2012 where she is working on reducing the illegal trade in ivory and rhino horn that is decimating Africa's elephants and rhinos. She divides her time between being a mum to her three year old son, Solo, lecturing in the environmental sciences, and undertaking freelance conservation work in Africa and Asia.

Also by Tammie Matson

Dry Water
Elephant Dance

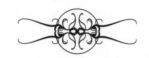

TAMMIE MATSON

PLANET ELEPHANT

MACMILLAN
Pan Macmillan Australia

First published 2013 in Macmillan by Pan Macmillan Australia Pty Limited
1 Market Street, Sydney

National Library of Australia
Cataloguing-in-Publication data:

Matson, Tammie K. 1977-author.

Planet elephant / Tammie Matson.

9781742612942 (paperback)

Matson, Tammie K.
1977 – Zoologists – Australia – Biography.
Wildlife conservationists – Australia – Biography.
Elephants – Conservation.Wildlife conservation – Africa.
Work-life balance.

591.092

Some of the people in this book may have had their names changed to protect their identities.

Typeset in 13/16.5pt Granjon by Post Pre-press
Printed by McPherson's Printing Group
Maps by Laurie Whiddon

Papers used by Pan Macmillan Australia Pty Ltd are natural, recyclable products made from wood grown in sustainable forests. The manufacturing processes conform to the environmental regulations of the country of origin.

For Andy, Solo and the flutter in my tummy

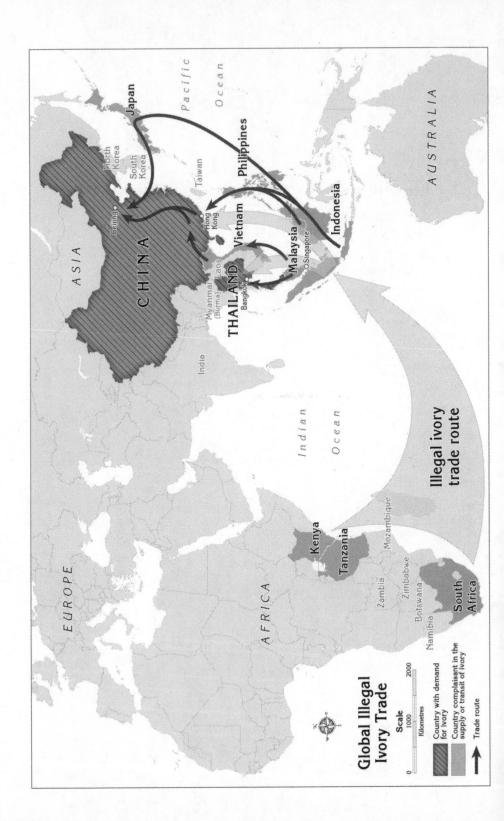

Global Illegal Ivory Trade

Scale
0   1000   2000
Kilometres

Country with demand for ivory

Country complaisant in the supply or transit of ivory

Trade route

Illegal ivory trade route

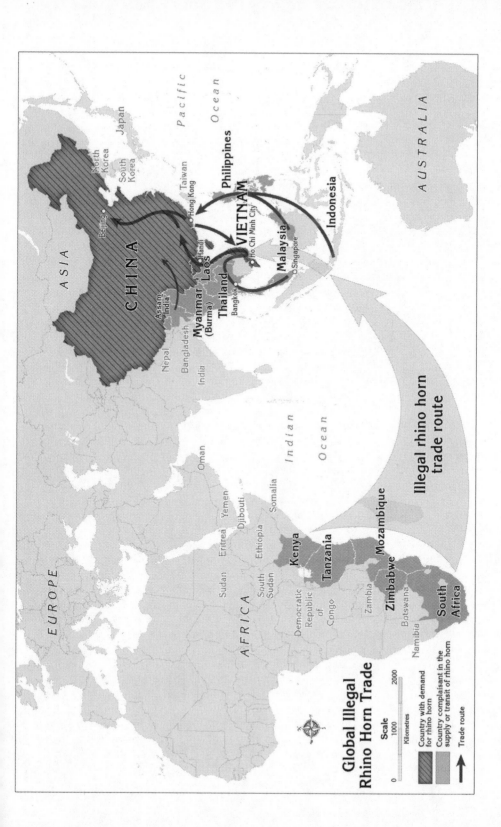

Global Illegal
Rhino Horn Trade

DON'T CALL ME PYGMY

Sabah, Borneo, September 2012

There are times to be brave. Times when life calls upon you to rise to the occasion, to find the honey badger inside you, to face your fears head on. This was not one of those times. This was a time to run.

At first it had just been the crackling of branches, a whisper of grey hide – blurry to the naked eye, pretty much invisible through a camera lens – in between a moving wall of green. It was barely a hint of the presence of an animal much bigger than me. Deep in the rainforests of Borneo, my untrained eyes couldn't see anything further ahead than leaves ten metres in front of me where, based on the rapid gesturing of my guide, Sulaiman, stood a two-metre tall pygmy elephant. But if my eyes were fooling me, at least my nose wasn't. The smell of elephant was all around me, wafting up like steaming tendrils of rotting cabbage. The elephant was there. I could smell him.

Pygmy elephants are the smallest of the Asian elephants, with bulls standing no taller than two and a half metres at the shoulder. That isn't really that small, at least compared to a midget like me, even though they are considerably more vertically challenged than their savannah-dwelling African cousins, which can grow to over four metres in height. But this elephant was no matchbox-sized critter, as his name suggested, and he could do a lot more damage than kicking me in the knee.

'He's not in musth?' I had asked Sulaiman a minute earlier, wanting to confirm that we weren't walking into a mega-disaster. Any bull in musth – the temporarily aggressive, high testosterone state in which males have only one thing on their mind: sex – was potentially life threatening if you got inside his personal space.

'No,' Sulaiman replied, smiling confidently, and walked on.

I had followed him closely, checking behind me at regular intervals, in my mind's eye plotting an emergency exit route back to the small dinghy we had arrived in, which was tied up to a sapling on the river bank. But within a minute of walking in the forest, I had lost my bearings. The thick rainforest was totally disorienting and I wasn't even sure which way the river was, let alone the boat. Then again, if the bull charged and I made it to the boat, an elephant could crush even that in an instant. Elephants are masterful swimmers, with trunks that function like snorkels, and so this one wouldn't be put off by a river.

It was mid-morning, barely 10 am, but in Borneo's oppressively humid heat, I felt like a prawn dumpling in a bamboo steamer. The back of my shirt was soaked with sweat as I stepped off the boat onto the muddy bank. Immediately my Scarpa boots, which had served me so well in the last decade in Africa across all sorts of terrain, sank into the earth that was spongy with decomposing leaves and vegetation. A melee of insects filled the air with a hollow drone, punctuated at regular intervals by the cry of cicadas, a sound so loud and completely insane that it was more like a shriek from a mental institution.

In my short time in Borneo I had learned that there were as few as one and a half thousand pygmy elephants left on the planet. Asia's most pint-sized elephants lived in a world of conflict. Very little of their natural habitat was left, and they were forced to survive in islands of forest in a sea of palm oil plantations and escalating human development.

I tried and failed to adjust my camera to focus on the elephant, growing increasingly more agitated as I failed to find anything through the lens. As I looked up from the camera to see if I could get a visual on him, the bushes in front of us started cracking and moving. It was only then that it occurred to me that we were very close to this bull, much closer than I would ever intentionally have got, at least on foot, to a wild African elephant. It was because of the thick rainforest vegetation that we were so close to him, ten metres away at most, a distance that he could cross in seconds.

And then he charged. A lot can happen in three seconds. In the first second, the bull was coming straight at us through the trees. He only seemed to take about three giant steps before he was there. And really *there*. In the fleeting moment that he charged at us, no more than five metres away, I could see every last elephantine wrinkle with infinite clarity. In the next second, Sulaiman stood his ground, clapping loudly and shouting at the bull to back down. In the third second, I swore, which seemed like a sensible thing to do at the time, and then I did what every self-preserving human does at moments like this. I ran for my life.

As I bolted, the elephant let out an unmistakable warning scream, a heart-shaking, ear-piercing, get-the-hell-outta-here screech. The terrifying sound of it at such close range reverberated through my chest and seemed to echo through the forest. Adrenaline surged through my body, giving my legs enough power to beat Cathy Freeman on the track. A moment later, a second elephant trumpeted in reply to him in the distance, deep and hollow. The way their voices echoed through the dense forest was otherworldly and eerie, almost like we were all under water.

I didn't slow down, although I wasn't going to beat any sprint race records running through this forest. Odd-shaped fallen logs and rambling vines tried to trip me at every step. As I tried to stay upright and cover as much ground as possible, my breathing sounded heavy in my ears, it wasn't my proudest moment. I must have looked like a cross between a sloth and a dancing lemur on speed and I was very glad no one was there to witness the unfortunate spectacle that was about to end in me being flattened by an irate pachyderm.

I swerved through the trees, leaping over fallen trunks and dung piles, my feet barely touching the ground as I ran. I could hear something running behind me – branches cracking – and I didn't know whether it was Sulaiman or the bull or both. I just kept running. I knew that if that bull wanted to catch up to me, he could easily do so. Elephants are not bumble-footed in the jungle as I am. They can push down trees in their path that I would have to take a wide berth around.

As the blood coursed wildly through my veins, the thought occurred to me that my number could be up today. This could be it. But I couldn't afford to die. I had a child. Solo wasn't yet three years old, and he needed his mum.

Let me go, elephant. Let me go.

CHAPTER 1

EYE OF THE ELEPHANT

Assam, India, late November 2008

Four years earlier I was working for the global organisation the Worldwide Fund for Nature (WWF) when the opportunity arose to become involved in making a documentary about human-elephant conflict in Asia and Africa. The idea of a film documenting the wars that were taking place between elephants and people, as well as some of the solutions being put forward across their range in Africa and Asia, was a subject that was very close to my heart. As a conservationist I had seen the human-elephant conflict in north-east India and southern Africa first hand, and I felt strongly that the more people there were telling this story, the more action there would be to solve the problem. The Sydney-based production company, Animal Media Australia, led by film-maker Stephen Van Mil, had just received an award for its film on Birute Galdikas' pioneering work with orang utans.

Not long after I first met Steve, I left full-time work at WWF to write a book about my own experiences working on human-elephant conflict – *Elephant Dance* – which allowed me time to contribute to a film on the same topic. One late spring morning after several months of planning, I found myself in a queue at Sydney airport, waiting to get my boarding pass to India for the first part of the filming. Steve had arranged for me to meet Sydney artist Nafisa Naomi there as she was on the same flight and would be joining the crew to document the behind the scenes action of the film through her photography and art.

A woman with long dark hair and ebony eyes lined with kohl, wearing tight long pants and with an impressive cleavage, waved to me from across the check-in area. I waved back, feeling suddenly underdressed as she joined me in the line.

Nafisa was bubbling with excitement, not having been back to India, the land of her birth, since her childhood. I was happy to let her do the talking. My mind was ticking over with concerns about whether the producer and crew would get their visas in time to join us in India in a couple of days and whether we would get enough footage in the short time frame. I had a little time before they arrived to touch base with my contacts at various conservation organisations in Assam and set up the best places to film. It was going to be a tough ask to film everything we needed to in just over a week. We would have to film day and night to capture enough footage. On top of that, I needed to be clear in my own mind about what I was going to say on film regarding the very serious plight of Assam's elephants, so that I didn't come across as a total idiot or, worse still, a boring, rambling scientist.

On the flight to India I learned pretty much the entire life story of my travelling companion. The daughter of a Dutch mother and Indian father, she spoke with an Australian accent but had spent her early childhood in Hong Kong. Nafisa had studied medicine for three years before giving it up to work in fashion, and only much later in life, following a divorce, had decided to dedicate herself to art. I had seen some of her wildlife art and I had to admit it was incredible, but it was her human portraits and botanical art that had won her both Australian and international awards.

It was the middle of the night when our plane landed in Mumbai. As we collected our luggage, every eye was on Nafisa and her fabulous figure. I wasn't sure whether it was because by local standards she wasn't covered up enough or if they thought she was a Bollywood film star – or both. I was just glad that it was taking the attention off me with my blonde hair and it didn't seem to worry her.

As we slept in our twin hotel room, we were oblivious to the history unfolding across the city at other tourist hotels just kilometres away. That night's coordinated attacks by Pakistani terrorists would hit international headlines in the days to come because their targets had included famous hotels – like the Taj Mahal and Oberoi Trident – frequented by foreigners. While we slept soundly, at least 166 people were killed in these bombings and shootings, including 28 foreigners, and dozens more were taken hostage, some of them Australian.

It wasn't until the next day, after flying to the capital of Assam, Guwahati, and driving for four hours to the town of Tezpur, that we heard anything about it. We hadn't seen the news since we'd left Sydney, and it was only when checking emails a day after the bombings that we were alerted to the disaster that we had narrowly missed. Among my emails there were several urgent messages from loved ones asking if I was okay, as no one had any idea whether I was alive or dead. No one had been able to phone me because my cell phone didn't work in Assam. I had learned on my last trip to this part of the world that the government controlled communications and made it pretty much impossible for foreigners to buy a local phone. I figured it had something to do with keeping on top of the ULFA, the United Liberation Front of Assam, the rebel movement that had a tendency towards bombing public places in this part of the world.

Tezpur, which means 'city of blood' in Assamese, was 175 kilometres and a long, slow drive from Guwahati's national airport. Assam's fifth largest city was a long way off the beaten track in one of India's most remote and lesser known states. Few tourists came to this part of India, which is way up in the north-eastern corner, wedged between Bangladesh to the south and China (Tibet) to the north. It was my favourite part of India because of its incredible national parks, such as Kaziranga, home to greater one-horned rhinos, elephants and tigers. In the Assam jungle you felt like you were in a scene from *The Jungle Book*. Like the rest of India, it was heavily populated, but nowhere in Assam was quite as crazy and polluted as the bigger cities like Delhi and Calcutta, and the rice paddies and tea plantations along the heavily potholed roads gave it a more sedate, rural feel.

From the back seat of the Mahindra (an SUV) I watched women in sparkling saris of azure blue, flamingo pink and every other colour of the rainbow as they glided along the side of the road like flocks of radiant birds. Belching buses barged past, their roofs loaded up with mountains of luggage and the occasional forlorn-looking goat strapped on with rope. Barefoot children wearing dirty underpants with gaping holes ran along the streets and begged for rupees when we stopped by the road. Blasé Brahmin cows ruminated in the middle of the street, forming carefree road blocks that everyone seemed to accept as the norm. A man lay face down on the dirt by the road edge, his legs and two shoes sprawled across the tar road as if he had just stepped out of them and fallen flat on his face. Our driver didn't slow down, just hooted and swerved like all the other vehicles going past him.

'What is wrong with that man?' I asked, worried that he had been hit by a car. People and cars were just ignoring him. .

'He have been drinking,' our driver said, and pressing down on the accelerator.

Physical labour was still the way of things in Assam. Beyond the manifold towns lay a patchwork of custard-coloured rice paddies, most of it already harvested by this time of year, with just a few people picking rice by hand with nimble fingers. Neat piles of precious harvested rice plants, resembling stalks of long dried grass or hay, stood alongside the rows. Wearing only knee-length fabric wraps around their waists, usually barefoot but sometimes in well-worn leather sandals, skinny boys and older men alike pulled wooden carts loaded high with rice husks. Their backs shiny with sweat, these human machines were all pumping sinew and muscle on protruding bones. Four ducks waddled across the road to a pond with red algae forming a scum on the surface. An old man sat out the front of a ramshackle hut while watching children bathe playfully in the water. I viewed it all whizzing by from the back seat of the Mahindra, present but not truly there, an observer rather than a participant, as if watching television.

That night at the Hotel Luit, a Kingfisher beer brought some relief. Nafisa, who apparently didn't usually drink, downed a stiff local vodka. After that drive, she said she needed it. The hotel was dirty and ratty, just as I remembered it. It smelled of yesterday's curry and stale smoke. On our arrival an Indian man with greasy hair had taken us to our room and in his limited English combined with hand gestures and a suggestive smile indicated that we might want our beds pushed together. Clearly they didn't very often get two women unchaperoned by a man sharing a room together in this part of the world.

'He thinks we're lesbians,' Nafisa exclaimed with amusement.

The man didn't understand a word she said, just grinned sleazily back at her as he stood by the door.

As hotels went, there wasn't much to choose from in Tezpur, and according to my conservation colleagues this was one of the best, but I decided immediately that there was no way we were going to spend more than one night there. I had a vague recollection of an eco-lodge next to Nameri National Park that I had driven past last time I was there, about half an hour from town. I was sure it would serve as a nicer base for us and the crew than the Hotel Luit, where I figured we would either catch typhoid and die or be stoned for suspected lesbianism. I wasn't sure whether it was illegal to be gay in Assam, but I wasn't taking any chances.

The next morning, we packed our things and asked our driver to take us to Nameri. Nestled in the forest adjoining Nameri National Park, the eco-camp was everything I had hoped it would be. Huge trees with broad dark leaves towered over quaint cabins that seemed to have been absorbed by the jungle, covered as they were in vines sporting bright pink flowers. I breathed in all that green and felt my lungs sigh with relief as the fumes of Indian towns were expunged. A tightness in my chest that until then I hadn't even noticed was released. Living in the city, I realised I had missed the sense of peace I always feel in places with lots of big trees. How easy it is to forget what gives you peace of mind when you are caught up in the hustle and bustle of fast-paced daily life.

Early the next morning, on the way to the WWF office in Tezpur, our driver stopped at a bridge blocked by Assamese army trucks. The military were a common sight in that part of India, as the national army had been deployed there since 1990 to keep on top of armed separatists groups like the ULFA, who were seeking to establish Assam as a sovereign state.

Two weeks earlier I had been listening to the BBC news when it was reported that seventy people had been killed and three hundred injured in at least eleven separate bombings before noon on 30 October across Guwahati, probably by the ULFA. Now, watching stern-faced soldiers scanning the bridge with bomb detectors that looked like the metal detector I once used as a kid to search for coins on the beach in North Queensland, I was reminded of the risks of being in this part of India.

An army officer came over to our vehicle, peered conde-scendingly at Nafisa and me in the back seat, and began firing questions at our driver in an authoritative voice. I should have been pleased that the soldiers were checking that there were no bombs on the road, but I really didn't feel comfortable with the eyes of this officer on us, glaring as if we might be spies. He didn't look like a particularly friendly guy, with a rifle slung over one shoulder and a moustache big enough to threaten a ferret perched on his upper lip.

As a foreign, blonde woman in Assam, it was impossible to blend into the crowd, and that made me nervous. But it didn't seem to worry Nafisa. She wound down her window, smiled win-ningly, leaned out with her camera and asked to take his photo. The officer didn't seem to know what she was saying and was more interested in her cleavage, but he also wasn't comfortable being confronted in this way by an overtly assertive woman, and I could see him getting riled up at the idea of having his photo taken.

'No, no, no!' he barked gruffly.

He spoke limited English, but his hand gestures demon-strated that it was obviously *not* on to take photos of army officers.

I didn't know Nafisa well enough to be able to tell if this was fearless bravado or naivety or both, but I was growing increas-ingly anxious. The last thing I wanted in this situation was to get into an altercation with the Assamese army. We were two women from Australia who were a long way from home and without the compulsory male escorts that this part of the world demanded. India was not necessarily a place where women could rely on the police to get them out of trouble; indeed, they could end up causing more themselves. Assam was still an extremely sexist place by western standards. The majority of people were Hindu, but with recent mass immigration from Bangladesh, a growing part of the population was now traditional Muslim. Women here were expected to cover up and shut up.

It entered my mind that Nafisa might get arrested – and get me arrested too, by default. I really didn't want to see the inside of an Assamese prison cell. I gave her a look that said please stop. I slunk lower into the seat as the driver tried to take back control of the situation. The officer stepped up his serious act, glaring at us while grabbing regular eyefuls of Nafisa's cleavage. As our driver attempted to placate him, there was a yell from one of the army trucks on the bridge. In the hubbub of raised male voices, the officer waved a nonchalant hand at us, now distracted by something else that was going on in his domain. I breathed a sigh of relief as finally we were able to go on our way.

The following day we left in the wee hours before dawn to visit a village that WWF conservationist Soumen Dey thought might be a good one to trial chillies. These humble red fruits are an effective deterrent to elephants and an excellent cash crop for local people. On a previous trip here when I had worked for WWF, it had taken me a long time to convince anyone in India that chillies were worth a try to help reduce the human-elephant conflict, based on their success in Africa, but Soumen had finally agreed to give it a go.

In Zambia, the Elephant Pepper Development Trust had shown that elephants didn't like chilli and across numerous sites in Africa they had demonstrated how the use of chilli fences, chilli briquettes (bricks made of elephant dung and chilli, with a hot coal on top that produces 'chilli smoke') and chilli crop buffer zones could deter elephants from crops. The other great advantage of chillies as an elephant deterrent was that the fruits themselves could be sold as a cash crop, providing an alternative livelihood for people living on the poverty line. While I knew chillies alone were not the solution to the problem of human-elephant conflict, I believed they were a very useful tool for local people to minimise the serious negative impacts and maximise the benefits of living alongside the planet's largest land mammal.

It didn't take much to convince Steve that filming the chilli projects, both the functional ones in Zambia and the one that WWF was planning to test in India, would make a great addition to the film. It would show one of the positive options that existed to combat human-elephant conflict, and also would provide a good contrast to the heartbreak around the conflict itself.

In India at that time, the mortality toll on both sides of the human-elephant conflict was severe. Elephants were killing at least four hundred people annually, while more than a hundred elephants were killed every year by being caught in low-hanging power lines, hit by trains and poisoned. The conflict was a direct result of habitat loss. Almost two-thirds of the natural forest cover north of the Brahmaputra River in Assam had been destroyed in the last couple of decades, leaving elephants with no choice but to move through the tea plantations, rice paddies and villages that had replaced the trees. That was often where the conflict occurred, and particularly during the rice harvest season, when elephants raided rice paddies for food.

Our arrival in this village, three hours east of Tezpur, was no small thing. Soumen told us that many of these people had probably never seen foreigners. A crowd quickly gathered around us as we visited local people who had started growing chillies in their back yards. Soumen showed us where he wanted to help this community cultivate it on a larger, more commercial scale, in a nearby paddy field.

As Soumen and I talked with some village leaders, I noticed Nafisa eyeing one of the motorbikes parked nearby. The next thing I knew, she was riding it down the corrugated dirt track heading off into the distance. Now a huge crowd gathered around, running after her and cheering at the entertainment value of seeing a foreign woman tearing off on a motorbike. Oh no, I thought, so much for the professional reputation I was trying to maintain. The men might be impressed, but I was sure that the women would be shocked and ashamed by such an act of boldness. But when Nafisa returned in one piece (thankfully), the women as well as the men gathered around her, in awe, it seemed, of her courage in a place where women have little status. To my amazement, to them Nafisa's behaviour appeared to be empowering, perhaps showing them that it was okay to be different. They didn't think she was crazy at all. It was like she was a Bollywood star. I reflected that I might have been too harsh on my travelling companion, too quick to judge through my conservative, scientific goggles.

These poverty-stricken people put on a huge curry feast for our lunch, and through Soumen they asked us questions like how old we were, whether we were married and had children. When Soumen told them that I was in my early thirties and Nafisa in her mid-forties, the women responded by saying that this could not be right as Nafisa looked much younger than me. Although she was clearly foreign, Nafisa's Indian blood was a matter of intrigue. And I realised that while we had come here to share the story of these people and their battle with elephants, they too now had a story to tell.

'What's that?'

It was early in the morning, just before dawn, and my cohabitant was clearly more awake than I was.

'Don't worry,' I reassured Nafisa, 'it's probably just a cow.'

'Really?'

'Definitely,' I said, in my most serious zoologist voice.

We had heard the strange, high-pitched sound at all times of day since we had been at Nameri. As the daughter of a cattle farmer, I knew that cows bellowed like that sometimes. But when we went to investigate shortly after, we discovered that it wasn't a cow at all. It was a baby elephant, tethered to a tree not far behind our hut. Later we were told that she had been orphaned in the annual floods and rescued by Department of Forestry rangers. She would probably be raised there by the rangers to become a working elephant like the adult elephants nearby. Elephants were on the payroll in this part of the world as they were used to patrol the dense national parks along jungle trails more suited to them than to jeeps.

I am always cautious around wild animals and prefer that they come to me on their terms rather than the other way around. But this young elephant appeared to be desperate for interaction, reaching out her trunk to try and grab the nearest person's hand. As I squatted near her, she drew my hand into her mouth and sucked on it. When I pulled it away, she reached out with her trunk and pulled it back in again. It was like she was saying, 'Hold my hand.'

This little elephant was one of so many babies orphaned in Assam, not just during the floods but as a result of the escalating human-elephant conflict. During the conflict, babies can get separated from their herds, sometimes falling into wells or tea garden trenches. Gods they may be to many of India's people who worship the elephant-headed deity Ganesh, but you sure wouldn't want to be reincarnated as an elephant living in modern-day India.

Now that the film crew had arrived, we would be able to start filming the stories of the people who lived in this part of the world, like the children who slept in a tree house because they were too scared to sleep in a hut after their father was killed by an elephant, as well as the elephants themselves who were battling for survival.

The crew consisted of four men. In addition to Steve, there was Adam Harper, at that stage a co-producer, with whom I had worked at WWF, and South Africans Greg Nelson behind the camera and Kenny Gerharty on sound. Steve, Greg and Kenny had all flown in from the western side of India where they had been filming whale sharks for one of Steve's other films, and Adam was still on his way, delayed by airport closures in Thailand. They were a day late, cutting into precious filming time, as their camera had broken and had to be replaced in the biggest city they could find in western India within twenty-four hours.

There was no time to waste. Within five minutes of arriving, the crew started testing the camera and setting up shots of sunset over the river against the awe-inspiring backdrop of the snow-capped Himalayas. After a quick curry for dinner, Steve decided that they would try and get some night footage in the paddy fields near camp. It didn't sound like a particularly big deal, and it wouldn't have been except for the fact that there were a couple of vital things missing in this scenario.

One was torches. The night was pitch black and the paddy fields on the border of a national park were full of pissed-off elephants, giant dried-mud potholes where the elephants had walked, rice paddy trenches and other things that you could fall, twist or pirouette into in an ungainly fashion. There was also the not inconsiderable chance that we could walk right into armed poachers or, more exciting still, the occasional terrorist.

The other missing item was a local guide. One thing I'm not is an adrenaline junkie. I've never wanted to bungee jump or swim with great white sharks. Whenever I went walking in the bush among lions and elephants in Africa, I never carried a rifle, but I always, *always* had a local tracker or guide with me (and sometimes he was armed). His job was to watch not only my back but also to check the spoor (tracks) and signs of the presence of other animals. Local people always know the area better than I, as a relative new-comer, ever could. On this night, we were just half a dozen foreign idiots walking around in the dark without a torch.

It's a good thing to be a little bit scared when walking through the bush on foot. It fine-tunes your senses, helps make you just that little bit more alert for when an elephant does charge out of nowhere. But there's a thin line between courage and reck-lessness. As we staggered through the darkness that night, we wouldn't even see an elephant, let alone hear it coming, until it was too late. After a couple of hours of tramping through the completely unfamiliar dark forest, I was relieved to hear Greg say that we had to go back because the replacement camera wasn't working properly. After all that, none of the footage was usable anyway.

The next morning, I insisted that we buy half a dozen torches as a bare minimum before doing any more night filming. If an elephant or a terrorist was going to kill me, I damned well wanted to look it in the eye.

In the days to come, the crew filmed scenes of the devastat-ing forest destruction at the base of the Himalayas, the lens capturing incredible old jungles eaten away by the human settlements of primarily poor people who lived traditionally. Villagers re-enacted their experiences of elephant attacks, showing us the places where elephants had charged and people had been killed. The crew filmed the brewing of rice beer, which the elephants (and people) get supremely drunk on. It's an evil brew that elephants will knock down houses to get to. They interviewed an old lady in a white sari (the colour worn during mourning) who was a widow of conflict. Her husband had been killed by an elephant right in front of her house and she now relied on the kindness of family to take care of her in her old age. We filmed until the early hours of the mornings to capture the war on elephants, with dozens of men camped out by fires beside their rice paddies preparing for that night's battle to keep herds out of their crops. The cameras rolled as a hundred or more men brandishing burning spears and homemade guns yelled at a small herd of elephants running for their lives across a crop, with firecrackers and gunshots ringing out across the night.

But one of the most extraordinary things I saw on this trip wasn't caught on film at all. It was nearing midnight, somewhere in the rice paddies, and we were bogged in a thick muddy ravine that doubled as a road. Outside, the dark night sky was lit up by a trillion stars, while here on earth the warring men's burning spears and bright torch lights flickered and flashed. When the vehicle had slid into the mud and didn't look like coming out any time soon, I was too tired to care about the dozen or so men outside the car whose job it now was to make a plan to get us out of there. Minutes earlier I had lain down, trying to curl into the most comfortable version of the foetal position that I could manage in the back seat of the Mahindra using my backpack as a pillow. I wondered what it must be like to be up there with the stars and the moon looking down upon this war zone in which neither side was winning. What would the stars think of us, fighting for space and survival? If there was a wager, which side would they back?

As I drifted off to sleep, I tried to block out the din. Punctuating the backdrop of angry, shouting men, firecrackers and guns was the harrowing sound of screaming elephants. Mothers, babies, grandmothers. The breeding herd of largely females was being forcibly pushed out of the ripening rice paddies that had drawn them in from what little remained of their natural home. They were hungry – and terrified. This was a normal scene in rural Assam and one at which the locals didn't bat an eyelid.

Some time later – maybe minutes, perhaps hours for all I could tell – I felt myself rocking in the seat. Let me clarify: something was rocking me or, at least, the car had moved. Only half awake, I opened my eyes. The car was still. Had that really happened or had I been dreaming? The answer to that question was clear a second later when the car jolted forward, almost knocking me off my seat. I sat bolt upright and spun around to look out the rear window. Staring right back at me was the eye of an elephant. In fact, not one but two elephants were giving the car a substantial nudge, while I had no choice but to sit there looking rather like a bleary-eyed meerkat caught in a sandstorm (and with hair to match). I had become an elephant's plaything. Surrounding the vehicle now was a huge crowd, all of them local men, and most of them talking and shouting at the top of their lungs.

Suddenly the driver of our vehicle, yelling in Assamese, jumped into the front seat and started accelerating while the elephants gave the car one more giant heave-ho. And then, in all the usual madness of India, we were off, driving into the night in search of more elephants raiding paddies to capture on film.

The long hours of filming may have been exhausting, but I had forgotten how emotionally draining it was being so close to the war on elephants. It's a bit like working in a place where you are surrounded by poverty – you somehow get desensitised to the horror, but it takes its toll nevertheless. Although I had witnessed it before, it still broke my heart to see elephants running through paddy fields, screaming in protest and fear, as people chased them away back to a forest that now barely existed. It just didn't seem fair. But the other side of the story was also incredibly sad. Assam had so many extremely poor, uneducated people in rural areas who were totally dependent on their rice crop to feed their families. There were some horrendous stories of elephants attacking people, including a ghastly one I heard of a pregnant woman being ripped apart.

I could understand why people wanted to retaliate, but it was also obvious why it was happening. The forests were disappearing and so elephants simply had nowhere else to go. The human population was increasing, which meant that the problem was only going to get worse. The more I thought about this, the more questions I had and the fewer answers. My brain was threatening to combust with all the cognitive churning that was taking place in its convoluted channels. The truth was, it all came down to habitat, really. The clearing had to stop, but it had gone so far that it was also necessary to recreate safe, natural corridors of habitat for the elephants so as to link the remaining islands of forest. And in my view, there had to be more opportunities for local people living with elephants in Assam to benefit from their presence through industries like ecotourism. It was a hard truth to face, but elephants had to be a part of this state's development or they would have no future there.

I've long held the view that much can be learned from southern Africa's approach to conservation. Countries like Namibia, for example, have experienced great success in combating poaching and increasing wildlife populations by mastering the art of community-based wildlife conservation. Communal conservancies provide truly local ownership of the animals that roam on their traditional lands. Those animals have a financial value and the community's ownership of them is legally recognised by the government, providing an engine for economic and social development that is truly sustainable. Wildlife-based industries like ecotourism and trophy hunting (where hunters pay for the privilege of a controlled hunt of certain selected animals as 'trophies') provided tangible benefits like jobs, income and food to communities who would otherwise be living in poverty. It isn't really that complicated. Some refer to this solution as 'what pays, stays'. In fact, management of the animals isn't really about the animals, but about managing people and their livelihoods. And as a way to increase wildlife populations, it works.

In the years that I lived in Namibia I watched incredibly successful conservation programs emerge since this country gained independence from South Africa in 1990, ending a long civil war during which poaching was rife and wild species were decimated. Now many local communities who once received no benefits from wildlife had entered into joint tourism ventures with commercial ecotourism companies like Wilderness Safaris, and were receiving training, employment in safari camps, and percentages of the profits. Wildlife populations there were on the rise because people living alongside them had a genuine stake in their future. Some communities, like the San Bushmen of Nyae Nyae Conservancy, where I ran a project on human-elephant conflict in 2005, had entered into a partnership with a trophy hunting operation, which gave them not only jobs and income for the community, but also much-needed meat. Whether or not I liked trophy hunting at an emotional level, the local people I had surveyed there did because of all the benefits it provided. To the Bushmen, meat in their bellies meant more than western ideologies about protecting elephants at all costs. Such sentiments were worth very little in the stern face of daily survival in the developing world.

When the locals were on board, anything was possible. People in Africa are really just like people anywhere else – they want a better life for themselves and for their families. I had seen in southern Africa that if wildlife helped people to achieve that, then it would be cherished and nurtured just like anything of 'value'. If elephants destroyed their crops and lions ate their goats, then they were considered the enemy. These people are no different from farmers in Australia who shoot the dingoes who threaten their livestock, or the American ranchers at war with wolves and coyotes. We may look different, have different religions and cultures, and speak different languages, but at a core level, we humans are still the same species. We are all just animals that need food, water and shelter in order to pass our genes on to another generation. No matter where you come from, whether you're a Himba nomad in the desert, a rice paddy worker in India or a farmer near Birdsville, everyone just wants to lead a safe, healthy and happy life.

From what I had seen of India, although many people worshipped the elephant-headed god Ganesh and revered elephants, there was still some way to go to convince villagers living with them that conserving wildlife was a smarter option for them and their families than driving it out and destroying the dwindling forests in which elephants lived. In Assam, people were so poor that any threat to their meagre crops was devastating. Much of the damage to Assam's natural habitats had been done decades earlier with the clearing of forests for tea plantations and commercial logging. Thankfully the era of intense commercial logging had passed, but the deforestation still continues as every day piecemeal bits of forest are removed by local people, who load up their bicycles with impossibly high piles of wood for local sale. All of these little bits add up, resulting in more human-elephant conflict as the elephants follow ancient migration patterns that no longer wind through old jungles but through human settlements.

The head of the Wildlife Trust of India, Vivek Menon, described the state of India's wildlife like this:

> In today's day and age almost every wildlife preserve in India is in danger. In danger from poachers waiting for the authorities to take their eye off the ball to enable a strike. In danger from fringe villagers whose idea of usufruct rights [rights in relation to common property] run counter to conservation imperatives. In danger from knowing and unknowing development lobbies. In danger from the ignorance of the Indian populace and its polity that overlooks the fact that our Protected Area system is actually a vital national heritage.

The year before, in 2007, when I had been in Assam with WWF to advise the state minister for the environment on some ideas that were working in Africa to reduce human-elephant conflict, my question to the WWF team in Assam was, if southern Africa was starting to have some success in realising genuine conservation outcomes, couldn't the same principles be applied to India? It seemed a valid question to me, but I met with huge resistance, perhaps because I was a woman, and a foreign one at that, in a place where women still had very little status and foreigners rarely visited. All of the conservation staff at WWF and the ministers I met were men. And, as expected, there were half a dozen reasons why most of the people I spoke to didn't think my outlandish ideas would work.

There were too many people in India, and too much corruption, too much political instability. India was *different* from Africa (if only I had a dollar for every time I heard that one). One argument put to me by one conservationist was that raising income for conservation through trophy hunting wouldn't work as a management option because most Indians were philosophically opposed to hunting. These reasons were all valid and fair. But I had more questions that were met with automatic no's. *What about tourism?* Not enough tourists were visiting Assam because they were scared of the rebel insurgencies and the bombings and, besides, the locals didn't want loads of visitors. *What about high end, low numbers tourism?* But that would just make national parks unaffordable for Indians, who constituted the majority of visitors to them (seventy per cent). *Why not increase the number of foreign visitors?* These things don't happen overnight, you know.

I was starting to get the picture. Clearly, I couldn't possibly understand (you aren't from here), and it wasn't that simple (you really should know your place, woman). India's problems were *complex*. How I grew to hate that word. Complex. Conservationists used it whenever they found it too hard to give me a straight answer or didn't know the right one. The reasons why Africa's approach wouldn't work went on and on. Some of the points were valid, but I couldn't get past the thought that negativity and a sense of being overwhelmed by the problem were inherent in the psyches of many of those working in conservation, creating a culture that was unable to see the wood for the trees. I wasn't suggesting cutting and pasting Africa's model onto India, because obviously there were differences and there had to be local ownership, but negativity towards ideas that weren't their own didn't stop me thinking that some of the approach that was working in Africa could in some form also be applied to India.

Thankfully, at least one of the staff at WWF had been willing to give the idea of chillies a go after the Assamese minister for the environment had spoken out in the newspaper about his support for it. But it was early days for Soumen and his chilli project and while I encouraged him from a distance, only time would tell if it would make a difference.

After filming the war zone and WWF's proposed chilli site, it was a mild relief to visit the Wildlife Trust of India's Centre for Wildlife Rehabilitation and Conservation (CWRC), near Kaziranga National Park, to film the orphaned baby elephants and other wildlife being rehabilitated there. I had met some of the elephant calves a couple of years earlier. They had been much smaller then, and interaction had been limited as a result. But this time was quite different. There were about six baby elephants there now, and each of them had a unique personality, one of the centre's resident veterinarians, Dr Boro, told us. We watched as Dr Boro and the keepers weighed the elephants and fed them with bottles containing special formula milk made specifically for elephants.

One of the youngsters, Deepa, was a little bit larger than the others. The oldest at just a few years old, she had taken on the role of matriarch for the group. In the wild elephant breeding herds are headed by a strong female leader known as the matriarch, whose commands are followed by the entire herd. What was astonishing about Deepa's assumption of this role was that she had not had any older elephants to teach her this behaviour, but had simply taken it upon herself to lead the group of babies. One of the calves tried to push me over playfully, nudging me with his fuzzy forehead, and pulled my hand into his mouth just as the young elephant at Nameri had done. With their hairy heads and innocent, observant eyes under long lashes I completely fell in love with them.

Dr Boro told us how one of the little females, Soni, had been separated from her herd when she was only four months old. Her herd had been raiding a crop when it was driven away by villagers. Soni was roaming alone in a tea garden, no doubt trying to find her mother, when villagers found and attacked her in retaliation for the damage that the herd had done to their crops. They cut her tiny trunk with a machete, leaving a deep wound, but thankfully did not cut it off completely before she was rescued by the CWRC.

Tikla, a two year old male, had fallen into a tea garden drain and become trapped. When he was eventually freed, he could not be reunited with his herd. His story was not unusual as elephants, particularly youngsters but also adults, often became trapped in these trenches.

The stories of these orphans were harrowing, but their characters were endearing. It was impossible not to be won over by their playful antics and obvious sense of humour. The goal of the CWRC was to help these elephants return to the wild, as they had successfully done with elephants in the past, relocating them, when they were old enough, to the World Heritage listed Manas National Park in northern Assam. I had never been comfortable with seeing animals in captivity, but these orphans had been rescued from situations that would almost certainly have led to their deaths, and the prospect of them being returned to the wild at some point was enough to give me a lot of hope for their future.

The bigger question was, if the destruction of the forests continued in Assam, would there be any 'wild' left for them to return to? It was a question that I would have to leave unanswered for now, because my time with the crew was coming to an end. Much as I had loved being out in the field and seeing the crew film one part of the bigger global story of human-elephant conflict, I had to get home. The other part of the story we had yet to film was in Africa. If the company's production funding came through we would film there the following year. But for now, it was a matter of urgency that I board a plane back to Sydney. Two weeks earlier I had married my boyfriend of the last year and a half, fellow conservationist Andy Ridley. In three days' time, the official post-wedding party for our friends and family in Sydney was on and my new mother-in-law, Lizzie, had already arrived from England for it.

But getting home might not be that easy, I realised. A little disturbingly, there were a few rather large obstacles in my path that hadn't been there before I left Sydney. There had been riots in Thailand so Bangkok had closed its airport, which I was due to fly through. The airline cancelled my flight and gave no indication when it might be rescheduled. Then there was the state of Mumbai, which I also had to fly through to get home, and which was in complete disarray after the terrorist attacks the week before. It was beginning to look like I was going to miss my own wedding party.

But Andy wasn't going to let that happen. He and a friend in Sydney managed to get me a flight home with another airline. Standing outside the CWRC after a morning with the orphaned elephants, one of the crew passed me the mobile phone lent to us by a local WWF staff member.

'I've got you a flight, babe,' Andy shouted over the crackling line, 'but you have to leave now.'

I could hear the stress in his voice. Torn between the elephants and the man I loved back in Sydney, there was only one choice to be made. I would really miss being among the elephants, but guys like this only come along once in a lifetime.

Very early the next morning, a driver arrived to take me to the airport at Guwahati, leaving the crew to continue filming around Kaziranga National Park. I left the jungles of Assam behind, wondering when I would be back.

CHAPTER 2

LOVE IN THE ANIMAL KINGDOM

I was born and raised in Townsville, in the 1980s a coastal town of about 100,000 people next to Australia's Great Barrier Reef. There was no shortage of adventures to be had in far North Queensland, where the ocean teemed with deadly saltwater crocodiles and box jellyfish, but on the cusp of my sixteenth birthday, a serendipitous twist of fate shifted the course of my life. In 1993, Dad took me to a land even more desolate and dry than the outback, and in two short weeks, Zimbabwe's dusty, parched lowveld captured my heart.

At the time my father could never have known how taking me with him on safari to Africa would alter the direction of his eldest daughter's life. That experience with him at a game ranch called Humani in the Save Valley Conservancy in south-eastern Zimbabwe changed my world forever and marked the beginning of an addiction that has never gone away. All the logical, rational arguments in the world couldn't have persuaded me to take another course. Once Africa bit me, I had the bug forever.

We were in a wildlife conservancy that was kept afloat by trophy hunting, something that to me seemed an enormous contradiction in terms. Conservation and hunting in the same place? Killing animals to save them? I could see that Humani was teeming with wildlife and that the meat from the animals was feeding us in camp as well as the locals who lived there. But it just didn't make sense. Nor did the fact that my father was a trophy hunter, and yet also the person I looked up to more than anyone else in the world. Dad *loved* animals as much as I did. It was because of him that we had grown up spending as much time in nature as we had. Why on earth did he want to hunt? It wouldn't be until many years later, when I saw the way well-managed trophy hunting can contribute to the conservation of species and their habitats that I really came to terms with it.

For now, I was hooked on Africa. I didn't understand why, but I had to return. At seventeen, I wrote a letter to Roger and Anne Whittall, the owners of Humani, asking them if I could volunteer for them in my gap year after finishing high school. To my great excitement, they agreed. And so, in 1995, after untold hours of working as a checkout chick at the local supermarket to pay for the plane ticket, I deferred university and was thrown into the deep end – the African way.

Within a week of arriving at Humani, despite having just finished school myself, I started an afternoon class teaching English at the local primary school to about twenty pupils, some of whom were a few years older than me. Some of the 'kids' in my class walked through the bush for ten kilometres to get to school each day, running the risk at any time of walking into elephants or rhinos.

At Humani anything could unfold on any given day. One second I would be taking a relaxing evening stroll at sunset, the next I would be holed up under an electric fence next to a mealie (corn) field in the dark, shivering while listening to the footsteps of some unknown creatures that potentially had me in mind for their dinner. I could be teaching English to a bunch of enthusiastic young people at the village school one day, and the next trying to stop the local witchdoctor from cursing the headmaster with malaria.

To survive in that part of the world – to *thrive* there – I learned that you had to accept that you were not really ever in control. It was liberating, in a way, if a little frustrating at times. I learned the African saying 'just make a plan', which is a saying the locals use on a daily basis to cope when things go wrong. If you get a flat tyre when you're two hundred kilometres from the nearest town, and you realise you don't have a spare or a jack, nor any mobile phone reception, you just have to make a plan. When you're peeing in the bush with your shorts around your ankles and a honey badger saunters up to you (this mild-looking creature is infamous for acts of genital mutilation and afraid of nothing), you make a plan because you have no other choice. Plans can take many shapes and sizes in Africa. The point is that you make one. This is based on the foolproof assumption that in Africa anything that can go wrong will go wrong at the worst possible time. If you fail to make a plan, there's a good chance something will make a meal of you. I came to see that I was capable of much more than I thought I was, simply because I had no choice but to make plans daily, from taking advantage of the company of a local Shona woman when caught out alone and on foot in the wild one night in the dark, to outsmarting a cheetah who was being hand-reared by the Whittalls to stop her sneaking up on me and practising her stalking and pouncing techniques. Thrown in the deep end, it was sink or swim.

By the time I turned eighteen I had decided with absolute certainty that I would become a wildlife researcher. This, I felt, was a job that would allow me to work with wildlife in Africa in the long term, a career of adventure, a life of excitement in the wild. I wasn't thinking about whether I would ever make any money out of it, whether it would ever complicate my life on that far-off day when I might have a family.

I had few of the prerequisites to study science, having up until then been planning to study law, so I found a side route to a science degree through the agricultural department at the University of Queensland. I then worked my butt off to miraculously pass high school chemistry and physics in my first year of the degree, before switching to science and getting back on course towards a major in zoology.

Then, in the new millennium, I was astonished to be offered an Australian government scholarship to study the behavioural ecology of common impalas in Zimbabwe. Finally, the dream was real. But there was a catch. This was, after all, Africa, where nothing goes to plan. Just as I arrived in Zimbabwe to start my field studies, the country began to fall apart. Across the agricultural lands, President Robert Mugabe's land redistribution program was forcibly and often violently evicting white farmers from their properties. No one knew for how long the instability would go on, but my university wouldn't support me staying there when there was a chance I could be caught in the crossfire. Devastated, and worried about my friends there, I left Zimbabwe and the Whittalls in search of a new research site.

Six months later, I ended up at Etosha National Park, Namibia, a harsh, arid place where stark white elephants covered in dust from the vast white saltpan strode across endless short grass plains peppered with zebras and springboks. Etosha was home to the threatened, arid-adapted black-faced impala, a subspecies of the impala about which very little was known, and therefore the ideal study species for my PhD.

In my first few months at Etosha, I got lost in the desert, was sized up by lions and almost trodden on by an elephant cow, things that you would think would cause most self-preserving humans to say goodbye to Africa and live a normal life. But those experiences just made me love it more. Why? Well, for some god-forsaken reason, in Africa I felt like I was the real me. Slightly insane, a kind observer might have suggested, but nonetheless, *me*. I looked for reasons to make sense of it. I really did. Was Australia once connected to Africa in the days of Gondwanaland? Was there an African in our family lineage somewhere? Had I been an African in a former life? None of the obvious or more obscure possibilities could be confirmed, so there was no choice but to accept it for what it was. A part of me. Eventually, it no longer mattered. I stopped asking the question. After all, if you want to get technical about it, a long, long time ago, we *all* came from Africa. The campfires, the animal tracks in the sand, the rich hues of sunset over the savannah, all remind us who we once were before smartphones and televisions and twenty-four hour a day McDonald's. At a basic, primordial level, when I stared into the campfire flames at night as hyenas whooped and jackals cried out, I was a part of Africa and I knew that it would always be in me.

Every morning that I woke up in Etosha National Park during the years I was collecting data for my PhD, I would do so with a feeling of excitement in my stomach at the prospect of facing the new day at dawn, a day that could bring anything from a charge by a black rhino to the birth of a baby zebra. I was studying the behaviour of the black-faced impalas in order to provide ecological data for Namibia's first national management plan for the subspecies, but being out in the field every day I not only got to know my study species very well, but also all the other species that shared the impalas' habitat. I felt like my life had a purpose and by being out in nature every day I felt a part of something bigger than myself.

By mid-2003 I had completed my PhD on black-faced impalas and was looking for the next adventure. That was how I came to start work on elephants, a species that I had always been fascinated by. It was partly because of elephants that I fell in love with another part of Africa in 2005 – Bushmanland. This magnificent region in Namibia's north-east and bordering Botswana's Okavango Delta was teeming with elephants, especially during the hot, dry months when they congregated at the limited man-made and natural water points. The chief of the Bushmen in Nyae Nyae Conservancy told me that they had a serious problem with elephants, which were causing a lot of conflict with the local people, and they needed help to find solutions.

Thinking that an impala expert had no hope of getting funding for a human-elephant conflict project, I was amazed when all the funding and the government research permit I needed to run a study materialised in the next two months. I was the first to admit I had a lot to learn about elephants, not to mention the fact that the species often scared me half to death, but this was too good an opportunity to pass up.

It didn't take long to work out that a few simple things could be done to reduce local conflict with elephants. Most of the human-elephant conflict took the form of damage to installations like water pipes, tanks and solar set-ups, and primarily occurred in the hot, dry season when competition for water was at its highest. Small herds – usually bulls, who tended to be the risk takers – were the ones doing the damage. But one factor contributing to the conflict could easily be manipulated to provide some relief from this problem, and that was the distance between elephant drinking places and villages. My research showed that the further wildlife waterholes were from villages, the less likely it was that conflict would occur. In the years following the project, several cement cribs were built, a couple of them by groups of young Australians like myself working with Ministry for the Environment game warden and old friend Dries Alberts and the local Bushmen, trying to take the 'problem' away from the villages. They helped, but human-elephant conflict would continue to be an issue that the government and the Bushmen would have to proactively manage.

The elephant project with the Bushmen didn't pay me a salary, so I was also working for Wilderness Safaris part time as an environmental consultant, travelling all over the country in a dilapidated short wheel base Land Rover that had more character than any car I've ever driven before or since. My environmental colleague Basilia Shivute and I covered thousands of kilometres in that tough old beast, losing ourselves in desert dunes far, far off the beaten track up near the Angolan border and ending up in some of the most luxurious safari camps imaginable. These places were so remote and so breathtaking in their natural beauty that often I didn't want to return to the civilisation of Windhoek. I had no intention of ever returning to Australia. With a great job and a PhD under my belt, the idea of leaving Africa was unthinkable. This was *it*. As good as it gets.

But Africa was about to teach me something new again – nothing stays the same forever. The end of my twenties loomed, along with some bigger questions about whether a life in the wild would always be enough for me. One night in the middle of the desert an elephant stood right above my tent for a couple of hours, scratching his butt on a nearby tree and farting to his heart's content. That night, thinking that this was it and my number might well finally be up at the grand old age of twenty-eight, I decided that I wanted more from my life than this. I loved the wilds of Africa and all my dreams had come true but, still, something was missing.

It can get pretty dark and cold when you're on your own in a tent in the desert at night, and I was pretty sure I no longer wanted to spend my nights alone being farted on by anything, let alone a six-tonne elephant bull. If there was going to be farting going on in my tent, it had better be done by me or else by someone who at least looked like Bear Grylls. So when the WWF offered me a job as head of the Australian threatened species program in Sydney, while I didn't want to give up my life in Africa, I also knew that I had to take the plunge. The time had come. Besides, after years in the bush living on baked beans and biltong, I was close to financially broke and it looked unlikely that the Namibian government would give me another work visa. So Saturn kicked me off the astrological cliff in my twenty-ninth year, sucked me out of Africa and spat me rather unceremoniously onto the thirteenth floor of a high rise in Sydney.

Australia's biggest city was another type of jungle, a concrete one, with its own predators and prey, and the instincts and skills I had learned to survive in the African bush hadn't equipped me for things like dealing with office politics and bullies; the business side of the conservation industry, which was less about animals than raising money and working out how to spend it, sweet-talking donors and corporates; and avoiding tripping over in high heels. But Africa had shown me that sometimes it's better to go with the flow than to continually resist it. Watch, listen and learn. Accept that you are not in control. Stay clear of the hyenas and the vultures. Above all, in the presence of predators, show no fear. Such lessons were ingrained in my psyche after years in the wild and they were surprisingly useful in big city life. I learned a lot in my two years at WWF Australia about the way the mainstream environmental movement works and it concerned me greatly to learn that despite this country's considerable wealth and resources, it still had the highest rate of mammal extinction in the world.

Then, in 2007, another new world opened up to me on my first visit to India, a land that I would learn had much in common with Africa. India too had big cats and mega-herbivores like elephants and rhinos. The big difference was the first thing that hit me about India the second I stepped off the plane – the sheer volume of people. Intertwined with the vibrant colours and potent smells of India, so vivid and intense they made me squint, it was a heady mixture. Unlike southern Africa where it was possible to drive for miles and not see a town for all the bush, India was a sea of towns, seething with humanity, with small pockets of forest crying out to be saved. That, I would learn, was why it had some of the worst human-elephant conflict in the world, because India's 25,000 or so elephants had no choice but to come out of what little natural habitat was left in search of food.

For the first time in more than a decade, I had begun to see that there were adventures to be had and a lot of work to be done to conserve wildlife outside Africa. But working for WWF also led me to a different kind of adventure. In my first week on the job I met the man who would become my husband. Unlike with all of my previous victims, and to my family's and friends' great surprise, this time there wasn't a shred of safari khaki in sight. Andy was then WWF Australia's head of communications. An Englishman by birth, he was mad about sharks – and, for that matter, anything to do with diving on coral reefs – which was why he had moved to Australia five years earlier. But after years of working on communications campaigns to protect the Great Barrier Reef and Tasmanian old growth forests, he had come up with an idea that would grow beyond what anyone imagined at that time: Earth Hour. Back in early 2007, no one had any idea that Earth Hour would explode across the world, becoming the largest environmental social movement to date. That year, Andy and his small team just hoped that everyone would turn their lights out in one city: Sydney.

Andy's passion and commitment to make a difference reso-nated deeply with me. Here was someone who was truly excited and motivated about turning around the damage we were doing to the planet. In truth, I had never met anyone like him before. He made me laugh more than anyone I had ever known, and I think I knew within a month of secretly dating him that I was serious about him. But Andy had never been to Africa. For any normal girl, this wouldn't have been a problem. But for me, it was *massive*. Would a life with him draw me further away from the wildlife that I loved? Or would he share my passion for it? I wasn't about to give up all I had worked for just for a man. But at the same time, I did have a strong sense that Andy had come into my life for a reason. He had opened up my world and, together with working at WWF, I came to see that perhaps I could do more for African wildlife from outside Africa than within it, using my communication skills as well as my scientific training.

I missed being in Africa all the time, but I was still manag-ing to get back over there often enough to satisfy the addiction. And I was enormously relieved when, on our first trip to Africa together, Andy loved every second of it. He then topped it off by choosing a remote island at the confluence of the Zambezi and Chobe rivers to propose to me while hippos honked in the background, the most romantic engagement that was humanly possible, surrounded by wildlife in Africa.

My time in Africa had taught me to always keep an open mind, to consider the other side of the story, to be ready to embrace a change in perspective, and to not be afraid to make a plan when it all went wrong. It had taught me to listen, and to look to nature for answers. The main thing was that I think I was now starting to ask some of the right questions.

Having worked for an international non-government organisation (NGO), I no longer had as much faith in the conservation world to deliver real meaningful change for species on the brink of extinction as I did before. In spite of some impressive efforts by truly committed individuals, it was going to take much more than the existing machinery of the environmental movement to fix these problems. I wasn't sure what the solution was, but I felt strongly that communicating these problems to a mainstream audience was going to be important.

By the time Andy and I tied the knot on a beach in the Yasawa Islands, Fiji, I felt very sure that my time in Africa had been the training ground I needed – in life and in conservation – for what I was going to do next. As I stepped out into the bright, South Pacific sunlight in my strapless ivory dress, clutching a posy of locally grown white, yellow and pink frangipanis, I trusted the feeling that I was on the right track. And something also told me that meeting Andy and the immediate connection I'd felt with him hadn't been a coincidence.

CHAPTER 3

BURPING FOR AFRICA

Sydney, December 2008

I used to say that I was never going to have children. In the 1980s and 1990s, society told women that we could have it all – marriage, kids and a career – thanks to the feminist movement, a message that was reinforced at the Catholic girls' high school I attended. But it was a career that I wanted, a life in which I made a difference in the world. The life of a housewife and mother was as far from that ideal as you could get, although I think deep down I always imagined that one day I would have my own family, and that I would make raising kids work with a blossoming, inspired career and a sense of purpose outside the home. I mean, how hard could that really be?

By my late twenties, it was evident that the most obvious thing wrong with my occasional hankering to have my own happy family 'someday' was when and how it would actually happen. As a career-focused woman living the relatively nomadic life of a roaming zoologist in Namibia, there was no sign of the kind of partner that I could see fathering my offspring, for a start. But also, because I was so focused on my work in wildlife conservation, all of my nurturing energies were channelled into animals, and the sight of other people's babies failed to produce much more than the slightest flicker of maternal instinct. Baby elephants were cute, cheetah cubs adorable, but baby humans? Forget it! Like many women working in wildlife conservation, I had other priorities.

As my thirties approached after returning to the relative civilisation of Australia, for the first time I began to think about what it might be like to have a husband, a hound and maybe even a child. After all that unintentional fighting against my inner nature (ironically as a result of my fight to save nature) a ticker signalling a biological imperative hardwired somewhere deep inside my brain kicked into gear. It turned out that I wasn't all that much more advanced than the average coelacanth, after all. Animals are preprogramed to reproduce and pass on their genes, and for all my good intentions to buck that trend, so, it seemed, was I.

Two vital triggers happened around this time that changed everything. Firstly, enter prospective mate, worthy of siring my precious offspring and sharing my gene pool with: Andy. Secondly, throw in a little pressure (the life-threatening variety): both of us had minor but alarming cancer scares in the one year. The result? The timing was as right as it was ever going to be.

Where my family now lived in rural south-east Queensland, I was considered positively ancient to be thinking about start-ing a family. My younger sister Kek had had her first beautiful daughter, Ella, in her early twenties while she was studying to be a vet (yep, the animal thing does run in the family). Many of my friends there already had a couple of kids or else one on the way. This was in stark contrast to my new life in the big city, where most of my new friends in their late thirties were still single and searching for the right partner, or only just thinking about starting a family, after having kicked some solid goals in their careers. Listening to the horror stories of friends in their late thirties or early forties who had tried IVF and others who had experienced heartrendingly disappointing miscarriages, Andy and I decided that we should stop *not* trying to have a baby and just see what happened.

Expecting it to take a while, we were shocked to find that I was pregnant within a month of being married. The suddenness of this revelation was both exciting and a little worrying. For a start, the timing of it meant that our baby would be due at the very same time that my book, *Elephant Dance*, was due to be released, right in the middle of two weeks of publicity. I imagined myself racing from interview to interview with the baby's head lodged like a rockmelon upon the delicate knot of my cervix, the giant orb of my pregnant belly barging ahead of me to photo shoots, then my waters breaking midway through a radio interview and drenching Richard Fidler's feet. Clearly, that wasn't going to work. My publisher would kill me. It was the first time that career-related things in my life would have to be shuffled around to fit in with family, a theme that would recur again and again, pretty much for the foreseeable future, although I didn't know it then. The compromises had begun.

I farewelled the gastronomic delights of soft cheese, sashimi and oysters, and kissed goodbye to booze and Nurofen just after Christmas at the end of 2008. On New Year's Eve, at a friend's party in Newtown, I hadn't realised how odd it would feel to be completely sober among loads of drunken, revelling party goers. I seemed to get more and more sober and awkward as everyone got increasingly addled until, at about 11 pm, just short of the fireworks, I kissed Andy goodnight and snuck out the back door.

I wasn't enjoying myself and I was tired of explaining to people why I wasn't drinking on such a festive occasion, unable to tell them the truth this early on in the pregnancy. But I needn't have worried about that. A few days later, I miscarried.

We blamed it on watching the movie *Marley and Me* on the morning of New Year's Day, which had us both sobbing uncontrollably in the cinema. The trailer had sold us a light, funny story about a badly behaved dog, the perfect antidote for Andy's hangover and my reward for drinking lemonade on New Year's Eve. They lied. At the end of the movie, with tears streaming down his face, Andy sobbed, 'How could they make the dog *die*?' His tears just made me cry more, but the movie had hit a nerve with me for a different reason. After my depressing New Year's Eve, Jennifer Aniston's character really brought home the message that juggling marriage, children and career could get . . . well, complicated. Her life had been absorbed into everyone else's, her dreams sacrificed for her family's. Was I about to do that too?

I had worked incredibly hard to build a career in wildlife conservation, from slogging through my degree and PhD at the University of Queensland in a discipline that didn't come naturally to me, to fighting for my place in the hardened, male-dominated world of conservation in Africa. I had spent a long time working on who I was and now, in my early thirties, I was finally at a point where I was content with that. As ego-based as it was, my sense of identity was intimately tied to my career. Without that, who was I? After all those years of education and hard work, was I about to throw it all away? Like Jennifer Aniston's character in *Marley and Me*, was the 'I' in me about to just disappear? Were my dreams and aspirations about to melt away, replaced by a vision of a happy family in which I was defined by my mummy title rather than my doctorate? Frankly, that didn't seem fair.

As always, I turned to the animal kingdom for a dose of perspective. Things could have been much worse. I could have been a salmon. After their epic swim upstream against the flow of a river, salmon find calm waters to reproduce, the females laying their eggs on the riverbed before they are fertilised by the males. After that, the adults simply lose their zest for life. Both sexes slow down, weaken and die, not due to exhaustion but because of a chemical trigger in their brains, the same changes in hormones that drove them to reproduce on such a grand scale in the first place. But their golden moment is the act of reproduction followed by a rather spectacular mass die-off. What a way to go.

We humans (and most mammals, for that matter) live for a long time after reproducing. Most mammals look after their offspring for a long time before letting go, producing multiple sets of offspring in their lifetime. It's quite common for female elephants to still be with their mothers as adults, simply because the females tend never to leave 'home' or the natal herd. Far from reproducing and dying, elephants live long lives similar to human life spans in developed western countries. I knew I was more elephant than salmon, and while I wasn't planning to die after giving birth, I wondered whether a part of me wasn't about to.

Before I could answer any of the questions swirling around in my head, the pregnancy ended. I felt a strange sense of personal failure around the miscarriage. We were both disappointed, but we were also aware that almost a third of pregnancies ended this way in the first twelve weeks for no apparent reason. We had been fortunate that ours had ended early, before it had a chance to grow beyond a clump of cells. Due to our ages we still had time on our side. We could get back on the bandwagon and try again. Heck, it might even be fun!

I tried to put it into perspective, and began to think that maybe it wasn't such a bad thing not to be pregnant just yet. We could enjoy simply being married for a little while, and not rush into becoming parents. I would indulge in all the sashimi, oysters and white wine that I could get my hands on for now. I threw myself into my work, writing a report for WWF International and Earth Hour on the impact of climate change on ten of the world's most iconic species, making the final edits to my book, and organising the interviews and logistics of the next stage of the documentary filming in southern Africa.

To help pay for the filming, Steve had asked me if I could arrange for a group of investors and tourists to join the crew, offering them a behind-the-scenes experience while on safari in Africa. It didn't take long to find six interested people and sign them up for the trip in March 2009. They were a mixed bag of Sydneysiders and Brisbanites – a publisher, a children's book author, insurance brokers, an events coordinator and her son who had just finished school, plus Nafisa would come along to document this part of the story in art. Most were people who would probably never otherwise have met. By the end of the safari, I knew that Africa would either have made lifelong friends or enemies of them.

Two days before I was due to fly to Zambia for the start of the African shoot in mid-March, I was flattened by nausea. Leaning over the basin in the bathroom, burping and retching uncontrollably, the reason for it became clear. Two lines, clear and unmistakable. I was pregnant again. This time, after losing one, we were more cautious about our enthusiasm levels. As Andy said, we would pop the champagne after the twelve week scan. For now, the bigger worry was the fact that I was about to go to Africa for three weeks, a place not known for its high standards of hygiene, not to mention that I couldn't take any anti-malaria prophylactics and we would be there in late March, a time when there were still a lot of mosquitoes around.

I phoned Kek, who had been pregnant twice and was to me an authority on all things to do with babies. I asked her why I was feeling so sick. Surely this couldn't be right? No one would get pregnant if it was always like this.

'It's just morning sickness, Tam,' she said, as nicely as she could to a woman who has just been told she may well be ill for the next nine months. 'You're pregnant. You'll get used to it. Eat something.'

'But morning sickness is meant to happen in the mornings, isn't it? *Burp* . . . It's eight o'clock at night! Maybe this is just a virus?'

'Uh-uh, nope,' Kek said, in the kindly tone of someone who has already been through it more than once before. 'It can happen any time, sometimes all day. Just try and eat something, honestly. Dry crackers or something plain. As soon as you've got something in your stomach that should help.'

'What about drugs? These websites that say I can't take any anti-nausea medication at all are a bit over the top, aren't they?'

'I hate to tell you this but doctors won't give you anything because they don't know what effect it might have on the baby. The first few months are when the organs are developing, so it's a really important time for the growth of the baby and they don't want to be responsible if anything goes wrong.'

Early the next morning, feeling so ill that I told Andy not to worry about me going to Africa as I might well die before I even got to the airport, I headed straight for the doctor's surgery at Bondi Junction. I had no idea how I would be able to participate in the filming in this state, let alone manage a group of tourists on safari. The combination of nausea and anxiety was a killer, each compounding the other. What I needed was a nice, helpful doctor to tell me that everything was going to be okay, that my baby and I would get through this just fine as long as I looked after myself. What I wanted was a pill to stop the nausea. What I got instead was the complete A to Z of why I was an imbecile.

'You are not pregnant. It says here on the file that you miscarried,' he declared, staring at the file as though the contents of the cardboard folder knew more about my body than I did.

'Yes, I did,' I replied, like I needed reminding, 'but now I am pregnant again. I am flying to Africa tomorrow and I just need to know if there is any medication that I can take with me in case of emergencies.'

There was a long pause while the doctor took all this in. But he had only heard three words – Africa, pregnant and emergencies – and now he was on high alert.

'You miscarried,' he muttered. 'How do you know you are pregnant?'

I explained that I had done a test the day before. Two in fact. I burped violently, causing the doctor to shuffle uncomfortably in his seat.

'You cannot take anything but Panadol while you are pregnant. It is not safe for the baby. Anything else and you are putting the baby at risk.'

I had been pregnant for a day, and already I felt like a bad mother. This was not a good start.

As for malaria, the biggest risk for travellers in Africa, I would just have to cover up and use repellent, the doctor said.

'Better still, don't go to Africa until after the baby is born,' he concluded, waving me out the door.

Helpful. Now I was not only sick and anxious, I was also angry.

I left the doctor's surgery feeling significantly worse than when I had arrived. That night, packed and ready to go, still burping at regular intervals, I barely slept a wink. My stomach churned with nerves, exacerbated, no doubt, by what I would later learn was the emotional effect of pregnancy hormones. Andy, usually calm and balanced in situations when I was frazzled, was freaked out too faced as he was with the prospect of his ill wife and unborn child getting on a plane to Africa for three weeks. It was two weeks before Earth Hour, and that pressure alone was usually enough to elevate the stress levels in our house. As I waved him goodbye at the airport and headed for the line-up at customs, I was pretty sure this was the first time I had ever been to Africa feeling anxiety rather than excitement. But it was too late to turn back now.

Zambia, Botswana and Namibia, March–April 2009

Deep in the heart of Botswana's Okavango Delta, tucked into a sling bed in a small but comfortable dome tent on the banks of the Chobe River, I snuggled under my duvet and prepared myself for the opera of Africa's night. The density of wildlife in Chobe National Park was so great that I knew it wouldn't be long before I heard the deep harrumph of a lion, the eerie cry of a jackal or the *whoo-oop* of a hyena. This was one of my favourite things about being in the bush in Africa, lying in bed just listening to the night sounds. And then, the chorus began.

'Shut the f*** up, will you! I'm trying to sleep!' a woman's crackly voice exclaimed from the tent next to mine.

'Oh f*** off, Mum, and stop whingeing.'

This was supposed to be a mother and son bonding trip, but it was clear that neither mother nor son was used to spending so much quality time sharing a small dome tent in the middle of the bush and it wasn't bringing the best out in either of them.

The night chorus continued for at least twenty minutes, loud enough to scare any marauding predators off.

Finally, they settled down.

Then someone in a tent nearby started to snore. The nearest village was many kilometres away, but I was pretty sure they could hear it. I put my pillow over my ears and tried to sleep through what sounded like an earth-mover driving through the middle of camp.

Since arriving in Africa a few days earlier, I had been out with the crew filming almost constantly. We had started the filming in Livingstone, the Zambian border town at Victoria Falls, to get footage of both the conflict itself and the Elephant Pepper Development Trust's use of chilli to deter elephants from local farmers' crops. I had spent every night out in the villages with the crew trying to capture good quality images of elephants caught in the act of crop raiding, which we hadn't been able to in India. Very few film crews had obtained good footage of human-elephant conflict anywhere. Elephants tended to raid crops at night, which made filming it trickier than in the daytime, although not impossible if you had the right equipment.

The bigger challenge was that, even though the elephants were raiding crops a lot, we didn't know exactly where they would be and when on any given night. It would have been handy if our proboscidean friends had been equipped with mobile phones and could just have let us know the location and timing of a raid, because then we could easily have set up the cameras in readiness for the action. As it was, all the elephant phone lines were down and we were relying on random chance incidents. The likelihood of us being in the right place at the right time was about the same as spotting a shy, nocturnal aardwolf in the Kalahari in broad daylight. Even though we were maximising our chances by being there at the time of year when there was a lot of it happening, and by staying in farming villages that local rangers told us were currently experiencing a lot of human-elephant conflict, it really was the luck of the draw.

The nights were spent driving to potential elephant raiding sites and literally sitting in the HiLux waiting for an elephant to appear. At regular intervals a mobile phone would ring and it would be for Mr Zuma, our Zambian Wildlife Authority (ZAWA) escort, letting us know that elephants were raiding somewhere else (of course, they would be long gone by the time we got there). It was a game of sit, wait and hope for the best.

After the second long night of trying, unsuccessfully, to capture human-elephant conflict on film, we arrived back at our lodgings after midnight to find one of our safari guests half passed out outside the room, his head and face covered in blood. The guy looked like he had had a serious run-in with a honey badger. My first thought was where on earth I would find a doctor at that time of night in Livingstone. I had a first aid kit in my luggage, but his injuries looked beyond the healing powers of that. Had he been attacked by someone while we were out? The man was slurring and not making much sense. The producer, who was a friend of his, soon worked out that the guy had drunk too much whiskey and had walked into a wall. Before I could think any further about finding a doctor, he had passed out again.

By the third night, the crew were growing uneasy about the fact that we still hadn't been able to capture any human-elephant conflict on film. The area around Livingstone was the place where my conservation colleagues had told me we were most likely to succeed. If we didn't get footage in one of the villages there, we probably wouldn't anywhere else, and without it, the film would be missing a vital component of the story.

So on the third night, when we did, by some miracle, happen to be near a farm where an elephant bull was trying to enter a maize field just after dark, the crew sprang into action as if they had just been poked with an electric prod. Mr Zuma had asked the villagers in that area to allow any elephant that entered their crop to eat a few plants so the crew could film it. The local farmers agreed to this, on the condition that the producer compensate any affected farmer with a bag of maize meal or the equivalent of what was eaten or trampled by the elephant. The reality was, if the crew didn't set this up, the film would never be able to show how elephants damaged crops.

All these years of watching wildlife documentaries and I had always thought that the cameras simply filmed what unfolded naturally. It was a revelation to me how much had to be 'constructed' in order for a story to be told on film. I was learning a lot about how to tell a story through the lens of a camera, and it was an entirely different process from writing a book: both presented a narrative, but film-making was more about 'showing' than 'telling', making sure that you had all the visual components so that your audience went on the journey with you.

The cameras rolled as the conflict unfolded before our eyes. A raiding bull was eating maize plants, and the farmer had come out of his hut and was banging on a drum to try and get the elephant out of his crop. The ranger let the scene unfold for a few minutes before shooting his rifle into the air. The drumming had had little effect on the bull's foraging, but the gunshot did the trick and the elephant moved off quickly. The conflict was all over in less than ten minutes and, I noticed, with a lot less of the crazy violence and drama of the elephant raids in Assam.

In Zambia, as in many other parts of Africa, it was a matter of individual villagers fending off elephants with drums and fires, and the elephants were mostly individual bulls, whereas in India, men went out in huge gangs armed with fire spears and homemade guns to push entire breeding herds of elephants out of the paddies. Zambia's human density was markedly lower than Assam's, at fewer than twenty people per square kilometre compared with Assam's several hundred, perhaps accounting for the different levels of intensity of conflict. But Zambia had a lot more elephants than Assam, around the twenty thousand mark compared to Assam's five thousand or so.

But right next door to Zambia was a country with even more elephants, tens of thousands more, in fact. Botswana was an important country for the film because it had more elephants than any other country in the world, somewhere in the realm of 130,000. With all those elephants much higher than average levels of human-elephant conflict might have resulted, and it certainly had problems on that front, but not as many as might be expected. Botswana was a big country, of which about seventy per cent was desert. Sparsely populated, its human population of about two million over such a vast space gave the country a population density of fewer than three people per square kilometre. The high value placed on ecotourism in the national economy, especially the kind that paid communities dividends, made it economically viable for many people to conserve elephants through wildlife-based tourism and not be entirely dependent on agriculture. It was a successful development model both for conservation and community development. There was also the stable political situation and the country's wealth by African standards, both factors that must have aided wildlife conservation in general. A key influence had to be the relatively high value of the national currency, the pula. The Botswana government was one of just a few African countries rich enough to pay hundreds of thousands of pula in compensation to local farmers who were negatively affected by elephants every year.

We were going to Botswana to film Chobe National Park's famously large population of elephants and also to hear from two experts on elephants in this part of the world, Elephants Without Borders' scientist Dr Mike Chase and his partner Kelly Landon. Headquartered in an unostentatious office near their house on the outskirts of Kasane, a few kilometres' drive from the borders of Namibia and Zambia, Mike and Kelly were conducting the largest study of radio-collared and satellite-collared elephants that had ever been attempted. They were following elephants crossing up to four countries in one season, covering much bigger territories than previously thought and continuing to expand in range.

What had begun as Mike's PhD study of northern Botswana's elephants had grown way beyond that, extending into the neighbouring countries of Zambia, Namibia, Angola and Zimbabwe. Mike and Kelly's research revealed that northern Botswana's elephants were actually part of a much larger, contiguous population of elephants across the southern African region, an area that was part of the emerging Kavango-Zambezi (KAZA) Transfrontier Conservation Area that Dr John Hanks had first drawn my attention to years earlier when I was working on human-elephant conflict in north-eastern Namibia. The KAZA was an ambitious project, bringing five governments together around a table to discuss the future of both its human and animal inhabitants. The idea behind it was that it would lift people out of poverty while also providing a safe haven for wildlife, in particular the world's largest elephant population. This was an important part of the bigger elephant story and so I was really pleased when Mike and Kelly agreed to spend a couple of days with the crew showing us their work and being interviewed.

Mike was humble and unassuming, not at all what I expected of an elephant researcher with such a large mandate, while Kelly was a strong, well-spoken American woman who clearly shared Mike's passion and played a pivotal role in their operation. As we sat at a table outside their house, Mike was every bit the diligent, passionate scientist as he shared his research findings with me on his laptop. I leaned over to look in detail at the comprehensive digital maps of the elephant home ranges across the southern African subregion.

'You see,' Mike said, pointing to one particular elephant home range which zigzagged across the borders of Namibia and Botswana, 'elephants don't have passports. They cross international boundaries all the time.'

I could see how elephants in Namibia's Caprivi strip moved down into Khaudum National Park, just north of my own previous study site where I had worked on human-elephant conflict with the Bushmen. These maps made it impossible for any country to truly claim ownership of these elephants because 'Botswana's elephants', for example, moved seasonally through Namibia into Angola, or east into Zimbabwe's Hwange National Park, and so could have been claimed by any of those countries depending on the season. Elephants were a natural resource shared between countries and the repercussions of that for their management were substantial. It meant that the development of the Kavango-Zambezi Transfrontier Conservation Area across these five countries was essential and that joint management by all five nations would be a key part of the survival of elephants in this region.

But the most exciting result from these findings was the evidence of elephants moving back into Angola. Angola had been a no-go area for elephants for decades because of the long civil war, which meant that much of the rural land was scattered with landmines, maiming people and elephants. Elephants soon learned that it wasn't safe to go there anymore, and simply stayed south of the border. Now, with the end of the war and extensive efforts to remove the landmines in south-eastern Angola, some of Mike and Kelly's satellite-collared elephants were returning.

This was really exciting news because it meant that a whole lot of former elephant habitat would now open up and take some pressure off the burgeoning populations in places like Botswana and Zimbabwe. In a time when habitat destruction was the norm, now we were seeing habitat resurrection on a grand scale, a rare event in this day and age. The south-eastern corner of Angola would be part of the emerging Kavango-Zambezi Transfrontier Conservation Area, enabling people living there to benefit from all sorts of wildlife-based economic initiatives in the future.

While the crew filmed Mike and Kelly at work radio tracking elephants, Steve asked me to spend some time with the safari group on a game drive. After all the long days and nights being out with the crew filming, I was happy to have a little down time. It also wouldn't be a bad thing to keep an eye on certain members of the group. A couple of days earlier, when a few of them had taken a game drive in one of our hired HiLuxes while I was elsewhere, the teenage boy had taken it upon himself to walk up to a herd of irascible Cape buffalo, which, while looking like a glorified cow, is actually one of the most dangerous animals you can encounter in the African bush. I was horrified when this story was relayed to me. I wasn't sure what was worse – the boy not knowing how dangerous that situation was, or knowing and just showing off. Either way, he had been lucky, but I didn't want him trying any stupid moves like that with any other animals.

Being the wet season, Chobe was still quite moist and green and there were literally elephants everywhere. At every turn, it seemed, a herd would appear. These elephants were relaxed in Chobe's safe and plentiful environment, obviously aware that tourist vehicles posed no kind of threat and carrying on with their natural behaviours around us. It was incredible and I could have spent hours just watching them. Most of the group felt the same way, but the sentiment wasn't unanimous.

'Oh no, not another bloody elephant! Where are the lions?' one woman exclaimed, clearly unimpressed.

'Look, baby baboons!' I exclaimed back, sighting some cute youngsters playing on a log.

If the hilarious antics of baby baboons didn't amuse this woman then nothing would. The rest of the group clicked away on their cameras, ecstatic to be capturing such great, close-up footage of Africa's wildlife.

After a few minutes, a solitary voice broke the silence: 'Is it time for a drink yet?'

Back at Baobab Camp, this particular woman was finally happy once she had downed a few strong gins and tonic, later on providing the best entertainment the camp staff had seen for a long time by dancing and doing headstands on the table.

It was harmless fun, and I'd heard of plenty of crazier things happening on safari, but it reinforced the reason why I could never be a good tourist guide, and why I have so much respect for those who do this for a living. For me, much as I wanted others to be spellbound by Africa and viscerally immerse themselves in its wonders, I loved being in the bush on my own, or just with one or two other people who shared my passion for it. I was a wildlife nerd. But on this trip, probably due to the pregnancy hormones giving me something akin to permanent PMS, my patience was thinner than usual.

I seemed to get increasingly tired as each day went by, reaching a level of exhaustion I had never experienced before. First trimester tiredness seemed to gnaw at my bones and all I really wanted to do was curl up on a bed in the tent and rest. I was constantly burping and retching, and tried my best to hide it from the group, who probably just thought I was extremely impolite. I felt like a social reject being unable to drink and having to go to bed early each night, and I knew that my behaviour stood out in a group whose other members were all on their trip of a lifetime and making the most of the camp bar. But I knew that with each bit of filming we did we were one step closer to having the footage we needed to tell Africa's side of the human-elephant story. And I was glad that I stuck it out, because one of the scenes the crew managed to film stayed with me for a long time, capturing in a nutshell the reality of life for modern-day elephants.

It was about 8 pm and dark as we sat in the HiLuxes by a waterhole and salt lick just a few kilometres from the Elephants Without Borders' base on the outskirts of town. A few hundred metres away was a highway, the main route linking the town of Kasane, only about a kilometre away, with the border post. I watched cars and trucks whizz past at high speed, their headlights beaming up the road into the darkness. And then came the elephants, ethereal grey wraiths bathed in harsh artificial light.

A stretch of several hundred metres across the highway was right in the migration path of every elephant in the vicinity, drawn by the water and the salt in the pan. They would come through all night, Mike told us, in the relative protection of darkness. I watched breeding herds with small babies run across the road, their giant bodies lit up by the headlights of cars as they crossed. A solitary bull stood on the road some distance back, blocking traffic while another herd of females with youngsters crossed. Soon there were dozens of elephants at the salt lick, perhaps a hundred or more, and the highway simply had to be traversed to get there. Here in the middle of Africa, a town and a national park converged on the borders of three other countries, and jostling for space to cross a highway thick with vehicles were elephants in their hundreds. To me, this was the face of the human-elephant conflict in Africa. People and elephants simply had to find a way to coexist. There was no other choice.

From Botswana, and the modern-day African challenge of managing a large and growing population of elephants, we headed to Namibia's Caprivi strip to film the long-reigning Chief Mayuni, a local hero in conservation. The Integrated Rural Development and Nature Conservation's (IRDNC) Richard Diggle was my contact in this part of the world. The Caprivi wasn't the sort of place where a film crew and a bunch of Australian tourists could just pitch up and say g'day. It was an incredibly traditional place where chiefs ruled and ancient laws set the tone.

Richard explained how Chief Mayuni had taken the human-elephant conflict problem into his own hands in this part of the Caprivi. His village had been on the banks of a riverbed where elephants frequently came to drink and feed, causing irreparable damage to his community's crops. Quite sensibly, the chief decided that rather than making the elephants move (by calling on the Ministry for the Environment and Tourism to remove or cull them), it made more sense for the village to move, and so he convinced his community to rebuild their village away from the river. By taking the initiative and relocating away from the problem rather than fighting back against the elephants, the chief became a role model in conservation circles.

I was excited to meet this local icon, but also a little nervous. Richard explained that there were certain formalities we would have to adhere to in his presence. His hut was a royal area and any visitors were allowed by invitation only. It was like visiting the Queen of England – except this monarch would be dressed in leopard skins. We would have to kneel before entering the area outside his mud and brick house, which was surrounded by a solid wall, and wait to be asked in by his minders. When we were in there, the tradition was that before speaking you had to clap your hands. The chief always spoke first. Women had to be completely covered up and long pants were not acceptable, which meant wrapping a sarong around my legs, covering my long cargo pants. Apparently, all symbols of female independence were considered offensive. By the time Richard finished telling us about all these preparations, I had begun to feel very unworthy of the chief's attention and much more nervous than before.

'Are you ready?' Richard asked Steve and me as we approached the royal hut.

'Ready as we'll ever be!' Steve replied jokingly, and I nodded anxiously.

The three of us and Nafisa went first, with Greg and Kenny filming us from behind. I hitched up my sarong and knelt down at the entrance to the hut, then waited for the command to enter. Two men came out and beckoned us in. I wasn't sure if one of them was the chief but, judging by the way they ushered us to a circle of chairs, I guessed they were his assistants.

'He will be here soon,' Richard said in hushed, reverential tones.

We waited for several minutes before the chief appeared, resplendent in his leopard-skin hat and pressed suit. We all stood as he entered. Inappropriate as it might have been, I wanted to shout, 'All hail the chief!' but I kept my mouth shut. People probably got speared for doing things like that here in the Caprivi.

I clapped my hands twice before I spoke, feeling like I should follow it up with a rendition of the hokey-pokey. But this was a formal discussion, and there would be no random dancing here – unless, of course, the chief kicked it off. He looked mildly nonplussed by it all, less interested in our questions about elephants than in the video cameras filming him.

During the hour or so that we were engaged in our discussion with the chief about human-elephant conflict, Nafisa had been busily drawing his portrait. As we all got up to leave, she asked if she could approach him to present it. The chief's face beamed when he saw what she had produced. It was an incredible portrait with an unmistakable likeness, and it was clear that the sitter was struck both by Nafisa's artistry and by his own handsomeness.

Before we left the Caprivi, there was one very important thing we had to do. On the opposite side of the world my husband was heading up what was about to be the second record global Earth Hour. The campaign that had begun in Sydney now involved eighty-eight countries and more than four thousand cities worldwide, ten times the number of cities as the year before. At a petrol station in a nearby town I picked up the national newspaper, *The Namibian*, which had Earth Hour on the front page. I was astonished. Here I was at a petrol station in a remote, rural area in the middle of Africa, picking up a newspaper in which the campaign that Andy's small team had started just two years ago was the lead article.

Then the cameraman, Greg, said to me, 'I just got a text about Earth Hour from WWF, Tam. Is that your hubby?'

I felt incredibly proud of Andy and wished that I could share the moment with him. A few of us decided that we had to do something to celebrate Earth Hour, despite our extremely remote location. Greg and Kenny grabbed their gear, Nafisa gathered up her art equipment and the four of us shot out to a hippo pond at sunset to spend an hour contemplating the beauty of our planet. Moments like these were rare, taking time to just stop, think and talk about how we could make our lives more sustainable, how we could, in our own lives, help to turn things around for wildlife. This was really what Earth Hour was about – the conversation.

Like all things that are successful, Earth Hour had received its share of criticism. Some said it was purely symbolic and did little to nothing to save energy. They were right about that, but they were completely missing the point. Earth Hour wasn't just about turning out the lights and saving energy. It never had been. It was about taking that time to talk about these issues with family and friends, creating a global interconnected community that could create real, unified change on all sorts of issues related to living in harmony with the planet we all share.

As we sat by the pond listening to the insects and the frogs and the hippos honking, it really sank in how much we all need to take that time to think about what we are doing to the planet. If we don't do that soon, there won't be anything left to save. It isn't just the wildlife that will be in trouble if we don't change our ways. Humanity is well on its way towards its own suicide. Most people living in cities are completely disconnected from the natural world that provides everything we need to survive. In a beautiful natural setting like that African pond at sunset, it all made complete sense, but I realised that many people didn't have the luxury of that reflective time in such an awe-inspiring environment. An hour to stop and think at Earth Hour – no matter where you were – was the beginning of a bigger conversation that we needed to have across the planet before it was too late.

After a few days in the Caprivi, our two heavily loaded HiLuxes headed in the direction of Rundu to overnight at a camp on the Okavango River. This mighty river, which originates in Angola (as the Cubango River), drains through Namibia's northeast before ending up in Botswana's Okavango Delta. We were headed to Kaisosi Camp, seven kilometres east of the town of Rundu, where the river formed the boundary between Angola in the north and Namibia in the south.

Unlike most of the other places we were visiting for the documentary, I had never been to this camp and only had some rough instructions for getting there. I had lost sight of Steve's HiLux, which had the crew in it, so I presumed that he had seen the turnoff to the camp and gone on ahead. The only problem with this scenario was that after a short while of driving down the gravel road, it disappeared into the Okavango River. Being late wet season, it was still raining in Angola and the river had swollen up over its banks and literally swallowed up the road. There was no sign of a camp anywhere in sight; nothing but fast-flowing water and the tops of trees and bushes caught up in its swirling force.

I got out of the car and assessed the situation carefully. I had a vehicle full of paying tourists who I wasn't keen to put at any kind of risk. It was impossible to tell how high the water was and whether it was running too fast for the HiLux to avoid being swept downstream. I knew the Okavango River was full of crocodiles and hippos, animals that regularly killed people in this part of the world. This was one place you didn't want to go for a leisurely swim, or even wade in to see how deep the water was. I waited there for a little while, hoping that someone from the camp would turn up to tell me whether it was safe to go on. But no one did, and after twenty minutes, I knew I had to make a decision.

I could see roughly where the road was probably supposed to go by the open water in the gap between the trees. Theoretically, if I just followed that I would eventually end up in camp – assuming we didn't get swept away. The only problem was that I didn't know how far the camp was from where we were standing. It might have been just around the corner, a few hundred metres away, or it might have been a couple of kilometres away. The water might have been shallow all the way, or completely the opposite.

I took a deep breath and mustered my courage. 'What do you think, guys?' I asked the group. 'Should we do it?'

There was resounding agreement from my passengers, who apparently had more faith in my ability to get them through this predicament than I did, or perhaps they were simply spurred on by the prospect of a refreshing cider at the other end of a long drive. So I engaged low ratio 4 x 4, put the car into second gear, began to recite a silent prayer, and plunged into the shallows of what I hoped was the road. I wouldn't be able to turn around once I started, so this was a one-way track to somewhere, even if it meant floating downstream into the town of Rundu in a HiLux doubling as a dinghy.

I knew from driving 4 x 4s in fast-flowing water in other parts of Africa that I needed to maintain a little bit of speed to go against the current, so I kept the engine's revs high and my foot firmly on the accelerator. At first the water was fairly shallow, just covering the tyres. Although my heart was racing, I knew we would be okay if it stayed at this height. But a few hundred metres down this ever deeper river-road, it was taking all of my concentration to focus on remaining in the gap between the trees as the water began to rise. In it came, drenching my boots and splashing up onto the bonnet. Mechanical things were not my strong suit. I could change a tyre, should the need arise, but I had no idea what happened when a HiLux's engine was saturated like this. Would it just cut out, leaving us stranded in the river, or, even worse, without any acceleration, floating downriver? Water was now flowing amply over the bonnet of the car and I was saying prayers quicker than a nun on Good Friday. I tried to look calm and collected as I didn't want to distress the tour group, but this situation was way outside my control and no sign of the camp was in sight. I didn't even know if we were still on the road. The HiLux was on the verge of becoming a boat.

Just hold your foot down, Matson, and keep it there, a little voice in my head said. *Keep your cool.* There was no choice now but to plunge on through the rising waters. Ignoring my soaking feet, I just kept my foot planted hard on the accelerator and tried to smile with more confidence than I felt. The current was strong, causing the HiLux to keel slightly towards the passenger side. In my wildest dreams I had never imagined that the camp would be this far away from dry land; we seemed to have been driving through the river for at least five minutes. It felt like five days.

And then, defying all odds, as suddenly as it had risen the water began to drop. A cheer rang out from my passengers, reflecting my own enormous relief as an apparition appeared – the thatched-roof entrance to the camp. I thanked all the gods of rivers and HiLuxes that I could think of and it took every bone in my body to resist the urge to kiss the ground underfoot. A close inspection of the contents in the back of the HiLux showed that, amazingly, the only things that were wet were the HiLux and my feet. All of our luggage was completely dry, despite the water that had surrounded it up until a few minutes ago. It hadn't leaked into the cabin at all.

Geez, I sighed inwardly, still slightly nauseous from anxiety. If it was that hard getting to this camp, what on earth was tomorrow going to be like? Driving through a swelling river was one thing, but I knew the next day would bring an even bigger challenge – eleven hours of serious soft-sand 4 x 4 driving on a track that few attempted. The northern track from Rundu to Khaudum National Park wasn't on most tourist maps because it was known locally as the road through hell. The only reason I knew about it was that my old friend Dries Alberts, the government warden of this area, had told me about it. When I asked him if he thought I would be able to handle it, he had been too polite to say no, but he had added a number of cautionary notes along these lines: *If you break down there, no one will find you. The area is full of lions and elephants, so chances are if you do get found eventually it will only be your bones. But don't worry, Tammie, I'm sure you'll be fine.*

I had never driven this route before, so I was privately nervous about it. It would be a long drive for the tour group even if we didn't get bogged. I wasn't sure they would all be up for it. But this was by far the fastest way from Rundu to Tsumkwe, the small town that functioned as the capital of Bushmanland, avoiding a much longer route around the national park on tar and gravel roads. This route would take us through the Khaudum National Park, so although it would be rough riding, there was the incentive of possibly seeing some elephants and other wildlife. Dries agreed to meet us at the northern camp in Khaudum and to escort us from there through the park down to Tsumkwe.

Once we got through the first part of the drive and joined Dries, this was the part of the trip that I had most been looking forward to. It had been a couple of years since I had seen Dries and his partner Stacey, friends from when I worked in Bushmanland on human-elephant conflict. I was told that my former translator and son of the chief of Bushmanland, Leon, was now working at the Tsumkwe Lodge guiding tourists for a living. I was excited about being back in this special part of Africa and seeing my old friends. It felt a little like going home.

I took off first, with Steve's HiLux behind me, turning off the tar road near Rundu and onto an almost nonexistent sandy track with a blink-and-you'll-miss-it sign to the national park. A little overzealous, I put my HiLux into low ratio 4 x 4 and set off. I could tell immediately that we weren't going to get very far. Even at speed, the HiLux was struggling not to sink into the soft sand, and within a hundred metres, we were bogged. Steve's HiLux charged up behind us, revealing the gloating grins of the all-male crew.

'Bogged already, Tam? That didn't take you long.'

In my enthusiasm to get started on the long drive I had forgotten to take some air out of the tyres. I swallowed my pride, and started letting the tyres down. As soon as that was done, we were on our way, driving in second and third gear at most, riding on the sand like a boat on undulating waves. The journey went smoothly after that, with my HiLux full of girls singing mad freedom songs as we barged over some of the roughest tracks in the country, miles from civilisation. Many hours later, Khaudum Camp appeared around a bend in the track and there was Dries, chatting nonchalantly to his staff next to his official Ministry for the Environment and Tourism LandCruiser.

I handed over the keys of my HiLux to Kenny and jumped in Dries' vehicle, looking forward to a catch-up after so long away. It wasn't until we reached a waterhole a couple of hours later that I realised that Kenny wasn't driving my HiLux. Nafisa was. And her female passengers (the ones who had been joyfully singing freedom songs a short while ago) were now as stern-faced as bullfrogs in a drought. They looked like angry pandas ready for kung-fu, their make-up smothered beneath layers of dust from Dries' LandCruiser, leaving white circles where their sunglasses had shielded their eyes.

Not having driven in this kind of environment before, Nafisa hadn't known that you have to stay a long way back behind the vehicle in front of you to avoid swallowing all of its dust. Either that, or she'd just felt the need for speed behind the wheel of one of Africa's most fun off-road vehicles. Suffice it to say, there was a grim-faced rush for the showers when we finally reached the lodge in Tsumkwe, followed by an equally rapid rush for the bar.

Over the next couple of days, the crew filmed the large flocks of flamingoes in the Nyae Nyae pans south of Khaudum National Park. The birds came there seasonally to raise their chicks, providing a pink and white spectacle that dazzled the eyes on the glaring hot pan. The crew also interviewed people like Dries, who had seen so much of the history of this area and played a massive role in its conservation, and arranged to film a special dance by the Bushmen, which brought back so many memories of drifting off to sleep on a swag in my tent while listening to the locals sing at the nearby village. Hearing the singers made me nostalgic for the life I had once had in Bushmanland, as well as aware of just how much things had changed. Only a few years earlier, I was based in a one-bedroom flat in Windhoek and spent most of my time in a HiLux or a Land Rover traversing this great desert land, cooking Afrikaans sausages (*boerwors*) and gem squashes over a campfire, falling asleep to the beat of African drums and Bushmen singing.

After almost three weeks filming across southern Africa, I felt like my feet hadn't touched the ground. I had never had such a mad experience of Africa as I did on this trip. An incident one morning at breakfast pretty much summed up the lunacy of it when Nafisa appeared, parading around the camp with a chameleon balanced precariously on her head.

'Look at me, Steve! Look!'

Half of the group was too hungover to care. A few looked up and watched her antics with mild curiosity, their expressions bemused, like they were watching a hyena trying to mate with a honey badger. The rest of us just focused on our eggs.

I had given up trying to keep the peace by now. It was better to split the tourists up into different HiLuxes. On the bright side, the mother and son who had been about to kill each other initially had actually bonded and seemed to be treating each other with a new respect. Now, as the trip neared its end, I just longed to stop and breathe Africa in, to spend some time chewing the cud with Stacey and Dries and Leon about old times, to smell the campfire smoke. I wanted to be completely selfish about being in Africa, to not share it with anyone, to not have to convince anyone of its pure, unadulterated majesty. But there just wasn't time. And to my own enormous disappointment, when Dries and Stacey came to camp for dinner on the last night, I could barely keep my eyes open. I wished I could tell them why I was so tired, to share this secret that would explain why I wasn't myself. I would only learn later that Stacey had a secret that she didn't know herself then either – in her early forties, she was pregnant too.

The next morning, feeling a little short-changed and mentally preparing to pack my bag to head for Windhoek and my flight out the next day, I blundered into the shower. That was when I discovered a rapidly enlarging black tick in the vicinity of my nether region.

'Oh crap, I've got a pepper tick!' I exclaimed, more to myself than anyone else.

It must have crawled onto me when I was sitting under a leadwood tree during my interview the day before. Any tree which provided shade in the bush attracted wild and domestic animals in the heat of the day, making it a hot spot for parasites like ticks. As I tried to work out how to get it out, I wondered whether a tick might affect my baby. The stinging warnings of that awful doctor in Sydney who'd made me feel like a bad mother just three weeks earlier sprang to mind. *God, maybe I am a bad mother already!*

Before I could chastise myself further, Nafisa burst into the bathroom where I was standing stark naked. I shrieked and reached for a towel. Friends we might have been, but even so it was a bit early on in the relationship for a complete strip show for this Catholic-raised prude.

'Where is it!?' she exclaimed, with something akin to glee, clearly hoping for the opportunity to put her three years of medical school into practice.

To my horror, she bent down to investigate at close range. I pulled the towel around me and leaned back, almost tripping over and into the toilet in an effort to escape.

'I'm going next door to get one of the boys to help,' she declared, running out of the shower and into the room next door before I had time to protest.

'Nafisa, no! I'm fine!' I called after her, locking myself in the shower.

After three weeks in the bush (so to speak), a delicate shave was in order to pull this small creature off its new home in my lady garden. Very gently, I began to shave around it. The body of the tick was tiny at this stage, but its head was well and truly lodged in my skin and couldn't just be pulled out without leaving the head in there. It had to go. Ticks in this part of the world could cause horrendous diseases like tick bite fever if left unattended.

I could hear Nafisa in the room next door, telling the boys what was going on, and I could also detect their hesitation to become involved in what was clearly 'women's business'. In a panic, I shaved it off by accident before anyone else had a chance to investigate, and astonishingly, the head of the tick appeared to have come out too.

The death of the tick also heralded the end of the filming in Africa. For producer Steve, it meant the start of the process of finding the money to go into post-production and complete the editing stage. For Nafisa, it was the start of a whole new artistic cycle, creating the elephant artworks inspired by the trips to India and Africa. Her plan was to donate the proceeds of this art to elephant conservation. And for me, it was the beginning of a different kind of journey, one in which I would have to learn to be okay with no longer being in control of the steering wheel. Having spent the best part of my twenties in Africa, you would think that letting go of control would have been second nature to me by then. Well it turned out that I still had a bit to learn.

CHAPTER 4

HELLO BABY, GOODBYE BRAIN

Sydney, June 2009

At four months pregnant, I was a pear on steroids. My thighs had exploded while my stomach hadn't yet grown enough to look noticeably pregnant. A kind observer might have described me as 'just a little bit fat' – but that was the least of my worries. Much more disturbingly, I was losing my brain. My precious cerebral matter seemed to have been sucked down through my body and deposited in my lower half. That would explain the thighs. That, and the bucketloads of Cheezels I was craving. I recall thinking what a godsend it was that I wasn't an elephant; compared to my nine months of pregnancy, elephants had to deal with almost two years!

Lost in my thoughts, one day I drove down to the local Blockbuster DVD store in my ancient Barry Barina (also known as The Silver Bullet) to get some afternoon entertainment that didn't involve alcohol. We clearly didn't need two cars now that I wasn't working away from home but, in a last ditch attempt to keep what remained of my independence, I was clinging on to Barry, who had been with me since I returned from Africa two years earlier. I knew it was a bit silly and really not good for the environment to keep him, given that Andy and I could easily share a car, but if I let Barry go, I figured I was entering the land of complete marital dependency, a prospect that scared me more than a drooling, rabid honey badger in my kitchen having a conversation with a deadly black mamba. *That* much. Several days later, we drove past the Blockbuster in Andy's Subaru on our way to the beach.

'Isn't that your car, babe?' Andy enquired, pointing out a silver Barina parked out the front of the DVD store.

I glanced at it momentarily. It did look like mine.

'There're a few around here. It must be someone else's,' I replied with complete confidence. 'It's not mine.'

'Babe,' Andy said, in a gently amused tone of voice, 'it's yours. It's got Queensland *Smart State* plates.'

'Oh my God . . . '

Andy burst out laughing.

Earlier that week, I had accused him of using up all the butter, only to find it, a day later, completely melted in the third drawer down in the kitchen, along with the cling wrap and the tea towels. God only knows why, but I must have put it there. Andy was as perplexed by my random acts of forgetfulness as I was. His wife – at least the girl he married just a few months earlier – was super-organised, efficient and in control of every aspect of life, from paying the electricity bill on time to developing strategies for the conservation of endangered species. This imposter in my body had driven to the DVD store and walked home, leaving behind her car for several days in a one-hour parking spot. To this day I don't know how it wasn't towed away. Then I would really have been confused. I probably would have phoned the police to register a stolen vehicle. Sheepishly, I pulled the keys out of my bag, got out of the Subaru and retrieved Barry from outside the DVD store, before driving him home in a haze of mystification and shame.

Soon after I left my job at WWF, the goalposts shifted. The world was shaken by the global financial crisis and charities had to buckle down, cut budgets and retrench staff. At about the same time, after more than a decade of John Howard's Liberal leadership, Labor's Kevin 07 took the helm of Australian federal politics. Even though I thought that was a good thing for the country, it was disastrous for the species program at WWF. The Threatened Species Network had been completely funded by the Liberal federal government and it was one of the first things to go under the new government. Although we had made provisions for alternative funding sources from corporations and trusts, these didn't materialise after I left, and within a few months most of my former staff were on the street looking for jobs. Even if I had wanted to go back to WWF at some point, that option was no longer open.

I had been so busy for so long that I had forgotten how to live at a normal, more sedate pace in which there was time to breathe, to think and to simply be. And so, with the book written and the filming complete, I suddenly had a whole lot of time on my hands. That should have been a good thing, but rarely do we A-type personalities embrace such periods with the enthusiasm they deserve. Instead, I began to worry.

I started to think about the prominent women working in the male-dominated field of African conservation that I had known over the years, women like Save the Rhino Foundation founder Blythe Loutit, the Cheetah Conservation Foundation's Laurie Marker, and the Turgwe Hippo Trust's Karen Paolillo in Zimbabwe, and others whose names I had been in awe of as an aspiring conservationist, women like Dian Fossey, Cynthia Moss, Joyce Poole and Jane Goodall. And then something significant struck me. I realised that they generally had one thing in common – very few had children. I don't know why I hadn't noticed this before. I began to wonder if the grand passion of conservation seemed largely incompatible with family life, at least for women.

Self-doubt crept in through a crack in the door, an unwelcome visitor that nonetheless made itself comfortable on my couch. What would make *me* more able to juggle both than these amazing female pioneers? Were the issues all that different now for female conservationists than they had been fifty years earlier? By falling pregnant, had I just committed career suicide, resulting in the end of my work in the field and the start of a life of mundane office work? Fifty years after the feminist movement gave women so many more options, had we really come that far in conservation?

Perhaps African wild dogs had it sussed, I mused. They didn't give all females the *choice* to reproduce. In African wild dog society, generally only one female in the pack has the babies – the alpha female. The rest of the pack operates as babysitters, keeping the pups safe from predators, and as hunters, providing food for them. When the hunters return from a successful kill, they will provide the mother and pups with freshly regurgitated meat.

In truth, I appreciated all the choices that feminism had brought about for women like me, even if those choices made my life more complicated. It just didn't seem fair that it was still only women who had to make them. There were plenty of studies showing how married men tended to have higher incomes than their single counterparts, compared with a negative or nil effect of marriage on women's salaries. A career in science particularly affected choices around family life, according to a 2011 study of 2,500 scientists. It showed that twice as many women scientists as men had fewer children than they wanted as a result of what was perceived as the constraints that their scientific careers imposed on family life.

With a baby on the way and Andy going great guns in his career, now coordinating Earth Hour globally, I couldn't exactly just run off to Africa and find a job there like I would have in the past. In any case, in a few months' time the airlines and insurance companies wouldn't let me travel anyway. I could have started applying for conservation jobs at other Australian organisations in Sydney, but my heart wasn't in it the way it was with African conservation. I knew I wouldn't be able to do as much travelling after the baby was born, and that, combined with the level of time commitment required when working in a senior role for an environmental charity, was going to make it very hard to juggle both roles well.

Unable to see a clear way forward, I decided to do something totally different for a while. I started doing some course development for Macquarie University, putting together the background materials for their first undergraduate Science Communication unit, which would be led by the well-known climate scientist, Tim Flannery. There was a job up for grabs lecturing the subject when it was done, but I hit a snag there too. The start date coincided almost exactly with when my baby was due, making it pretty much impossible for me to go for it.

The more time on my own I had to think about my job prospects in Sydney, the worse I felt. A persistent little voice in my head just wouldn't shut up. *What have you given up for this? Was it really a normal life you wanted? What about the adventures, the freedom, the career you love, working with animals in the wild?* At that point, all these things seemed like they belonged in the past. And that was a very big problem, because I wasn't sure I could live without them. I had to keep working as a wildlife conservationist somehow, but how could I constantly travel to the back of beyond where the wildlife was with a baby in tow? How could I work in places where hazards like elephants and lions were part of the job? How would our fledgling marriage survive that time apart? How would we survive if I didn't?

I was terrified of becoming a statistic, but for the first time in my life, I felt powerless to change my fate. I was four months up the duff and it seemed like my life was over. I had to find a way to keep my hand in wildlife conservation that wasn't going to compromise my ability to be a good mother.

Finally, I did what I had learned many years ago in Zimbabwe – I stopped complaining and made a plan. If I couldn't be working on the ground in Africa, the next best thing was helping from afar. Around the middle of 2009 the idea to start a small conservation organisation came about, the aim of which would be to raise funds for and awareness of conservation, focusing on human-elephant conflict. Nafisa had produced dozens of beautiful elephant artworks from her trips with the film crew and she wanted to donate the profits to elephant conservation. I wanted to start something that could enable donations to be taken in Australia for the projects I knew were making a difference on the ground in India and Africa, as well as being a vehicle to spread the word about what was happening to elephants and other species throughout their range.

At the same time, after filming human-elephant conflict in India and southern Africa, Steve was struggling to find the funding to commence the post-production stage of the film, and as he started to take on new projects, I was beginning to worry that after all our hard work, he wasn't going to attract enough funding to get it to air. Someone suggested that linking the film to a charity might make it more attractive to donors so, in October 2009, a month before I was due to give birth, Nafisa, Steve and I launched the organisation, which we called Animal Works, at an event at Sydney's Arthouse Hotel. Wilderness Safaris together with Epic Private Journeys in Brisbane generously donated a safari that we used in an online competition in the lead-up to the night to raise over $6000. Nafisa's detailed elephant artworks were displayed around the venue and we showed the crowd of about three hundred people the short trailer of what we hoped would become the film 'Elephant Wars'. Although no artworks were sold on the night, the event raised enough funds to kick-start the organisation which, as a result, was able to provide a large donation to the Wildlife Trust of India's orphanage in Assam.

Encouraged by the funds raised during the first event, I started the time-consuming process of applying to register Animal Works as an Australian not-for-profit organisation and to have it listed with the Tax Office so that donations would be tax deductible. Professional website designer and volunteer, Kathrin Longhurst and I worked together to develop the organisation's website, using Nafisa's art to illustrate it. We established a small committee and the organisation's mission of making conservation everybody's business. The elephant art was put up for sale on the website and I started building a community of supporters and followers on Facebook and Twitter, linked to my own Facebook site. Then, having got the ball rolling with Animal Works, my contractions began in earnest.

November 2009

'I . . . can't . . . It's . . . too . . . much . . . ' I panted, as another contraction threatened to kill me.

'Come on, babe,' Andy encouraged me calmly, as he had been doing now for almost thirty-six hours of labour. 'You're almost there.'

By the time our son's little head appeared, covered in dark brown hair, I was so exhausted that I didn't care if I lived or died. I never, ever wanted to give birth again. How on earth did women do it once, let alone go back and do it again?

Andy had tears in his eyes as he cut the cord and the doctor put our son on my chest. We had decided to call him Sol, which was a shortened version of Solomon and means 'the sun' in Latin, but from the beginning he was known as Solo. Immediately I was overcome with an intense sense of protectiveness towards him, a feeling that would grow even stronger in the days to come. I had never felt anything like it before. There was fierceness in this mother love, complete with the knowledge that if anyone came too close or in any way threatened him, I would literally scratch their eyes out. Such emotions were completely foreign to me. In those early days with a newborn I felt closer to my animal nature than I ever had.

In my work I had seen animal mothers in such a state just after birth, but until I had my own child I never really understood why they got so tetchy when they had newborns. For example, there was only one situation in which you would ever see a female impala on her own, and that was when she had recently given birth. Impala mothers separated from their herd to give birth alone and they keep their youngster isolated for about a week. These super-smart animals realise that a newborn impala is more likely to be taken by a predator than any other impalas in the group, so the newborn is safer if it is away from the conspicuousness of a large herd in those first, most vulnerable days. The tiny lamb lies low, bedding down in the grass and resting while its mother feeds. Impalas all have their babies at the same time of year so that with the glut of simultaneous babies, at least a few will survive the predator feast if they are scattered far and wide.

And regardless of the species, mothers in the animal kingdom always keep a greater distance between other creatures and themselves when they have very small young. In a study I did on common impalas in Zimbabwe, I found that the distance to which female impalas allowed me to walk directly towards them before they fled (flight distances) increased when females had young, as did vigilance for predators. Now, with my new baby in my arms, I finally understood why. I was acting the same way.

The famous chimpanzee researcher Jane Goodall described it beautifully in an interview for CBS Extra's *60 Minutes* when she said, 'After I'd had my own baby I then began to understand mother chimps much better . . . I was always surprised to see a mother chimp get so agitated and angry if another individual, another chimp, came too close. But then when I had my own child and somebody would shut a door loudly and start waking up little Grub I'd get this surge of real anger which I couldn't quite understand . . . then I understood the female chimps.'

If I felt an affinity with any animal in the early weeks, it wasn't an impala – it was a dairy cow. The round-the-clock breastfeeds, which involved waking four or five times a night, just about killed me. I remember thinking at 3 am one dark night how common and underrated motherhood was when it was really *extraordinary* that any woman survived the newborn baby stage once, let alone wanted to do it again! My mum had made it look easy and she told me she'd *enjoyed* it. There could only have been two possible explanations for this remarkable claim, I figured. Either she had experienced a memory blackout about how awful it was, or she had lied to get grandchildren!

Ten days after Solo was born, Andy flew to Copenhagen for a special Earth Hour as part of the UN climate change meetings. Conservationists were pinning a lot of hope on these meetings of global leaders at the Conference of Parties (CoP) to make some positive decisions and plans to combat climate change. With such a tiny baby, the timing was awful for us as a family, but we had agreed long before the birth that it was important he go. This was a cause we both believed in and I fully supported Andy's need to be there. But the endless waking at night every two hours had given me the head space of an inmate at Guantanamo Bay, even with the help of my mum initially and then, when she left, my sister.

I'm not very good at asking for help, and on the seventh night of pretending that I wasn't really losing it, that I was okay, I phoned Andy in tears, past breaking point. He was on a bus somewhere in Copenhagen in the middle of a raging blizzard talking to a top BBC correspondent about Earth Hour, which was due to be held the next day. Listening to his wife on the phone cracking up, I can only imagine how completely powerless he must have felt.

When he arrived home a few days after my call, having been delayed at Copenhagen airport by the arrival of Barack Obama on Air Force One on the final day of the CoP, he had woken up to some hard realities. So much hope had been pinned on global leaders reaching a decision that would see some tangible action on climate change, but it was not to be. All of the non-government organisations (NGOs) had been kicked out of the Bella Centre where the meetings were being held and there had been some early signs that no deal would be reached.

The global Earth Hour team had collected online 'votes' for action on climate change from hundreds of millions of people from around the world from Earth Hour nine months earlier. They had saved them all onto a hard drive and placed it inside a chrome orb to be handed over to United Nations leader Ban Ki Moon at a special Earth Hour event in City Hall Square. With the world's media poised to broadcast his acceptance speech, a

WWF staff member liaising with the UN leader's office phoned Andy at the last minute with the devastating news that the talks had run into serious problems. The UN leader would not be coming.

There was a huge amount of disappointment around Copenhagen, but for Andy the great lesson learned was that the green movement had overestimated its level of influence on global decision makers. Having several different campaigns from different organisations competing for the same space instead of presenting one unified voice had probably undermined them all. Then again, some forces at play at this conference were way beyond the ideals of those fighting for action on climate change. This was about politics. In the aftermath, the Americans were blaming the Chinese for the lack of an outcome. Others blamed the Americans for demanding much of others but not doing enough themselves. And amidst all this political posturing, a legally binding treaty never emerged, and still, nowhere near enough was being done to stop climate change.

Andy got home to a wife melting down from sleep deprivation, so there was no time to recover from either the experience or from the epic journey home over two days' worth of flight delays and airline transfers. But holding his three-week-old son in his arms, what was most important in life became abundantly clear. Parenthood provides clarity in a way that nothing else can. Solo was now the most important thing in our world.

CHAPTER 5

RETURN TO ZIMBABWE

Harare, May 2011

It was almost ten o'clock at night in the capital of what had recently become one of Africa's more infamous countries, and about twenty-four hours since I had last slept. The interminable flight from Sydney, via Johannesburg, to Harare was finally over. After waiting for half an hour to pay my US$30 entry fee to Zimbabwe, then being berated by the customs official for allowing my eighteen-month-old son to pour water on my passport, I loaded up a rusty trolley with our mountain of belongings and plopped Solo on top like excess baggage. It was reassuring to know that my old friend, Roger and Anne Whittall's daughter Sarah, would be there waiting for us. I was the last person to go through, so I hoped she hadn't arrived too early. But when a porter finally helped me wheel the trolley into the waiting area, there was no sign of Sarah. In fact, there wasn't anyone in sight other than a couple of porters. All of the other passengers had already left. My heart sank. Where was Sarah?

Solo chose that opportune moment to have a full-scale meltdown. Frankly, I knew how he felt. After so little sleep and a long journey on my own with a very busy toddler, I considered bursting into tears myself. It had been more than a decade since I had last been in Harare and a lot of bad stuff had gone down here since then. After a decade of dictator-led intimidation and violence against the public in order to secure votes, many rigged elections and beatings of those who didn't support the ruling party, failed crops as a result of the takeover of most of the white-owned farmlands by war veterans and subsistence farmers, compounded by drought and famine, as well as a completely collapsed economy, there were a lot of desperate people here now. Tourists had long ago stopped coming to Zimbabwe, and the problems had gone on for so long that even the media had lost interest. This wasn't the sort of place you wanted to be at night on your own with a small child.

What had I been thinking, coming here without Andy? He was working in Switzerland and wouldn't arrive for a few more days. It was fine taking chances when it was just me to think about, but we had Solo now. Was it safe to get in a taxi in this place at this time of night? I doubted it. Looking outside, it was almost pitch black on the street and there was nothing resembling a taxi rank anyway.

Returning to Zimbabwe had been my madcap idea. Eleven years earlier, in 2000, I had left in a terrible rush when President Robert Mugabe first sanctioned the invasion of white-owned farms by veterans of the war for independence. Humani, which was at the centre of the Save Valley Conservancy where I had been working, was right in the firing line for war veterans wanting land as it was then predominantly white-owned.

The turn of the millennium heralded the beginning of a decade of madness in Zimbabwe. In the Save Valley Conservancy, it meant widespread poaching by war vets and settlers alike, using snares taken from the conservancy's wire fences. It meant brutal intimidation of both black and white residents by political wranglers determined to see the ruling party stay in power at any cost. It meant that the habitat of elephants, rhinos and giraffes in the private wildlife conservancies had to make way for human settlements, most of them completely sanctioned by the government. With the political insecurity there – and the chance that I could be caught in the crossfire – my PhD supervisor, Anne Goldizen, wouldn't hear of me staying there to do my planned research on impalas. But I hadn't forgotten Zimbabwe, Humani or the Whittalls, who had played such a pivotal role in my early development as a conservationist.

In 2008, I had returned briefly to Zimbabwe to introduce Andy to the country that was so special to me, but we had only visited the 'safe' tourist destinations of Hwange National Park and Victoria Falls. Humani and the Save Valley Conservancy were still in the thick of the craziness, struggling to get fuel and food in from outside. The Whittalls were spending their days trying to keep the dollars flowing in through their safari business, while being on the front line of a war on poachers that had just started to go beyond petty snaring for meat and into the violent, criminal world of the lucrative rhino horn trade, driven by the rising demand for horn from Vietnam. The Whittalls hadn't been able to tell me exactly what was going on because phones and emails were tapped. As always, the only way to really know what was happening at Humani was to go there.

A few months after I had visited Zimbabwe with Andy, there were signs that things were improving. There was the historic power-sharing agreement signed by Movement for Democratic Change opposition leader Morgan Tsvangarai and President Mugabe in September 2008, which effectively took some power away from the ruling party. It wouldn't work forever, but it was better than the dictatorship that preceded it. Then in February 2009, Morgan Tsvangarai was sworn in as Prime Minister, another good sign. A few months later, the Zimbabwean dollar, worth more than the US dollar at Zimbabwe's independence in 1980, was replaced by the US dollar, following years of political instability and hyperinflation. Before it was consigned to the history books, the highest denomination of the Zimbabwean dollar was 100,000,000,000,000,000.

Friends in Zimbabwe told me that the replacement of the Zimbabwean dollar with the US dollar meant a return to business in the country, at least to some extent. Food and groceries were back on the shelves, and rebuilding had begun. I was told that there was an increasing Asian presence in Zimbabwe now, which was helping rebuild the economy, but at the same time probably fuelling the demand for ivory and rhino horn for Asian markets.

I didn't know much about why the demand existed in Asia, for either ivory or rhino horn, but I had heard that it had something to do with Traditional Chinese Medicine and the false belief that rhino horn was an aphrodisiac. One thing I did know, however, was that as long as the demand for rhino and elephant products existed, the poaching in Africa was sure to continue. The question was, did Africa have the capacity to stem the tide before the animals were all gone?

The need for support for conservation in Zimbabwe was probably greater than ever, as some of the big funding organisations had pulled out of the country when it became unstable. Despite the best efforts of the Save Valley game managers in the last decade to stay on top of the escalating poaching, the wildlife had taken a hammering. With the demand for rhino horn increasing in Vietnam as the species became rarer – worth twice the price of gold and even more than cocaine – the conservancy was going to need all the help it could get. When my friends at Humani assured me that my little family would be perfectly safe if we were to visit, I decided to take their word for it. They were fighting one hell of a battle there, and I owed it to them to try and do something to help.

When I left them in 2000, I had been a twenty-one year old, budding researcher about to start my PhD. I didn't really have anything to offer the Whittalls then. But a lot had changed since. Animal Works had been growing slowly but surely in the past year and a half. We were still run entirely by volunteers, not raising enough money to justify paying anyone a salary. Steve Van Mil was no longer involved as his filming pursuits took him in a different direction and new committee members had joined. One of them, Meli Souter, came to play a major role in the organisation's early development. A graphic artist with a passion for Africa and elephants, she volunteered to develop an elephant adoption program for Animal Works to support the cost of raising the elephant orphans at the CWRC in India. In less than two years, Meli's online adoption program, in addition to Nafisa's art sales and the original start-up funds from our launch, had resulted in Animal Works being able to transfer substantial funds to the Wildlife Trust of India's elephant orphanage.

With the Indian part of the organisation on track, I wanted to see what Animal Works could do in Africa. Although we were in Zimbabwe on holiday this time, establishing an African project for Animal Works was my ulterior motive. I wanted to know if this country – and in particular, the Save Valley Conservancy – had turned a corner enough to justify fundraising for conservation projects there. I knew from previous experience not to believe everything the media said. There was really only one way to find out what was going on in Zimbabwe and that was to go there in person.

Now, stranded at Harare airport on a major sleep deficit and with a screaming toddler in tow, I was seriously wondering if this had been such a good idea. After ten minutes there was no sign of Sarah, who we were supposed to be staying with in Harare for the next couple of days. With a rising sense of panic, I remembered that Sarah had emailed me before I left Sydney to say her mobile phone wasn't working and to phone her sister Debbie if for some reason she wasn't at the airport. I fumbled around in my bag to find the scrap of paper that I'd scribbled the number on at the last minute, then pleaded with a sympathetic porter to let me borrow his phone. Hearing Debbie's familiar voice on the other end of the line brought some relief, but she, like me, had no idea where Sarah was, only that she was meant to be there.

'Just hang in there, Tam, and if she's not there in half an hour call me back and we'll come get you,' Debbie said.

A few minutes later, an old Toyota Corolla pulled up outside the airport, and to my great joy, Sarah's smiling face popped out of the driver's window.

'Sorry, Tam, I didn't want to pay for parking!' she exclaimed. 'I've just been waiting outside.'

Relief flooded through me as we piled the luggage into her car and headed through the dark, eerie scene that was Harare at night. With no streetlamps, Sarah's car's dim headlights barely lit up the road enough to see the potholes. Only some of the traffic lights seemed to be working, so the few cars that were on the road had to play a game of Russian roulette to decide who got right of way.

While Sarah and I caught up on the last decade, Solo fell asleep on my lap in the back seat, oblivious to where he was in the world. What a blissful time of life it was to be one and a half, needing only your mum there to make you feel safe and happy. I had been preparing myself to face a world that might not be the same, but I still wasn't sure how I would cope with it if things really were as bad as the media suggested.

Solo and I spent the first couple of days in Harare staying with Sarah, catching up with old friends, drinking lots of Zimbabwean Tanganda tea and visiting the surprising array of new cafés and restaurants that had sprung up across town. It was heartening to discover that what I had been told was true; Harare was open for business again, bustling with activity, and there were no signs of the chronic shortages of groceries in the shopping centres that there had been a few years ago. Much had changed in my life and those of my Zimbabwean friends since the late 1990s, but it was wonderful to step back into old friendships as if I had never been away.

A few days later, a herd of common impalas bounded in front of our vehicle as Andy negotiated the dusty gravel road, which wound its way from the north of the Save Valley Conservancy to the south like a crooked spine. It was late May and already the lowveld grasses had faded to dried brown husks of their former luxuriant selves. The day was baking hot, even though it was almost winter, and the belligerent sun for which this semi-arid part of the country was famous showed no signs of easing off any time soon.

As we rounded a bend that led to the concrete bridge over the Turgwe River, we stopped to watch a monitor lizard lounging on the hot cement, warming up in the sun's rays. Beside him, an iridescent blue kingfisher, waiting for an opportunity to grab a quick meal with his long beak, perched on a gently swaying reed by water that sparkled as it rushed by. The kingfisher and the lizard seemed to have reached a truce, because neither appeared to be bothered by the close proximity of the other as they got on with their daily business, one hunting, the other sunbaking.

I must have crossed that bridge a hundred times when I lived at Humani in my late teens, and later when conducting studies on common impalas. In those days, the river could be a wide, febrile, flowing monster in full flood or a barely there creek that didn't flow at all, its hydrodynamics always changing in response to the unpredictable rainy seasons. Now the water itself was barely visible as a thick bed of reeds had grown up around the bridge.

Familiar memories flooded back as we drove across the cement bridge and up the other bank. We passed the place where I had once gone with Roger and Anne to rescue a baby kudu, which later died of shock in my arms in the back of the LandCruiser, then drove past the turnoff to Turgwe Camp, where we would be staying in a small manager's cottage. The same old 'Humani' sign greeted us as we headed towards the buildings of the Whittalls' property, its paintwork on cement looking a little the worse for wear, a sign of the times perhaps.

I reminded myself not to get my hopes up, that people and places change, that I had changed too, and that everything could be different at Humani after the preceding decade. But even so, I couldn't help my excitement mounting. I was looking forward to seeing Roger and Anne after so long, but I grew increasingly anxious as I took in the once familiar sights of the ranch.

The Humani 'compound', where all the local staff from the safari and agricultural operations lived now, had a big wire fence around all of the thatched roof rondavels. It looked to be electrified, but the wire was broken in places and it didn't look live. The obvious conclusion I had to draw was that it had been erected to keep the settlers away from the local staff's homes, for their own security with so many 'outsiders' now living there.

As we neared the Whittalls' house there were signs of decay and disrepair everywhere. The old butchery, where game meat was processed and sold to the local people, looked like it hadn't had a fresh coat of paint in ten years. Old scrap metal and rusty car bodies littered the entrance to the property, and just inside the gate to the house scrawny chickens scratched around in the dirt.

Beyond the tall wire fence that had always surrounded the house, the dwelling where I had lived with Roger, Anne and Sarah all those years ago, it was like taking a step back in time. As we pulled in, I could see that the weather had taken its toll, the dust and the rain leaving rusty brown stains on the walls, and the paint was peeling, but it was the same house, with the same old fireplace outside the front door, and the same wooden door at the entry. It occurred to me that it could have been intentional to let the house look rundown, to hold at bay war vets with gleams of assumed riches in their eyes. But it also could have been that every spare cent in this place was going into keeping things afloat. Besides, there probably wasn't much sense in investing in renovating your house when you knew it could be taken from you at any moment.

Andy parked the car next to a battered, open LandCruiser in the yard, upon which a beady-eyed vulture glared at us from a comfortable, padded bench seat. The bird of prey took one look at our pint-sized son and began to show a little too much interest in him for my liking, jumping over to him and trying to give him a quick nip. Andy hastily picked up Solo before any damage could be done, and we all walked together to the front door.

It was completely quiet, as if no one was there. Even the radio, which used to blare incessantly from the lounge room, was silent. We had radioed from the boom gate at the entrance to the conservancy an hour earlier, so I presumed that Roger and Anne knew we were coming.

Through the mesh screened louvres, I spotted a hunched-over figure with her forehead in her hands. I realised it was siesta time, post lunch. Roger and Anne were now nearing their seventies and probably appreciated an afternoon rest after rising early.

'Hello? Anne?' I said.

Anne sprang to her feet, as sprightly as ever, and her smile engulfed a kind and generous face that had weathered so many of Africa's storms.

'Ah, there you are, my girl!' she exclaimed.

We embraced, and I felt tears prickle my eyes for reasons I can't explain. Perhaps it was knowing that I had had the freedom to leave this place when the going got tough in 2000 while, unlike me, the Whittalls had no choice but to soldier through it. Perhaps it was a sense of guilt coming back. Maybe I was just happy to see her.

'Roger!' she called outside.

I scanned the lounge room. The same old painting of lions lapping water still overlooked the round, wooden dining table that had always been the focus of so many meals and rich conversations. The television looked like it hadn't moved from its position in the timber cabinet for more than ten years. Where before the walls in this room had displayed wildlife art and trophy animal heads, they were largely empty now, except for a few new photos of all the grandchildren who had arrived in their lives in the last decade. It was the same old fabric lounge suite, now showing signs of wear and tear. As they always had, several dogs lolled on the lounge room floor, providing footrests for visitors.

Roger emerged from the other side of the room, where the office and his bedroom were located beside their back yard. His cheeky, sparkling eyes greeted us as he gave me a shy, awkward hug, then shook Andy's hand. For some reason I had forgotten Roger's half-eaten ear (devoured by a lion in an attack many years earlier), which just added character to this man in the standard khaki collared shirt and shorts that he had always worn.

Solo stared at him for a moment, intrigued by the dominant presence in the room.

'You want to see a buffalo?' he said to Solo.

We followed Roger outside to where a rather sad-looking baby buffalo with a large callus on her leg was lying by a bed of flowers.

'She was attacked by a lion,' Roger explained. 'Anne's looking after her.'

I could see the teeth marks of the lion on the leg by the abscess. It looked like a serious wound to me, but Anne had raised all sorts of animals over the years – a baby lion, a cheetah, many antelope species and, very recently, a black rhino called Jimmy – so I knew this one was in good hands.

Anne returned with cold bottles of Coke for us all and a small bowl of grain, which she placed on the grass. On cue, a duiker with a particularly ragged tan coat (covered in parasites by the look of her) appeared and began eating from the bowl. She must have been another one of Anne's orphaned babies. Solo was delighted to have something his own size around and instantly leaned down to try and give her a pat.

'You'll see some big changes here, Tam,' Anne said. 'The road out to Turgwe Camp is full of settlers now. There's been a lot of clearing. But come, you can see for yourself. Let's get you settled in at camp.'

We downed our Cokes and followed Anne out to the cars. There we found that the vulture had vented his rage at not being able to nibble on our son by eating the windscreen wipers of our hire car instead. Andy drove as we followed Anne's car out to Turgwe Camp. Along much of the track, what was previously wild animal habitat had now become cleared fields, some with the remnants of maize crops, most with one or two small rondavels nestled under a stoic baobab tree. Settlers' kids watched us drive past without the friendly waves I remembered from people in this part of the world. Blasé African cows stared unseeing into the surrounding thornbush. The tracks of cows were all along the road. A bullock-drawn cart led by a local man pulled off the track to let us pass as we took the turnoff to the camp. I love African scenes of villages with grass roofs under baobab trees, but not here, in what was prime wildlife habitat. There is enough room in Africa for both. This was not the wilderness I remembered and it felt like something special had been lost.

Later that evening, Roger and Anne joined us for a sundowner in the main lounge of Turgwe Camp, perched up on the river's high bank. The view overlooking the winding river was just as breathtaking as ever. The position of Humani's Turgwe Camp remains to me one of the best in Africa. Kudus and nyalas fed on bushes in the riverine scrub on the other side of the river, picking up seeds and leaves that had fallen from the trees. It was a magnificent scene as the sun sank behind the thornbush across the river, but the conversation in camp was of more sombre things.

'About half the conservancy has been taken over by settlers,' Roger explained. 'You remember Sambornyai Camp, Tam, where you stayed with your father?'

I nodded. That was the beginning of my African journey, and I had fond memories of Humani's first safari camp. It had been a very basic safari camp – or 'rustic', as Sarah preferred to call it – consisting of just a few thatched-roof rondavels with cement floors, geckos in the bathroom, and chicken wire and mosquito mesh instead of glass windows.

'Gone. Burned down. And the area's surrounded by settlers now.'

Roger took a big gulp of his whiskey and water before revealing that only two of their previous four camps were still able to operate. Tourists had completely stopped coming since 2000 and the only way they were able to stay afloat was through the income from trophy hunting. Hunters weren't deterred by the political instability. If anything, perhaps, it made places like Zimbabwe a little bit more of an adventure.

In situations like this it was clear that without the income it provided there would have been no wildlife left at all in the Save Valley Conservancy. Safari operators like Roger and Anne would have had to leave at the first sign of trouble because there would have been no money coming in, and that would have been the end of any kind of anti-poaching program. There would have been no game scouts getting paid to catch poachers, no one to take the culprits to the nearest police station in the nearby town of Chiredzi, and no one to make sure they were convicted.

'Can you do anything about the settlers at all?' I asked, feeling rather naive.

'Some of them have official letters. Those we can't touch. But a lot don't have letters and we'll probably be able to force them to move somewhere else,' Roger replied.

I was surprised to hear Roger speaking with a hint of optimism in his voice. These were not the words of a broken man. He was still thinking about the future and making plans.

'And what about the poaching?'

'Since 2007, things have been better. Some of our species are actually increasing now . . . buffalo, eland, giraffe . . . most of the plains game. But it's the rhino we're worried about these days. These guys are really serious.'

What Roger wasn't saying carried as much weight as the words coming out of his mouth. These weren't your average local poachers killing animals for meat to feed their families. From what we had been told, they were violent criminal gangs, incredibly well armed, with the ability to slay the rhinos, take their horns (often while the rhinos were still alive) and get them out to buyers across the border. They had no feelings whatsoever for the animals. They just wanted the money.

'It's incredibly hard to stay on top of these guys,' he went on. 'They're tapped into our radios so they know where we are. And they're much better equipped than our guys are. I give out rewards for information and when my guys get poachers or their guns. Hard cash. That's the only way we can find out what's going on.'

The rhino horn trade was so lucrative that Roger and the other managers in the conservancy were being forced to play the crooks at their own game. But he was up against stiff opposition. The game scouts were being paid a basic monthly salary plus rations, and rewarded when they caught poachers, but a single rhino horn fetched tens of thousands on the black market. How could you trust your guys to stay straight when so much more money was on offer, enough to put your kids through university, enough to buy a house?

Soon after dark we were joined at Turgwe Camp by two safari clients. They were a wealthy, childless American couple nearing retirement. The woman told us that her husband had fairly recently had a complete heart transplant. He told us that he was there to hunt buffalo and various other species, and proudly bragged that he had a dream to fulfil. He wanted to be the first person in the world with a heart transplant to shoot 'the big five' (elephant, rhino, buffalo, leopard and lion).

Andy's jaw dropped. It was the first time in my life that I had ever seen my husband lost for words. I had met some fairly extreme hunters in my time, but this couple from the far south of America really took the cake. Over dinner, when the conversation turned to American politics, our open support for Barack Obama was met with complete horror from their side.

They wanted Donald Trump to be president and made it clear that we were a pair of idiots for not agreeing with them.

Later that night I tried to explain to Andy that there were different types of hunters. There were guys like my dad and other guys I had known who hunted because they loved to be in the bush and they saw it as part of conservation. There were others – in greater numbers than I wanted to think about – who were simply arseholes, hunting to show off their 'trophies' and gain bragging rights with their equally arsehole friends. Such people, in my opinion, didn't deserve the privilege of being in Africa, even if the money they paid was used for conservation. But the arguments around whether trophy hunting was okay or not meant little when you were confronted with the reality on the ground and your own emotional response to it.

The next morning Andy and I left Solo with Fungai and Lucia, two of the local women in camp, so we could take a look around Humani with Roger. Fungai, a mother of four, was the eldest daughter of Stella, who had worked for Roger and Anne for decades, running the butchery and the house. I felt like I had known Stella forever. She had been the one to warn me not to talk too much back in 2000 when she thought war veterans might overhear me and put me in a dangerous position. Lucia was the sister of Junior, who now worked as a carpenter for Roger but had been a teacher at Humani Primary School when I was teaching there in 1995. I planned to spend some time with these women later, learning more about what had been happening from their point of view, but the first thing we had to do was see the extent of the settlement. As we drove off, I saw Lucia tie Solo onto her back just like she would have a little African.

Andy and I squeezed into the front seat of Roger's LandCruiser and we drove out past the staff compound, with its non-operational electric fence, and the remains of the old shop, which was now without a roof and completely burned to the ground. I remembered the old man who had always sat out the front of the shop using an ancient treadle sewing machine to repair people's clothes. He always had a smile for me, but he and his old machine were long gone.

As we drove out on the main road that used to lead to Sambornyai Camp, Roger pointed out the vast areas that had been cleared to make way for villages. The mopane woodlands that had dominated this landscape for so long were now being whittled away and there was nothing Roger could do to stop it. It occurred to me that Roger must have lost his temper on more than one occasion. I couldn't imagine that he would simply have sat back and let this happen. This was a man known to the locals as *shumba*, meaning 'lion'. He must have been a wanted man among those who coveted his land.

'Have any of these guys had a go at you?' I asked.

'What?'

I knew it wasn't the question he was objecting to. Roger's hearing had never been much good, but it seemed worse now and with the roar of the LandCruiser he couldn't hear a thing I was saying. Sarah had told me he now wore a hearing aid – some of the time.

Feeling very disrespectful but seeing no alternative, I yelled into the ear that hadn't been inside the mouth of the lion: 'Have any of these guys had a go at you?'

'Oh *ja*, they've been trying to beat me up for years,' Roger joked, but I knew he was serious.

I stayed silent, hoping he would elaborate.

Andy asked him, 'What happened, Roger?'

As we drove through some of the remaining woodlands looking for fresh rhino tracks, Roger told us the story of the day a gang of war veterans came after him with sticks and other weapons, wanting his head on a platter, trying to intimidate him and his family enough to force them to leave.

'I heard they were coming, so I made a run for it out the back door of the house and headed into the bush. I just kept going, as far as I could.'

Roger had formidable bush tracking skills and he knew he could find his way home, but it wasn't himself he was worried about. He knew that Anne was shopping in the nearby town of Chiredzi that day and would soon be on her way home, walking unknowingly right into the hands of the irascible gang. He desperately radioed the boom at the northern gate of the conservancy to tell them to stop her coming through, but it was too late. The guard told him she was already on her way. Roger calculated that this gave him less than an hour to warn her. He had to think of another way to stop her returning to the house. This was Zimbabwe, after all, where the unofficial national motto was 'Just make a plan'. His eyes widened as he spoke about Anne, and I could tell that for all his good humour he must have been very concerned for his wife's safety.

Unable to do anything directly to help her, Roger radioed one of his game scouts, Chimeni, and sent him on a motorbike to stop her returning to Humani. But as the scout headed out towards the gate, an angry crowd prevented him from going any further.

Roger's brother, Richard, who had once run a successful agricultural operation at Humani, was the next to receive a call for help. Richard and Arthur, his brother-in-law, were by then at Roger's house, having heard that there was a drama going on. Roger told them to get out straight away and to try and warn Anne, but by then it was too late. The angry crowd had arrived at the house, along with Anne with a *bakkie* (utility) load of groceries.

Roger knew there was no point in him returning to the house as it would just rile up the crowd, so he lay low in the bush into the night and just waited for news from the house. I tried to imagine what it must have been like for him, how powerless he must have felt as night closed in around him, knowing that it was him they wanted, but that his family had been taken instead.

It wasn't until the next day that I heard the rest of the story from Anne. Along with Richard and Arthur, both of them also senior citizens, she was made to stand on the grass in their back yard for hours while the gang chanted political slogans and threw insults at them, jabbing in the air at them with sticks. What happened that night would have terrified most mortals, especially given the violence that had ensued on other white-owned farms around the country under the current regime. The gang slaughtered Roger's goats and sheep and cooked feasts for themselves on bonfires in the yard, then raided the liquor cabinet and helped themselves to the contents, clearing it out.

'I never felt in any real danger,' Anne said, smiling as if it was the most natural thing in the world to be captured by war vets while your husband hid in the bush, with the threat of lions and elephants lurking nearby.

I raised an eyebrow.

She laughed. 'It was actually quite funny the way they were treating me. They asked me how old I was, and of course I said, you don't ask a lady her age! They were making us stand up, and after a while, my legs wanted to give in so I just sat on the grass. Well, as soon as they saw that, one man leapt up and gave me a chair!

'Then Arthur needed a rest,' Anne went on, 'so I offered him my chair, but they wouldn't hear of that and they gave him one too! It was all just a big show, you know. They were poking sticks at us and throwing insults, but it was Roger they wanted.'

Anne chuckled. 'After a while Arthur stood up in a hurry to stretch his legs and the crowd got such a fright that the one closest to him almost fell backwards over himself to get away, thinking they were being attacked by these *old* people!'

'At one stage I was so desperate to go to the toilet that they let me go and when I got in there I found two of our house staff huddled beside the toilet bowl! They were so scared, you know. I just told them to close their eyes and ears. I really had to go!'

I burst out laughing, imagining Anne emptying her bladder while her two African staff squatted beside her, terrified of the gang outside, and trying not to watch. It amazed me, listening to both Roger and Anne speaking about the daily realities of their lives under pressure. They seemed without malice or negativity, which I thought was both astounding and impressive.

'There's no point holding a grudge,' Roger had said earlier in the LandCruiser.

'But do you think the whole conservancy will eventually be taken over?' I asked him, vocalising the worst case scenario for the wildlife.

'No,' he replied decisively, 'things will straighten out before that happens.'

The wisdom Roger and Anne had gained in almost seven decades of life in this country shone through in everything they said. What they were experiencing now was tough, but things had been worse. They had been through the war for independence, known as the Rhodesian bush war, then turned this semi-arid patch of former cattle country into a functioning wildlife ranch as part of a nineteen-ranch-strong conservancy. They had raised four children in this far-flung part of Africa, and now, in the last decade, against all the odds, they were still there when most of the white farmers in Zimbabwe had suffered terribly and been forced to leave, if they weren't killed first.

Roger was a hardened man of the bush who had seen a lot of blood shed in his life, both human and animal. He had one hell of a temper and could completely and ferociously lose it. He was notorious for it. But now more than ever, I admired his tenacity, his sense of humour even in the most adverse of circumstances, and his capacity to soldier on with those around him. Together with Anne, a pillar of strength and optimism, they were a formidable force. Without them there, and the local people they employed, Humani wouldn't have any wildlife left now, let alone any rhinos. It really put into perspective the lengths that some people in the world were prepared to go to in order to protect their livelihoods and the wildlife that sustained it.

Lucia, who managed Turgwe Camp, summed up the recent history of Zimbabwe even better, I thought, when I sat with her and Fungai in the kitchen chewing the cud the next afternoon.

'In 2000, when this started, people were really scared,' Lucia said.

'Scared of who?'

'The war vets,' she went on. 'They forced people to do things, go to political rallies, and if they didn't go they would beat them.'

'What about the school? Were the teachers affected?' I asked, knowing that Lucia had put her own children through Humani Primary School.

'*Ja*, most of the teachers ran away! They really disturbed the school . . .'

'The war vets?'

'*Ja.*'

Teachers, I later learned, were considered people of influence, so they were seen as important patrons for the ruling party to have on side. But many of the teachers supported the opposition party, leading to severe beatings by thugs supporting ZANU PF (Zimbabwe African National Union – Patriotic Front).

'You know, one time there was an MP who came here . . . '
Lucia went on.

'An MP?'

'A politician. He came to Roger's house and Stella was
expected to make lunch for him. He started saying to her, "Why
were you not at the rally? You must support the opposition
party." '

Stella, Lucia's mother, had been working for the Whittalls
for much longer than I had known them, and she was a formidable force to be reckoned with too. As Lucia told this story, I saw
the same inner strength in her.

'She say to him, "If you are MP, we want to see you every
day. Farm workers and war vets must be treated the same." She
said to him things like he is not giving them meat like Roger is.
"If Roger is looking after us and you are never here, who is more
powerful here to these people?" '

A week catching up with longstanding friends and
introducing my 'old' family to my new one flew by. Andy had
been overwhelmed by what had been his first encounter with
Zimbabwe behind the scenes, and I appreciated having his
level head there to help me assess things more clearly. We had
seen enough of the ranch to know that it had huge problems
with illegal (and somehow officially 'legal') settlers destroying
wildlife habitat, as well as the widespread poaching that came
with the increased human population, but it was encouraging
to learn that some species' populations had started increasing in
the last few years. Since the end of 2007, the unity government
and change of currency had definitely shifted things in
Zimbabwe for the better. Things couldn't have got much worse
before that. But now the Whittalls seemed confident that a
corner had been turned, and their relatively positive attitude
was heartening.

The rhino population in the Save Valley Conservancy, however, had almost halved between 2004 and 2011, and the signs on that front were not promising. It was an even worse story in South Africa, where almost two rhinos a day were being poached to supply the demand for horn in Asia. Roger was also concerned that the elephant population seemed to be declining in the conservancy. I hadn't even seen any elephants on this trip, which was a little worrying.

It was obvious that they needed more support on the anti-poaching front if the conservancy was to make any kind of headway against the rhino poachers. The game scouts were just not equipped or trained sufficiently to confront criminal gangs like those poaching for what had become one of the world's most valuable commodities, and their lives were at risk every time they came up against these guys. Across Africa, not just here, the battlefield on which the last of the rhinos were being fought for was littered with human bodies as well as rhinos.

Just as we were leaving, Roger said to me, 'Tam, do you think you could get us some laptops . . . for the kids at the school?'

In the past week, I had been so busy seeing old friends and trying to investigate as much as possible of the ranch that I hadn't even had time to visit the school. When I asked the camp staff about my old 'pupils' I learned that some of them had gone on to work in safari businesses in other parts of the conservancy, but no one knew where most of them had ended up.

Roger's request for the local children had come out of left field, but I nodded. 'Let me see what I can do.'

Not all of my friends from this part of the world were still alive. Sadly, Ipheas, the man who had worked in the bush with me as my eyes and ears when I was studying impalas in 1999 had died some time ago of what people believed to be AIDS. His wife had moved back to the communal lands bordering the

conservancy, where things had been really tough in the last decade. Brenda, my dear friend and Anne's niece who had been just
a few years older than me, had left a husband and two young
boys behind after succumbing to cancer a few years earlier. Their
faces were branded into a part of my brain – or perhaps my
heart – that had made me who I was. I missed their smiling faces.

Being back in Zimbabwe had inspired so many happy
memories, but the rawness of what we saw there took me on an
emotional roller coaster. In spite of the parts of the conservancy
that had been cleared to make way for people, and the hammering
that the wildlife had taken as a result, my overall impression was
encouraging. This was a country that was moving forward again
and I wanted to be a part of it. Although our time at Humani
had been short, I had enough information about what was happening to know that Animal Works' support there would be
worthwhile. It was time to start moving towards the future, just
as the Whittalls seemed to be doing, and to use my networks to
do something for the people – and the wildlife – that had given
me my foot in the door to Africa.

Up until then, Animal Works had been all about raising
funds for Indian elephant conservation. While our support for
the Wildlife Trust of India would continue, this would take
things in a new direction – to a project helping to conserve rhinos
in Africa. But before I could think any more about what could
be done from Australia to help stop the poaching in Zimbabwe,
there was something I needed to do first in India.

CHAPTER 6

HOPE IN INDIA'S ELEPHANT WAR ZONE

Manas National Park, Assam, November 2011

I have always felt that it's important that both organisations and individuals stay connected to the projects that they're sending their donations to – and these days organisations can keep their supporters connected too through YouTube videos, blogs and social media. When you're spending supporters' donor money on behalf of an organisation, I think you have an even greater responsibility and an obligation to be sure that your donations are getting the conservation outcome that was intended. So it was important to me that before Animal Works started our first project in Africa, I return to India to see how our funds were being used.

The Centre for Wildlife Rehabilitation and Conservation (CWRC), which was located next to Kaziranga National Park at the eastern end of the country, provided a vital service in Assam by saving baby elephants that had been attacked by people and separated from their herds, fallen into tea garden trenches or orphaned in the annual floods. The centre's first action was always to try to return a baby elephant to its herd, but when that wasn't possible, the baby was raised by dedicated keepers, who fed, weighed, walked and slept with the baby until it was old enough to be taken back to the wild.

Meli Souter had been voluntarily running Animal Works' elephant adoption program to raise funds for the Wildlife Trust of India for over a year when we heard about plans to reintroduce some of the rehabilitated elephants to the wild. In early 2011, veterinarians at the CWRC decided that six of the orphans were ready to be returned to a natural habitat to fend for themselves. They decided the best place for the six elephants, aged from three to six years of age, would be Manas National Park, where they would be part of the park's 're-wilding' program.

With support from the International Fund for Animal Welfare (IFAW) and the Assam Forestry Department, the Wildlife Trust of India began the process of sedating the small family of orphaned elephants at the CWRC and boarding them into trucks for the twelve-hour drive to Manas. But tragedy struck almost immediately. Deepa, the oldest elephant who was like the young 'matriarch' to the others, died of heart failure in what the veterinarians believed was a stress-based reaction to the sedatives.

I knew from seeing wildlife translocations in Africa that such operations were inherently risky and there were almost always casualties. Sedating and putting wild animals into a truck and keeping them confined in order to move them to another location, even if that location offers them a better chance of survival, puts them under huge amounts of stress. Deepa's death at just six years of age shocked us all and I was worried about how the remaining five calves would get on without her leadership.

Thankfully, we soon received the news that the five calves had made the journey without any problems and had been released into an electric-fenced area deep within the boundaries of the park. The plan was to keep them there for a couple of months of acclimatisation before letting them roam freely in the park, a technique that conservationists call a 'soft' release. But the oldest male, Hamren, had other ideas. Within a week of being in the enclosure, one night he found a way to escape. Unfortunately, he hadn't been radio- or satellite-collared before he performed his Houdini act, which made subsequent monitoring of his movements by WTI staff incredibly difficult. They would just have to rely on sporadic sightings of him by park rangers to know that he was still alive.

One can never underestimate the intelligence of elephants and their ability to get what they want. Four days later, following Hamren's lead, the remaining four orphaned elephants felt the call of the wild and escaped as well. Luckily, some of them were collared and so WTI staff could immediately begin monitoring their movements. Soni, the young female, had a radio collar which could be manually tracked using triangulation equipment, while the three young males, Sikom, Tikla and Tinku, had satellite collars, meaning that theoretically they could be remotely tracked using GPS technology. Since then, a small team of field-based staff of the Wildlife Trust of India had been tracking the five elephants as best they could.

It was ten months after the orphans had been released that Nafisa and I met in the bustling Guwahati airport, where we were joined by the Wildlife Trust of India's veterinarian Dr Bhaskar Choudhary, to see how the re-wilding elephant project was progressing. As we drove north towards Manas National Park, this quietly spoken and humble man told us a little about where we were going and what to expect over the next few days.

Manas National Park was declared a UNESCO World Heritage site in 1985, famous for its endangered tigers, elephants, greater one-horned rhinos and clouded leopards, but particularly unique in its rare and endemic species, like pygmy hogs (a groovy little pig with fewer than one hundred and fifty individuals remaining in the world), golden langurs (one of India's most endangered monkeys, known for its black face surrounded by spiky, wild golden hair) and Assam roofed turtles (a freshwater turtle with a raised carapace on its shell).

The park was contiguous with its sister park in Bhutan, the Royal Manas, effectively creating a much larger transboundary conservation area between India and Bhutan. Animals like elephants and tigers with large home ranges could move freely between the two countries. Heavy poaching and terrorist activity in the 1980s and 1990s had caused a serious decline in the population of many species, including tigers, elephants, ungulates like swamp deer and, most devastatingly, the complete extinction of Manas' population of a hundred greater one-horned rhinos. Consequently, UNESCO declared the park a World Heritage Site In Danger. It wasn't until 2011 that this status was removed following significant efforts by local conservation organisations and government to bring back the wildlife.

The Wildlife Trust of India had played a major role in rebuilding the critically endangered greater one-horned rhino population by providing three rhinos, hand-reared at the CWRC, to the park in 2008. There were now believed to be ten greater one-horned rhinos in the park, providing a vital third geographic population for the species to increase its overall chances of survival (the other two small populations being at Kaziranga National Park in Assam and Royal Chitwan National Park in Nepal).

I couldn't wait to explore Manas. Indians I had met in other areas of the continent thought Assam was a pretty wild part of the country, but it was when Assamese people started telling me that Manas was the truly wild part of the state that I became interested in going there. If the Assamese said that, it meant it was *really* wild. Manas attracted few tourists because of its remoteness and reputation for terrorist activity – perfect for folks like me who liked to experience wild places without throngs of people. I was looking forward to being back in one of India's rare old forests and seeing some wildlife, but what we were really interested in were elephants.

'So how are the orphans doing now?' I yelled to Bhaskar from the back seat, over the din of honking vehicles.

I had been coughing almost constantly since we left Guwahati due to the fumes from all the trucks on the road. As we dodged sacred cows, army trucks and irreverently lopsided, honking buses on the road north to Bhutan, Bhaskar explained that the post-release monitoring of the orphans hadn't gone to plan.

'The only elephant we can reliably follow right now is Soni, the one with the radio collar. For reasons I don't understand, the satellite collars don't seem to be transmitting,' Bhaskar said, shaking his head in obvious frustration. 'We do know that Soni is being followed by Tinku, another of the young males, so we can keep track of both of them while they are together. I think they might be following a wild herd.'

Bhaskar had overseen the translocation of the elephants per-sonally and it was clear that he wanted it to be successful. He couldn't guarantee that these five young elephants would grow to a ripe old age, given the number of threats that elephants everywhere in India faced on a daily basis, but he was hopeful that they might join a wild herd and have a better life in Manas National Park than they would have in captivity.

'What do you think our chances are of seeing them?' I asked, now feeling less certain about the likelihood of that happening.

Prior to leaving Sydney, in emails from Wildlife Trust of India staff, I had been told that we stood some chance of finding the orphans. There were no guarantees, of course, but a small chance was enough for me to make the journey.

'Pretty good, I think,' Bhaskar replied, to my surprise. 'We see them regularly. Our trackers are out there looking now. They saw Soni just a day ago, near the border of Bhutan.'

It was dark when we arrived at our hotel bordering the national park and, shortly after, a power failure left me standing alone in the hallway outside our room in the pitch black, wondering whether it was a genuine electricity problem or if we were about to be invaded by the Bodo rebels for which this area was infamous. I had reason to be cautious. Just nine months earlier, in February, six WWF volunteers, half of them women, who were counting tigers and elephants in Manas National Park, had been taken hostage for a couple of weeks. They were not harmed, but it must have been a terrifying experience for the young conservationists as they were held against their will in the jungle. The police blamed the National Democratic Front of Bodoland (NDFB) for the kidnapping.

This north-western part of Assam was traditionally held by the Bodos, a minority indigenous group which had been seeking sovereignty from India since the mid-1980s. The NDFB was very active in the 1990s, attacking Indian security forces and civilians, but hostilities had died down since 2005 when a ceasefire was agreed to between the NDFB and the Indian government. Still, attacks were not entirely uncommon in this part of Assam and the NDFB had been blamed for a series of explosions in 2008 that had killed about a hundred people and wounded many more. The recent targeting of wildlife conservationists in Manas National Park was enough to make me a little more wary than usual.

This was the first time I had been away from Solo for more than a night in the two years since he was born. It felt like a big deal.

Months of maternal anxieties and guilt over leaving him had led to this, but now that I was here I was surprised to find myself feeling really glad that I had come. I had made the most of the rare 'me' time on the flight to Guwahati, watching girlie movies, eating food that I hadn't had to cook, reading a book for more than ten minutes undisturbed and writing in my diary to my heart's content. To be honest, after the mammoth, almost twenty-four-hour journey to Harare a few months earlier with Solo, a flight on my own was simply heaven. My head knew that he would be perfectly fine with Andy, my mum and his nanny, Alina, even if the hole in my heart didn't, and that my worrying would serve no purpose other than to ruin my time back in the wild. Sometimes you have to let the head rule the heart so the heart can grow.

The next day I woke long before dawn and waited in bed for the sounds of India to filter into the room. Millions of insects hummed and throbbed in the forest outside the Bansbari Lodge, their combined voices filling the night with palpable life. Inside the austere room, a mosquito-killing light buzzed. We had given up on using the ceiling fan the night before as it only had one speed – super high. I pulled the blanket up over my shoulders as the morning chill reminded me that we were in the foothills of the Himalayas, at least sixty metres above sea level. As the sun contemplated rising outside, the call of wild peacocks heralded the beginning of the day in Manas National Park, a day – I hoped – that would provide a rich reward for the long journey that had got me here. Elephants.

As the Assamese sun rose over its flourishing tea gardens, I felt excited to be back in the wild. It was still dark, but I couldn't wait to get up. Bhaskar and our driver were waiting downstairs for Nafisa and me soon after 5 am. Fortified by a strong cup of sweet Assamese tea, we were soon on our way out of the hotel's car park, past the sprawling tea garden opposite where several women were already plucking dark green leaves, and into the jungle of Manas, less than a hundred metres from the hotel's entrance. The Bansbari Lodge itself might have been basic with its hard beds, white walls and cement floor (not a wall hanging in sight), but it was clean, and locations didn't get much better than this.

The forest enveloped us in a jungle cuddle as we drove along the corrugated main dirt track, blocking out the sky with its dense roof of botanical splendour. Great walls of interconnected leaves, vines and gargantuan tree trunks hugged by hundreds of stag horns closed in around us. I was enchanted. Even if we didn't see a single elephant, it had been worth the journey for this alone. Goosebumps prickled my arms and it wasn't just because of the cool morning air in the back of the open jeep. At the risk of sounding like a tree hugger, old forests like this are soul food for me, tapping into a deep need at a primeval level that modern society simply cannot satisfy. There's no drug like it.

The forest soon opened up into vast dew-laden grasslands that Bhaskar explained would be burned annually. The burns had already started this year, creating new wildlife foraging grounds and enabling better viewing of the animals for tourists. In some places the grass by the road was so high that it towered over the jeep, easily concealing a rhino or a tiger, possibly even an elephant.

I had forgotten how much being in nature enlivened me. I could actually feel the energy in my limbs, my fingers tingling with it. It had been a long while since I had felt like this, completely present in the moment, not wanting to be anywhere else or planning what came next. I realised with a sense of relief that the part of me that awoke on my first trip to Zimbabwe as a teenager was still very much alive. All it took was a return to wild places like this, in this case to a forest vastly older than me, to reignite that little spark that made my eyes shine just that much more brightly.

Most of the time in the daily grind of city living with a family, I could barely remember that feeling. Having my own family had brought wonderful things into my life, things that I would never give up, but there was no replacing the buzz of raw nature. I couldn't help grinning inwardly. I was still that same girl who walked up to a fresh lion kill in Etosha National Park, who spent her days among the impalas and the elephants, testing the wind, checking the dirt for tracks. Even those old bush senses I thought I had discarded seemed to be kicking back in again in this environment, with my peripheral vision enhanced and my sense of smell intensified. I was on a high and I didn't want to let the sensation go.

As the suspensionless jeep jolted along, heading north towards the Bhutanese border, Bhaskar stopped the car regularly to take a closer look at birds with his binoculars, to examine fresh leopard and tiger tracks, and (mostly for my benefit) to investigate piles of dung laid by elephants and rhinos (it is part of the charm – or the curse, depending on your point of view – of being a zoologist that I couldn't resist such a temptation). We careered over rackety old wooden bridges and through stony rivers that flowed with shallow alpine water from the Himalayas. My awareness of being somewhere truly remote and wild was overwhelming. This was some adventure.

It had been ten months since the orphaned elephants had set themselves free and Bhaskar was taking us to the place where they had been held for their first week, a small Wildlife Trust of India camp in the heart of the park.

'Here we are,' he said as we drove across a stony road, visible only to the driver, that crossed a low-flowing tributary of the Manas River. 'We're quite close to the border of Bhutan here.'

Behind us were the verdant green mountains of Bhutan, their undulating shapes creating a mosaic of blue-green pastels with increasing distance from Assam. It felt like another world, a million miles from home.

'Why did you choose this spot for them, Bhaskar?' I asked.

'It is far from people,' he replied succinctly. 'Quite close to Bhutan but near the middle of the park.'

Bhaskar was a man of few words, the kind of guy who probably preferred to be on his own in the jungle rather than nurse-maiding two Australian women through it.

A Department of Forestry house was set on the bank of the almost dry river that we had just driven across. Beside it, near an unkempt cleared area, were two small huts that looked to be made of crisscrossed reeds and dried mud, with grass roofs and earth floors. Behind the huts, close to the river, was a wooden, handmade lookout tower. The forest grew all around the dwellings, trying to swallow them up.

'This is where we released them,' Bhaskar said, indicating the cleared area near the huts.

The fence had obviously been taken down and there was no longer any sign that there had ever been elephants there. And perhaps that was how it was meant to be. This had been an acclimatisation site, to 'soft' release the orphans and familiarise them with their new environment before releasing them fully into the greater forest.

Bhaskar and some of the local staff put a couple of plastic chairs out for us to sit on and we shared a spread of strong local tea, bread and jam, packaged muffins and boiled eggs wrapped in foil. After a short break to eat, it was time to head for the hills – literally – in search of Soni.

Bhaskar informed us that he had spoken on his mobile phone to some rangers working with WTI based just north of the park and they had informed him that Soni wasn't much more than an hour's drive north of where we were. They had found her the day before using the radio tracking gear. Soni had moved out of the national park, passing villages, ambling through rice paddies and crossing tar roads buzzing with fast-moving traffic. This was the real world for a modern-day wild elephant in India. Because of the rapidly growing human population, natural migrations through what was once only forest now included towns, roads and agricultural areas.

Judging by her general direction, Bhaskar said, it sounded like Soni was headed for the mountainous forests of Bhutan. We followed her, leaving the peaceful sanctity of the national park and hitting the highway, only stopping to pick up some rangers and their radio tracking gear.

We passed through a village where, on a white wall, someone had painted in red: 'Create Bodoland against the stepmotherly attitude of the Assam govt towards the Bodos. No Bodoland No Rest. Divide Assam 50/50.' Perhaps the sign was old, or perhaps the Bodos still felt they weren't adequately recognised. Soni's new environment was one ruled by humans and their politics and, unlike at the CWRC where she was lovingly cared for, not all humans in this environment would be kind to her.

The tar road meandered up into the hills as signs indicated we were less than ten kilometres from the border post. We stopped on a bridge to take a radio location on Soni's position.

'She might be in Bhutan already,' Bhaskar said. 'You brought your passports, right?'

We nodded, and I sensed that Nafisa was as excited as I was to be crossing into the foreign territory of Bhutan to finally see the young elephants. By now it was mid-afternoon and except for our short meal break we had been on the road all day.

Suddenly, there was Bhutan. The border post was more impressive than I had expected. A giant archway painted in red, yellow, white and blue cultural designs graced the entrance. A sign by the road said 'Visit us again. Play safe sex. Say no to drugs and alcohol.' I was reminded of crossing into Botswana one time when officials were handing out free condoms to encourage similar practices. One thing I knew about Bhutan was that it was a highly spiritual place with strong roots in Buddhism. The government's policy to measure Gross Domestic Happiness rather than Gross Domestic Product to indicate their success was a commitment to serve Bhutan's culture and people by allowing spiritual and material growth to occur alongside each other. Clearly avoiding unsafe sex and illicit substances was part of that philosophy!

There were some low-rise grey brick buildings to the right with an impressive barbed-wire fence around the outside. A couple of officers dressed in informal T-shirts and jeans emerged from a very basic office by the road and came over to our vehicle. Bhaskar handed them our passports, explaining who his group was and that Nafisa and I were joining them to look for their elephants. The rest of the team were obviously known to them as no questions were asked. Bhaskar had told us he had taken people over the border before, so there should have been no problem. Unfortunately, that wasn't the case today. The border guards' stern faces said it all.

'They won't let you through,' Bhaskar said, after a serious interchange in Assamese.

Apparently we needed visas. I knew there was no way we would get them that day; they usually took a month and had to be obtained well in advance. It crossed my mind that the guards may have wanted money, but I thought better of mentioning it as I didn't know this part of the world well enough. This was Bhutan, a Buddhist land, not the Congo.

'But didn't you take people through before?' Nafisa said, as shocked and dismayed as I was.

'Yes, but they were not Australian. They were Indian, so it was fine. I'm sorry, but you are going to have to wait here.'

'They won't even let us go just up the road?' I pleaded.

Bhaskar shook his head. He couldn't risk irritating the border guards as the WTI team needed to be able to pass through there often to check on the elephants.

Feeling utterly dejected, knowing that Soni and Tinku were probably in close proximity, Nafisa and I offloaded our bags of camera and art gear and sat on a cement wall by the road, watching despondently as the jeep drove off up the hill. I was so angry and frustrated that I couldn't even write about what was happening in my diary. To come all this way and not be allowed to see the elephants was beyond a joke. They probably got to look at those elephants every day. It seemed I never got to see elephants anymore. I wanted elephants and I wanted them now! In my head I was having a full-blown tantrum. Aside from that, I didn't know how safe it was for two conspicuously foreign women to be sitting at a border post between north-eastern India and Bhutan. It didn't feel like the most sensible thing I had done lately. Everything seemed to be going wrong and there was nothing I could do about it.

Nafisa started working on some watercolour pictures of the border post while I stomped around near the road trying to think of another way to convince the border guards to let us through. As Nafisa painted, a crowd began to gather around her, including one of the border guards, who suggested to her that she should do a picture for him, perhaps a portrait.

'Sure, I'll give you a portrait right now if you let us across the border,' Nafisa said, her face deadly serious.

The border guard laughed in a good-humoured way and walked back to his office. A short while later he returned, this time with a small orange.

'For you. Bhutanese orange,' he said, proffering the gift to Nafisa.

When she accepted it, the little gathering of men near the office burst out laughing, encouraging their colleague.

After an hour of waiting I was still angry, but I had started to feel less nervous about our safety, especially when an old lady carrying a little girl of about Solo's age on her back came out onto the road to take a closer look at us. The little girl had a strong will and wanted to run down the road. I didn't understand what she was saying to her grandmother, but some things are universally understandable and one of those things is a toddler tantrum when a two year old isn't getting her way. The grandmother chuckled, no doubt having experienced it all before.

Judging by the responses of passing motorists to our presence by the road, it was pretty obvious that people didn't very often see two foreign women in this neck of the woods. Several came over to say hello and ask if everything was alright. People were incredibly friendly. Even a scruffy-looking dog that pranced down the road seemed to be smiling, making his daily contribution to the country's Gross Domestic Happiness.

The border guard who had given Nafisa the orange returned. Had he received a call from his boss saying we could go through? Sadly not.

'Look here, you see the elephants. They came here the other day.'

What on earth was he talking about?

Then he showed us a picture on his phone of two small elephants walking under the archway where we now stood, followed by a small group of men. It had to be Soni and Tinku!

What a crazy world they now lived in, walking down the highway like regular tourists.

After a couple of hours I finally resigned myself to the fact that we weren't going to see the elephants. Now I just hoped the guys would hurry up so we could get back into the park where we at least had some chance of seeing other wildlife. Finally, we spotted the jeep returning.

'They're just up the road,' Bhaskar told us, a fact that did nothing to reduce our disappointment. 'Right here.'

Great, I thought sarcastically. Whether they were a hundred metres up the road or a hundred kilometres made no difference; we weren't allowed to cross.

He darted up to the office in a last-ditch attempt to ask for special permission to let us through, but although the guards appeared to want to help us, they didn't seem to be able to get through to the right person on the phone and this wasn't a decision they were authorised to make. I allowed myself a minute amount of hope, but when Bhaskar returned he was shaking his head.

'I'm sorry,' he said. 'I tried.'

Nafisa and I were collecting our bags to pack them into the jeep when the loud trilling of a phone rang out from the office. The guard who had been sweet talking Nafisa ran off up the road to get it. A second later, he called out to Bhaskar, who followed him into the office. After about five minutes he returned, this time with a dose of Bhutanese happiness in his stride.

'You won't believe it. We can go. You have to stay in the car and have a border guard escort you, but you can go. He said, "Are you telling me that these people came all this way from Australia just to see two elephants?" I think he was embarrassed! Let's go now before the elephants move too far into the forest.'

Elated, Nafisa and I leapt into the back of the jeep, followed promptly by our new friend, the border guard, who looked tickled pink to be our escort up the mountain. Clearly things like this didn't happen on his watch every day. I noticed him snuggle in close to Nafisa, probably still anticipating that gift of a picture – or a kiss of thanks.

By then we had been at the border for three hours and the sun was beginning to disappear as the jeep wound its way up into the mountains of Bhutan. It was much cooler there because of the altitude and I was awed by the extensive scale of the natural forests all around us. This was quite a different experience from being in India, where so much of the natural forest had been destroyed as a result of the high human density. There were fewer than twenty people per square kilometre in Bhutan, compared with almost four hundred people per square kilometre in Assam. Much of Bhutan's extensive natural forests were still intact, whereas almost two-thirds of Assam's natural habitats north of the Brahmaputra had been destroyed in recent decades.

About a kilometre up the road the driver pulled off to the side.

'This is where they were,' Bhaskar said, looking up into the hills. 'I think they will still be close by.'

A couple of the rangers jumped off the back of the vehicle and headed into the forest. I scanned the landscape with my binoculars, looking for a glimpse of elephant skin. Under strict orders, Nafisa and I were not supposed to get out of the car, especially with the eyes of our border guard watching our every move, so we had to wait on the road. I set up my tripod and camera in anticipation of their appearance. The light was rapidly fading, so any shots I got now would not be of the best quality, but anything would be better than nothing, I figured. This moment wasn't really about the photos anyway. I mean, it would have been nice to have some for the record, but in essence this was about seeing with my own eyes that elephants could be hand-reared and returned to the wild with some success. It meant that the money that Animal Works had been raising in Australia was making a difference.

After about ten minutes, the sound of the men's voices signalled that they were on their way back to the car. The question was, had they found the orphans? And then we spotted them, two healthy-looking little elephants following a path through the thick undergrowth not far from the road. The sighting was nothing more than a flash of grey hide, a brief glimpse of a little trunk, and a lot of vegetation shuffling aside to make way for them, but it was good enough for us. The photos were hopeless, but after the afternoon we had just had, seeing Soni and Tinku together was much more than we had expected.

The two young elephants looked so small in the forest as they moved off through the undergrowth away from the direction of the road, like small boats in a sea of green. Seeing them in the flesh, it struck me how vulnerable they were, without a herd to protect them and teach them how to survive in the wild. Aside from those basic survival challenges, they still had to overcome the threats that killed elephants all the time in this part of the world, from being hit by trains to avoiding the villages that had resulted in them being orphaned in the first place. My heart went out to them and to the people who were trying to give them a better life.

Despite these sad aspects, it was a hopeful moment. For one thing, these two elephants had crossed the border into Bhutan, with its lower human population and abundant forests. This was potentially a safer place for them to live than Assam. Hamren, the young male who had first escaped from the soft release enclosure, had also been sighted over here recently, which was encouraging.

The fact that Soni and Tinku were sticking together was a good thing too. Elephants were so family oriented that having two of them foraging together gave them a better chance of survival. And if, as Bhaskar suggested, they were following a wild herd, then there was a chance that Soni and Tinku would yet find a bigger family and perhaps some elders to show them the way. Time would tell what the future held for them, but with such a dedicated team keeping an eye on them, there was good reason to hope.

CHAPTER 7

A NEW CHALLENGE IN AN UNEXPECTED PLACE

Being in the forest in India had reconnected me to nature in a way that I had almost forgotten I could be. As a first-time mum, it also gave me the confidence to know that I could leave Solo for a week or so and not damage him for life. He had been perfectly fine with a combination of his dad, my mum, who flew down from Queensland, and his adoring nanny, Alina, and it turned out that I was not as irreplaceable as I had thought I was.

Seeing how Animal Works' funds had helped elephants in India also gave me the confidence to build on the seed of an idea that had germinated a few months earlier at Humani, to start supporting the rhino anti-poaching efforts in the Save Valley Conservancy. Some ideas start small and only get legs when you begin talking to people about them. Each small step you take leads to something bigger and suddenly you find you've gone much further than you ever imagined. This was the case when I contacted Peter Allison, an Australian safari guide who worked for my former employer, Wilderness Safaris, in South Africa, about something completely unrelated, and then in a casual sort of way asked him if he would consider doing an event with me in Sydney to raise funds for rhino conservation in Zimbabwe when he was next in Australia. Although we had never met in person, Peter enthusiastically agreed to participate and, as it happened, he was going to be in Sydney launching his next book three months later. With Peter on board, I asked a few other Australian authors who wrote about Africa to participate and within a short time, Tony Park, Sally Henderson, Frank Coates and Ace Bourke all agreed to be a part of it.

Tickets for the first 'Imagine Africa' dinner at Ripples Restaurant on Sydney Harbour sold out in a month, so a second one was arranged for two months later. With sponsorship from The Classic Safari Company and Epic Private Journeys, the Animal Works team of volunteers and authors raised almost $20,000 for anti-poaching efforts in the Save Valley Conservancy.

I was ecstatic with this result. Since my return from Zimbabwe, I had also been working on developing a tourist expedition to the Save Valley Conservancy for Animal Works' friends and supporters, giving people a chance to both go on an amazing wildlife safari and do some hands-on volunteer work while they were there. The trip would raise funds for Animal Works' Zimbabwean project and I hoped the expedition would be something we could repeat annually with different groups.

I also hadn't forgotten Roger's hopeful request for laptop computers for the kids at Humani Primary School and after putting out a couple of calls for donations on our websites and Facebook, I now had a dozen second-hand laptops for the school. Some were contributed by caring individuals, but the majority came from John Vickers, the South African CEO of a Brisbane company called Technology One. Animal Works' volunteer and

IT specialist Shirley Michael cleaned them up for us and installed the appropriate software to get them ready for the kids.

The pressing question for me was how to get the laptops to Humani. Posting them was risky because they might be stolen somewhere along the way, and even if they did make it, the school would have to pay an exorbitant duty to the government that they certainly couldn't afford. The only safe way to get the laptops there without paying tax was for people to take them there in their hand luggage. Using the Animal Works' expeditioners to get the laptops to Humani seemed the perfect answer. However, it wasn't as easy to convince people that Zimbabwe was as fantastic a tourist destination as I thought it was. People in Australia and beyond were still very wary about going there as Zimbabwe's image had become one of political beatings, wildlife poaching and corruption, a far cry from the friendly wildlife mecca it had once been famed for.

I had seen for myself that Zimbabwe had turned a corner since 'dollarising' and the formation of the power-sharing agreement between Morgan Tsvangarai and Robert Mugabe in 2008. Although it still had some way to go before reaching its former glory as the 'breadbasket of Africa', Zimbabwe was still one of the best places in Africa to see wildlife. In spite of all they had been through, the people were as warm as they had always been. But few tourists were returning, because either they didn't know that it was now safe again or those who had heard rumours of an improvement weren't sure whether or not to believe it. The only way for Zimbabwe to regain the trust of foreign tourists was for some of them to start going there and for word of mouth to spread the message.

Roger and Anne had run photographic safaris at Humani for many years in the 1990s prior to the political upheaval of the following decade, but with the exodus of the tourists in 2000, the only option they had for income was trophy hunting. I strongly believed that with Humani's magnificent savannahs, perennial rivers and floodplains, as well as the presence of the big five and many other species, the place had huge potential for running safaris once again. Other ranches in the Save Valley Conservancy offered tourist activities in addition to trophy hunting, although they too were struggling to get visitors to return, and some, like Humani, had completely shut down their photographic safaris due to the lack of participants.

In spite of the significant land takeover in the south of the ranch, Humani was still a place where you could walk right up to rhinos on foot, watch elephants bathing in the Turgwe River, experience hippos up close and personal with long-time hippo conservationist Karen Paolillo, and catch sight of something you see almost nowhere else in Africa – African wild dogs in reasonable densities. Humani wasn't Kruger. You wouldn't see leopard after leopard there, lions outside your tent after breakfast and an elephant's trunk in your bathroom. But the wildlife viewing was still very good, and in other ways it was better than the controlled and much visited environment of Kruger. The place had an authenticity about it, a unique history and wildness that made it feel quite different from any of the national parks I had been to. Humani was the real deal, a wildlife conservancy in which people lived and made a living from the industry of wildlife, and that made it quite a different experience from being in a national park. When you visited Humani, you felt like you were part of the community.

On top of that, I genuinely felt that any tourism experience in Africa was much more fulfilling when you got to know the locals or, better still, got involved and helped out while you were there. Humani Primary School needed computers, but it also needed a good coat of paint and new glass in the windows. These were simple jobs that could easily be carried out by a group of unqualified volunteers.

When I first suggested to Roger the idea of organising a group of Australians to come out on a photographic trip, with a dual focus on wildlife viewing and local volunteer work at Humani school, he was keen on the idea and told me to go for it. The question was, given Zimbabwe's more recently ominous reputation, would anyone go on the trip? Fortuitously, one of Animal Works' committee members, Anissa Lawrence, managed to convince half a dozen of her friends to take the plunge, and soon we had ten Australians lined up to go on safari. Still, I think Roger was as surprised as I was when it all came together in June 2012 and our twelve-seater plane flew into Humani airstrip. For many of the Australians on this trip, it would be their first African experience and something they would never forget.

I was nervous about what the group would think of Humani and whether it would live up to their expectations. After the last group I had taken on safari with the documentary crew, I knew that I couldn't expect everyone to feel Africa's magic to the same extent that I did. And then there was the fact that things always went wrong at Humani – such was the nature of the beast – and Turgwe Camp, though comfortable, was certainly not a five-star lodge. There were frogs in the cupboards and no doors on the A-frame rooms, so guests had to be at ease with the idea of really being in the wild. Leopards had been known to walk past the chalets at night, although they never came inside. Experiences like that give some people mild heart attacks, while for others, it is the best part of their safari. But until you put a person in that environment, you just never know how they are going to react.

There was also the worry that Humani vehicles were notoriously prone to breaking down and often lacked brakes and suspension. Water pumps frequently malfunctioned, meaning that showers might not always be readily available. How would the staff in camp cope with the special requests of photographic guests who were known for being much fussier than trophy hunters? One of our group, Disha, was a vegetarian. I wondered if the cook had any idea how to prepare a meal that didn't contain meat, which was the staple of the safari diet.

I wanted this expedition to work. It would raise a small amount of money for local projects, primarily paying for the installation of solar panels at Humani school, enabling the laptops to be charged on a daily basis. But it was more than the money. I wanted Roger to see that Humani still had great potential for tourism in addition to the trophy hunting that they had become so dependent on since 2000. Highly endangered species like black rhinos and African wild dogs could not be legally trophy hunted, so to game ranchers like Roger who could not operate a viable tourism operation, the two species really weren't paying their way. In southern Africa they have a saying about wildlife: what pays stays. In the case of black rhinos, Roger and others in the conservancy had spent hundreds of thousands of dollars of their own incomes protecting the rhinos from poachers, but without tourists coming and paying to see those rhinos, they represented a serious financial cost to the land-holders for minimal gain.

Roger loved his rhinos despite the financial burden, but it was harder to convince him to love the wild dogs. To him, wild dogs were predators and consumed the antelope species that he could sell to foreign trophy hunters. So, like the black rhinos, they had a financial burden associated with them. Roger was not alone in his attitude; a recent study by South African scientist Dr Peter Lindsay showed that compared to younger ranchers, older ones tended to be more negative towards wild dogs. But his studies also showed that where ecotourism provided economic benefits to ranchers, this offset most of the predation costs of wild dogs, with the result that local attitudes tended to be more positive towards the species.

The wild dogs in the Save Valley Conservancy had been studied by scientists for decades and their behaviour was quite well known. The primary species in their diet was impalas, the most common variety of antelope in the conservancy. But even the most hardcore scientific data to the contrary couldn't convince Roger that the dogs weren't knocking off *too many* of his impalas. Local wild dog researchers clearly weren't making any kind of impression and had given up on getting through to him. I felt that Roger needed a reminder that the wild dogs were potentially a unique golden egg at Humani that very few other places in all of Africa had, and the best way to do that was to show him, not tell him. I knew it was probably overly idealistic, but I hoped that when he saw the faces of tourists after they'd just seen their first wild dog at a den, it might help change his mindset a little towards this endangered species. It might not work, but it was worth a shot.

As our light aircraft soared over the Save Valley Conservancy in June 2012, an endless vista of green mopane trees dotted the pastel-pink soil like fields of fairy floss. The occasional rocky outcrops of granite created crevices and caves for lizards and snakes, and provided the ideal habitat for leopards, rock hyraxes and klip springer antelopes. This was the first time I had flown to Humani and seen it from the air and the experience was entirely different from driving. After flying from Harare over a landscape of agricultural fields for an hour, the sheer extent of the Save Valley Conservancy and all its splendid wildlife habitat made me realise how important this area was for Zimbabwe's wildlife. The vast wilderness was breathtaking.

When we landed on Humani's dirt airstrip, Roger and Anne and many of the staff from Humani were there to welcome their Australian visitors, who came from a mixture of financial, environmental, information technology and even cleaning backgrounds. After the last Australian group I had been with in Africa during the elephant documentary filming in 2008, I wondered what sort of mad antics this safari would bring. I crossed my fingers and hoped for the best.

Everyone was loaded into two LandCruisers, one of which I was pleased to see Roger had especially equipped with a roof and seats with backs, as we had requested. It was a big improvement on the ripped bench seat that usually came with the vehicle! As we entered Humani village just beyond the airstrip, all the children from Humani Primary School and their teachers were there to give the group a warm welcome with traditional singing and dancing. The kids were wearing maroon school uniforms and singing their hearts out as they stomped on the dirt and used wooden clappers to drum.

The welcome from the locals was a great start and it just got better from there. This group of Australians from Sydney, Geelong and Brisbane leapt right in, not wanting to miss a moment of being in Africa. They seemed to love every second of the volunteering experience, most of the group chipping in to paint the Humani school sign bright blue and yellow while two of the women who worked in IT, Disha and Chantal, provided basic computer training to the teachers. They walked up to an old white rhino bull known as Umgozi, meaning 'the boss', who was so relaxed that he actually lay down under a tree and fell asleep while they watched. They sat by an African wild dog den to witness one of the continent's rarest predators in its natural environment, the animals' patchwork coats glowing in the afternoon light as they whimpered and whistled to each other. With only five thousand African wild dogs remaining outside captivity, this was an amazing experience. They spent hours at Hippo

Haven with Karen Paolillo, enjoying a unique, up close and personal experience with hippos from the bank of the Turgwe River.

To my astonishment, neither of the vehicles broke down on the whole trip, which was nothing short of a miracle considering that I knew what it was taking behind the scenes to keep them going. Vegetarian Disha was highly impressed when the cook presented vegetarian meals that were tasty and diverse every day, while still preparing meals for the carnivores in the rest of the group. The guides, Limon and Gareth, were professional and warm, and got on well with everyone. Even when the water pump broke and a few of the rooms had no water, there were no complaints, and Roger's guys went into overdrive to sort the problem out within a day.

Five days passed and to my amazement the first part of the safari had gone off without a hitch. Humani's first photographic group in a decade left to spend a few days in the luxury of Wilderness Safaris' Davison's Camp in Hwange National Park, taking with them fond memories of Humani and an experience that had also left something positive behind for the local community – a newly painted sign at the school, funds to repair the cracked windows, the laptops and the money to install a solar charging system. The teachers now also had some new skills in computer programs like Word and Excel, which they would pass on to the kids.

One of the best things to come from this safari for me was the interaction with the kids, who now understood that the laptops and other gifts they had received from the visiting Australians had come to them because they lived in a special place, a wildlife conservancy with endangered species like rhinos. As they grew up, I could only hope that these new custodians of Zimbabwe would remember that their wildlife was something to be highly valued, a treasure which people from all around the world would pay to come and see.

I knew that one safari wasn't going to completely change the way Roger felt about the wild dogs, but I couldn't help but notice a flicker of acknowledgement on his face when a couple of the group said over sundowners on the last night of the safari, 'Those wild dogs were the most amazing thing I've seen. Just incredible.'

And that, for now, was a start. Sometimes you have to put something out there just in case it leads to something more. You never know when that might happen.

When I left Sydney for Zimbabwe at the end of May 2012, I knew that I wouldn't be coming back to Australia for a while. After almost five years of being based in its birthplace, Sydney, the Earth Hour global team was moving to Singapore where the government was providing principal operational funding – and so our family was moving to Asia.

In the aftermath of the climate meetings in Copenhagen and since becoming a father, Andy had become much more motivated to mobilise millions of voices across the world. Since 2009, he had handed over Earth Hour in Australia to the WWF team in Sydney as he was now responsible for the global program. Earth Hour expanded into 126 countries in 2010, and in Asia, Africa and South America the growth was particularly astronomical. By this time only half of the international Earth Hour teams worldwide were being run by WWF offices; the rest were operated by other organisations, individuals or companies. It really had become a people's movement. Andy's focus now was on increasing Earth Hour's digital reach and enabling people to go beyond the Hour itself by challenging their friends in a kind of dare for the planet, what the Earth Hour team called the 'I Will If You Will' campaign. The potential contained in this idea was enormous and celebrities like Australian supermodel Miranda Kerr immediately jumped on board to support it.

Although still relatively early days, there were now signs that Earth Hour could be used to generate some significant conservation wins. Australia's Prime Minister Julia Gillard had pledged to implement a carbon tax in Earth Hour 2011, and the following year it happened. The former president of Botswana had pledged to plant a million trees in his country for Earth Hour. And it was starting to look like the amassing of 120,000 signatures by the Earth Hour team in Russia might lead to new legislation that would prevent oil pollution in its seas. It was impossible to measure its impact on international awareness, but there was no question that by mobilising their interconnected global community, Earth Hour – through the efforts of its supporters – was starting to create real change. Now the global team needed to be in a place where it had strong support to continue to grow, both from the WWF office of the country in which it was hosted and from the government. Singapore met all their requirements and the funding from Singapore's Economic Development Bank made it possible.

On the way to Singapore we took a month off to explore Indonesia before this new chapter of our lives began. We explored Bali and the Gili Islands off Lombok, snorkelled with more turtles than I had ever seen before, and took Solo to meet the komodo dragons of Rinca Island. It was an incredible experience to be able to share with our two year old, whose adventurous, inquisitive spirit was already alive and well. Nothing really fazed Solo. To him, the deadly komodo dragons that were much bigger than him and whose saliva was filled with toxins that could kill you with one bite were just 'big lizards'. When our boat broke down several times in the middle of nowhere somewhere out in the Flores Sea, he simply slept through it, only waking up when we made it back to land. When an earthquake rocked our hotel as we lay in bed one night, terrifying the life out of Andy and me, Solo was more curious about the little sparrow that had flown into our room in a panic, its radar unsettled by the shaking earth.

'There was a bird in our room, Mummy,' he said excitedly, as Andy and I rushed downstairs, debating where the highest land point might be in case the earthquake resulted in a tsunami.

Thankfully the big wave never came, but I was about to get another kind of shake-up when we got to Singapore. I had planned to continue to run Animal Works from Singapore, even though the logistics of it would be tricky with the committee being in Sydney, but I quickly realised that this wasn't going to be possible. The high cost of living in Singapore meant that continuing to run a charity that didn't pay me a salary, as I had for the previous three years, was just no longer feasible. While I had a small income from teaching wildlife management and communication to Macquarie University students in Sydney and could continue this from Singapore for a while through an online program, it really wasn't enough to pay anything close to my share of the bills, and Animal Works took up most of my time.

And as the organisation had grown, I had begun to see that Nafisa and I had different visions of how it should move forward. We came from very different backgrounds and so perhaps I should have seen it coming. I had worked incredibly hard to establish the organisation and get it to a point where it had a solid following, and the last thing I wanted to do was walk away. Having organised the first Animal Works expedition to Africa and raised almost $20,000 for Zimbabwe's rhinos, I felt like we were just starting to make progress. In the first couple of years, as a result of Nafisa's elephant art and Meli's elephant adoption program, $15,000 had been sent to the Wildlife Trust of India's Centre for Wildlife Rehabilitation and Conservation in Assam,

In northern Kruger National Park, South Africa, this cheeky, young, wild elephant kept us entertained as he played with other young elephants, including a hilarious mock charge with his little ears flared.

Lily and Rani, two of the young orphaned elephants at the Wildlife Trust of India's Centre for Wildlife Rehabilitation and Conservation (CWRC) in Assam, India. The centre does amazing work in rescuing orphaned elephants and giving some a second chance at life.

Meli Souter, who ran Animal Works' elephant adoption program to raise funds for the CWRC, feeds one of the orphaned elephants during a visit in December 2011.

Dedicated staff feed special formula milk to the orphaned baby elephants at the CWRC, while a vet conducts regular health checks. Each calf has a unique personality and requires special nurturing from both the keepers and its new family, the other orphaned elephants.

Never suggest to a wild pygmy elephant that they're small! I learned this in Borneo when a not-so-little bull charged at me at close range in dense forest. Later that day, Andy, Solo and I watched the same elephant and another bull in a friendly jostle in the Kinabatangan River, Borneo.

Borneo's pygmy elephants are significantly smaller than other elephants, with baby-like faces and heart-shaped heads. There are only a couple of thousand left and Sabah is a great place to see them from the safety of a boat, if you're lucky enough to find some grazing on the riverbank.

RIGHT: A baby suckles from its mother in the safe confines of a breeding herd in Amboseli National Park, Kenya. Female elephants stay with their mothers, sisters and aunties for their entire lives.

BELOW: There are only about five thousand African black rhinos remaining and fine examples like this, photographed by a ranger in the Save Valley Conservancy, Zimbabwe, are a great prize for criminal gangs.

This lovely old white rhino bull at Humani in Zimbabwe is known locally as 'Umgozi', meaning 'the boss'. Sadly, a few months later he passed away. Despite the extent of poaching in the area, he died as a result of getting stuck in mud and appeared to be too old to get himself out.

It's a wonderful privilege to be up close to a wild African white rhino like Umgozi, knowing that he has the power to crush you. It's an adrenaline rush but it's also a deeply humbling experience.

RIGHT: Two of the dedicated game scouts working with Aggressive Tracking Specialists on rhino anti-poaching in the Save Valley Conservancy, Zimbabwe. These men risk life and limb on a daily basis for little pay in the war to save the last of Africa's rhinos.

BELOW: A dedicated keeper at the Nairobi elephant and rhino orphanage gives a thirsty baby a feed of special formula milk, the recipe for which has been developed by Daphne Sheldrick's team over the years through trial and error.

At Daphne Sheldrick's elephant orphanage in Nairobi, Asian celebrity Nadya Hutagalung (pictured) and I had the privilege to spend time with the orphans as they had their daily mud bath. Under the care of the keepers at the David Sheldrick Wildlife Trust, these elephants that have been orphaned, mostly due to poaching, form new families and are eventually returned to the wild in Tsavo National Park.

There's nothing quite so confronting as the carcass of an elephant. Head of Operations at the Big Life Foundation, Richard Bonham, myself and Nadya Hutagalung squat on the termite mound where this elephant bull died after being poached with a poisoned spear a few months earlier.

This incredible old elephant bull in Amboseli National Park, Kenya, known to the local researchers as 'Tim', is one of perhaps just a hundred left in Africa. Soaring prices and demand for ivory make bulls like this a prime target for poachers.

LEFT: Travelling with a toddler to remote regions in search of wildlife can be nerve-racking and exhausting at times, but it is totally worth it to be able to share special memories, like seeing my first pygmy elephants in Borneo, with the whole family. Andy, Solo (aged almost three) and me on the Kinabatangan River in Sabah, in 2012.

BELOW: Andy, Solo and I watch an elephant bull eating bamboo in Minneriya National Park, Sri Lanka, on holiday in January 2013.

RIGHT: Solo (aged one and a half) and one of Anne Whittall's rescues, a duiker, have an afternoon snack in the backyard at Humani, Zimbabwe, in 2011.

BELOW: I love this photo of Anne and Roger in their lounge room at Humani. It amazes me how buoyant and hopeful they remain, even in the face of such long-term adversity. They should be enjoying the fruits of their labour in relaxing retirement, not dealing with poachers.

ABOVE: At seventy, Roger Whittall throws oranges to a young elephant bull just outside his backyard in Humani. Despite ten years of political instability, a devastated economy, extensive settlement in former wildlife habitats and rampant poaching, the Whittalls have hung in there at Humani with characteristic determination.

LEFT: A pit stop on the highway near Manas National Park, en route to the mountains of Bhutan (in background) while radio-tracking Soni, one of five orphaned elephants rehabilitated and released into the wild by the Wildlife Trust of India in January 2011. It was an adventurous day that did not go as planned!

Bryce and Lara Clemence on their front lawn at Chishakwe, Save Valley Conservancy. This young couple and their hardworking anti-poaching team have a huge task on their hands, fighting gangs of well-armed rhino poachers in an area encompassing 3,400 square kilometres.

At a ceramics shop in Hanoi, Vietnam, Minh Nguyen from TRAFFIC shows me a bowl used to grind rhino horn into a powder. The powder is sprinkled into wine to take the edge off the toxins in alcohol. There is no evidence that this works.

Although there is some mobile phone reception in the Save Valley Conservancy these days, it's not always reliable, so most internal communication is still by radio. My friend Sid captured this image during the Animal Works' expedition to Zimbabwe in June 2012.

Undercover as 'tourists' with TRAFFIC staff Tom Milliken and Bill Schaedla (pictured), at the sprawling Chatuchuk market in Bangkok, Thailand. I was amazed at the buffet of ivory items for sale. A variety of jewellery, amulets, cigarette lighters and statues were included in the displays.

Large tusks are commonplace in Sri Lanka's Temple of the Tooth, adorning altars and worshipping areas for Buddhist devotees. Many of these tusks may have come from former domestic 'temple elephants' owned by local monks.

In Hanoi's Lan Ong Street, known for its traditional medicines, nothing was too strange a thing to ask for. Need a little dried seahorse for your impotence? Try the viagra of the sea!

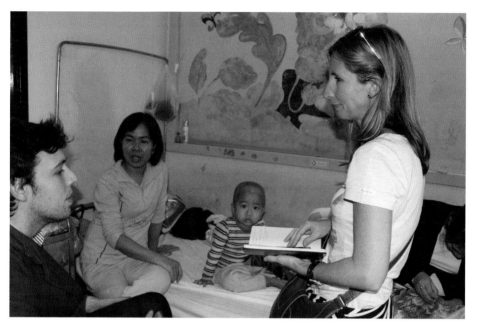

At the National Hospital of Pediatrics in Hanoi, I joined TRAFFIC staff, including Brett Tolman (pictured), to speak to mothers of children suffering from cancer about whether they would consider using rhino horn as a treatment if chemotherapy failed. Their desperation make people like this easy prey.

The happy, smiling faces of the kids at Humani Primary School in Zimbabwe, pictured in their classroom with teacher Fungai Chimsa in September 2012. They are enjoying their laptops donated from caring Australians and the new solar charging system to run them.

'One Tonne' stares us straight in the eye at Ol Donyo Lodge's waterhole, Kenya, causing all of us to freeze in awe and admiration. If the demand for ivory in Asia doesn't stop, elephant bulls like this will become a thing of the past. Let's hope – for our children's sake – that this doesn't happen.

providing funds that had helped get five baby elephants back to the wild. There was no question that everyone's efforts had been worthwhile and there was a lot more that could be done.

But you have to choose which battles are worth fighting. I had now worked for both a large global organisation and for a very small one, and I had come to realise that whenever human beings are involved there are always delicate egos to manage and politics to deal with. For me, I wanted to get back to my roots on the ground, and I needed to make a living. It was time to hand over the fundraising in Australia to others and to return to what I was trained to do, working as a freelance conservationist.

The timing made sense for another reason. Since 2008, poaching of both African elephants and rhinos had escalated to levels that hadn't been seen in two decades. My trip to Zimbabwe in June had really opened my eyes to the reality of the rhino poaching. Why was the poaching of Africa's pachyderms on the rise again? What had suddenly changed in the last few years? Were the threats the same as those that had decimated their populations in the 1980s, or were there new factors at play? I was determined to find out what was going on, initially by trying to understand the specific issue of what was happening, and why, to the Save Valley Conservancy's rhinos, and what could be done to stop it.

The funds that Animal Works had sent to the Save Valley Conservancy provided rewards and incentives for the anti-poaching scouts, anti-poaching equipment such as radios, and training for new scouts. I was really proud of what had been achieved, but I was under no illusions that these funds would come anywhere close to providing what was needed to stop the rhino poaching in Zimbabwe. Rhinos were still being slain in the conservancy and, tragically, in the first few months of 2012 another twelve were killed for their horns. This was a significant proportion of the rhino population of Zimbabwe, because Save

Valley had the second largest rhino population in the country. The illegal killing didn't look like slowing down any time soon. In neighbouring South Africa, where most of Africa's black and white rhinos lived, they were losing almost two a day to poachers.

In response to the escalating poaching crisis, in April 2012 the conservancy employed a new couple, Bryce and Lara Clemence of Aggressive Tracking Specialists. The family company had been training rangers in anti-poaching in Zimbabwe's national parks for years, so much hope was pinned on them to turn things around in the conservancy. But only time would tell whether their techniques would be able to stop the slaughter. It would take a while for Bryce to find his feet, read the situation and get behind the scenes, as well as train up sufficient loyal game scouts. In the meantime, the rhinos were still vulnerable.

With rhino horn being worth so much money on the black market, it was too easy for good guys to turn bad and get on the poaching bandwagon. Anti-poaching in Africa was just one part of the equation. It was a band-aid to help stop the onslaught, and a very necessary part of it, but it wouldn't stop the problem. I was beginning to see that preventing the complete extermination of Africa's remaining white and black rhinos meant attacking the trade chain all the way to Asia. This was not a battle that could be won in Africa alone. Stopping the demand in China and Vietnam had to be part of it. Penalties for poachers and traders had to be much stronger deterrents to the criminals involved in the trade. Authorities in Vietnam, from where the greatest demand was now coming, had to clamp down much harder on the enforcement side too.

The more I thought about all this, the more overwhelmed I became by the enormity of Africa's problem and how many levels had to be attacked to really make a difference. This was an international issue, not just a localised one. Asia and Africa were directly connected by a devastating trade chain that was driven purely by money.

It is a similar story for African elephants, with poaching in Africa higher in 2012 than it had been since the worldwide ban on ivory trading was introduced by the Convention on International Trade in Endangered Species (CITES) in 1989. Tens of thousands of elephants were being poached annually, especially in central and western Africa, as a result of the escalating demand for ivory in China and Thailand. Asia had decimated most of its own elephant and rhino populations and now buyers were turning to Africa for theirs. As we prepared to move to Asia, these were facts that I couldn't ignore.

As soon as I arrived in Singapore a fortuitous meeting with senior TRAFFIC officer Dr Chris Shepherd convinced me that I was in the right place at the right time. TRAFFIC is the world's largest wildlife trade monitoring network, at the front line of the illegal trade in rhino horn and ivory along with everything else, from soft-shelled tortoises to bears and pangolins. Over pasta at a bustling underground food court in Tanglin Mall, Chris told me that the next CITES conference was due to be held in Bangkok in eight months' time. Thailand was where a lot of the world's illegal ivory, much of it probably from poached forest elephants from Central Africa, was being sold to uninformed tourists as jewellery, phallic symbols and elephant carvings. Thailand was second only to China as the world's largest consumer of ivory, but it was number one in terms of the unregulated ivory market.

As I listened to Chris, a true veteran with twenty years' experience of working in Asia's wildlife trade, I realised I was entering a very shady, criminal underworld. Traffickers sold rhino horn as false cures for cancer or to flaunt wealth at drinking parties where it was the new 'drug of choice' to detoxify the body from booze. The wildlife trade was worth US$19 billion per year, the fourth largest illegal trade on the planet after narcotics, counterfeiting and human trafficking. Chris had the haunted eyes of a man who had seen it all, who had seen more than he wanted to. He spoke of witnessing cauldrons of tiger meat and bones in Myanmar, of bears in 'crush' cages on farms in other parts of Asia, living in abject misery their whole lives, and other horrors that I shoved into a dark part of my brain so I didn't have to think any more about them.

Singapore was a transit country for rhino horn and ivory, Chris explained, and an important link in the trade chain. The biggest illegal haul of ivory to date was seized in Singapore in 2002 – about six tonnes. Much of it was headed for China, the key country driving the illicit ivory trade, but it was also going to marketplaces in Thailand, where it was sold to unaware tourists, and the bulk of it was illegally poached from Africa. Other Asian countries like Malaysia and Vietnam also played a role as transit countries for illegal ivory, and there was a growing demand for ivory in the Philippines, where it was carved into Catholic religious icons. Central and West Africa were being hit the hardest by elephant poachers. This was the home of the rare forest elephant, which genetic research had recently suggested was a separate species to the African savannah elephant. No one even knew for sure how many of these unique, forest-dwelling elephants still existed, or where the cut-off point was for the species geographically, but these more diminutive pachyderms with their thin, straight, downward facing tusks and round ears were now under siege by poachers.

In one of the more recent and most shocking incidents, two hundred elephants were massacred in Bouba N'Djida National Park, Cameroon, by heavily armed poachers on horseback from Sudan and Chad. Entire families of elephants were killed. The poachers had moved on to Cameroon after decimating elephant populations in Chad and the Central African Republic. All this bloodshed was to fuel the demand for ivory trinkets, carvings and jewellery coming from Asia.

As for the rhinos in Asia, Chris told me that most of them had already been wiped out. Just the year before, Vietnam's last wild Javan rhino bit the dust in Cat Tien National Park, shot through the leg by poachers, its horn hacked off. There were fewer than a couple of hundred Sumatran and Javan rhinos combined left in south-eastern Asia, and only a couple of thousand greater one-horned rhinos remained in north-eastern India and Nepal. With so few of its own rhinos left, Asia was now turning to Africa for horn.

Most of the poached African rhino horn was headed for Vietnam, where demand was on the rise. Like many people, I had thought that rhino horn was used as an aphrodisiac in Traditional Chinese Medicine (TCM), but I now learned that was a myth. Rhino horn was, Chris explained, used to reduce fever and had been a part of TCM for generations, but not as a sex-enhancing drug. Due to its high financial value, it was flaunted at Vietnamese drinking parties as a way to help take the edge off a hangover, the perfect way to show off wealth and status among the nouveau riche.

'But why not just use Panadol?' I asked.

He nodded. 'It's more than a painkiller. It's status. And there are also guys out there selling the horn to people dying of cancer, telling them it will cure them. Of course it won't, but they'll try anything. They're desperate. And these guys selling it are real criminals.'

The more I listened to Chris, the more I realised how much I had to learn about Asia if I was to be able to make any kind of impact on the poaching problem in Africa. If something major wasn't done soon to stop the trade on the Asian side, we were headed towards a future in which both African elephants and rhinos would follow their Asian cousins, all of which were either extinct or almost gone.

Filled with dread, I knew that the world I was entering was going to show me things I didn't want to see. The sheer price of rhino horn made it more financially valuable in illegal trade circles than gold or cocaine, which meant that there were some dangerous criminals involved who cared nothing for human life, let alone the lives of animals. This was a far cry from the wild plains of Africa. In this part of the world, wildlife's only value was as medicine or as decoration. For me, as an animal lover, this was not going to be a happy place.

Before I could go any further on my journey into Asia's wildlife trade, I had a lot of reading to do to wrap my brain around what was happening. The situation in every Asian country was completely different and I needed to learn a little about all of them before I could even begin to understand why people were buying ivory or horn. I had no experience in this part of the world and it showed.

On top of moving to Singapore, handing over Animal Works, going freelance and researching the illegal Asian wildlife market, I still had to finish what I had started in Zimbabwe. Humani Primary School had laptops but lacked electricity to charge them. After months of looking for an affordable solar power system, a South African, Neil Bradshaw of Greensparks Solar-Electric, agreed to put something together for them with the money that had been raised from the Animal Works tourist expedition in June. In September the set-up was ready to install and so I flew to Zimbabwe to work with some of Roger's team to put it in.

Fungai and the teachers at the school were overjoyed with the new equipment as it would enable the Grade 6/7 kids to use the computers on a daily basis. The principal told me that to his knowledge this was the only rural school in Zimbabwe that had so many operational computers. To them it was enormously important to know that the outside world hadn't forgotten them, and that even if the media spotlight was no longer on Zimbabwe, people still cared.

Meanwhile, after a relatively quiet time politically, it had been an eventful couple of months at Humani. During August a small group of politically motivated officials from the nearby town of Masvingo had been causing a lot of unrest in the conservancy, undertaking their own land grab, dubbed the 'Masvingo Initiative'. The media reported that Masvingo's Governor Titus Maluleke, together with member of parliament Aaron Baloyi from Chiredzi South and others, had stormed into a technical meeting between the conservancy chiefs and the Department of National Parks that was taking place on conservancy grounds and attempted to vote down both the chair and vice chair of the conservancy. At the same time, the top level of the Department of National Parks withdrew the ranch owners' trophy hunting licences for the year, meaning that all of their clients booked for the 2012 season could not legally hunt. The Department of National Parks then handed out trophy hunting licences for the conservancy to several ZANU PF heavyweights, including Minister for Higher Education Stan Mudenge and the Masvingo governor.

With little to no tourism income, the prospect of losing their trophy hunting income was terrifying. It would have been the last straw for many of the ranchers in the Save Valley Conservancy who were already under serious financial pressure. For the wildlife it was potentially devastating as it also meant that there would be no spare cash to pay the anti-poaching teams. Fearing a wildlife massacre, the vice chair of the conservancy, Willie Pabst, the German owner of Sango, went to the media. The story made international headlines, with Mugabe's ZANU PF blamed for the hostile takeover.

Meanwhile, in the middle of all this uncertainty, Anne was mauled by one of the young female buffaloes she had once reared. The buffalo usually roamed around near the house and had never caused any trouble until this particular day when she knocked Anne over near a thornbush and repeatedly pushed her into it, ramming Anne with her horns. Unable to get back on her feet, Anne played dead while the dogs barked furiously at the buffalo. The animal continued to ram her but finally lost interest and moved away enough for her (sprightly at seventy!) to scramble up a tree. She stayed there calling for help, but no one was nearby and eventually, covered in deep, spiky thorns and blood, grazes and bruises, she staggered to the house of her sister-in-law, Jane. Several weeks later when I arrived at Humani, Anne's legs were still inflamed and raw from the thorns, some of which were probably still lodged in her flesh.

It was mid-September, the hot dry season in the lowveld, and I was up early. There was no such thing as a lie-in in these parts and, in any case, jet lag usually had me up by 4 am for the first week. Roger's voice boomed over the radio soon after five and it was the nicest time of day to watch the natural world awaken before the heat of the sun started baking the lowveld.

The day before, after the long drive from Harare with Roger and Anne's son-in-law Aiden, I had sat in their back yard under a baobab beside a Sabi star in full bloom, watching a young elephant bull munch on leftover oranges from this year's crop. He took his time, picking up the oranges one by one with the dexterous tip of his trunk, then inserting them into his mouth like delicious sweets. He was only mildly interested in the human sitting nearby taking photographs of him, eyeing me with occasional bursts of curiosity. When he was done eating, a herd of eland took his place, followed by a troop of baboons. All of them must have been waiting for the king of the jungle to move on, not willing to risk coming too close while the elephant fed, knowing their place in the hierarchy of the animal kingdom where size counts for a lot.

Now, next to where I had squatted with my camera, a bushbuck crept around the garden nibbling on Anne's flowers, looking up at regular intervals to make sure I was not a threat. It was one of the things I had always loved about Humani: that the place was surrounded by animals, some of them raised by Anne and never really leaving, others wild animals looking for an easy feed near the house.

'Come and join me, my girl!' Anne called from her bedroom. 'Pour yourself some tea on the way.'

The sun had not yet risen, but there was enough light to help myself to a cup of steaming black Tanganda tea from the teapot on the metal table in the yard. It was the same table that, many years earlier, Jessie the cheetah had always liked to lie on when no one was looking. I poured a drop of long-life milk into my tea and stirred in a healthy spoonful of white sugar before joining Anne in her bedroom. She was tucked up under the covers and gazing out at the bush framed by her bedroom wall – all that separated us from the wild world beyond was transparent chicken wire and mosquito mesh. The room had not changed in nearly twenty years, from what I could tell, although now there was one new addition: a thick horizontal log had been erected on posts outside the bedroom, providing some kind of security fence in front of the mesh windows.

'Is that to keep the war vets out?' I asked.

Anne chuckled. 'Oh no! We don't even lock up. It was for Jimmy!'

Jimmy was a black rhino that Anne had raised from a baby to adulthood, now roaming free somewhere in the conservancy.

'He was so cheeky, you know. He used to come into the bedrooms and sleep on the beds!'

I laughed, imagining a two-tonne rhino bull making himself at home in the Whittalls' house. When I had lived there, Jessie the cheetah had often been known to sleep on my bed when no one was looking. It didn't seem unbelievable that a rhino would try to do the same thing.

'Isn't the Sabi star beautiful?' Anne said, as we watched the sun rise. 'The flowers will drop off now after that *guti* [drizzly] weather we had.'

The Sabi star, a Zimbabwean endemic, was one of the most unusual flowering bushes in Africa. It flowered only when it was really dry and, unlike with other plants, it was the rain that caused the brilliant, hot-pink blooms to drop off. Everything in this place did things its own way.

Anne handed me a printout of an article from one of Zimbabwe's main newspapers that had come in via email the day before.

'You might be interested in this,' she said.

According to the journalist, Mugabe had allegedly told his cabinet that the Save Valley Conservancy should become a national park. From what we had been told by other landowners in the conservancy who were dealing directly with the government, the troublemakers from Masvingo had never had the president's support in the Save Valley Conservancy land grab and their actions were not in line with government policy. Mugabe and his political party, ZANU PF, however, had borne the brunt of the international media's criticism. The Whittalls' sources informed us that he had actually told them to step back, but no one knew for sure what conversations were really taking place. The future of the conservancy remained as uncertain as ever.

'Mugabe is the conservancy's patron, you know,' Anne said. 'Many people have forgotten that. Until now he hasn't really touched the conservancies.'

With Anne and Roger now overdue for a relaxing retirement, I wondered what the future looked like for this family and their neighbours in the Save Valley Conservancy. It was already two-thirds indigenised, with many of the landowners having indigenous partners, and the current chairman was also indigenous. But there were still greedy people high up in government who were pre-pared to take a chance to increase their own wealth, using their power and connections to bully for a particular outcome.

The last decade had already brought with it a great deal of change for the Whittalls. On the bright side, Roger and Anne now had nine grandchildren. On the negative side, two-thirds of Humani had been written off to settlers, and with it a huge area of former wildlife habitat had become subsistence farmland. What was still strong, however, was the Whittalls' belief that what they had was worth saving. That had not wavered, despite the enormous, ongoing costs of keeping the rhino poachers at bay, taking poachers to town to be prosecuted, and undergoing expensive and lengthy court cases to see them convicted.

Understandably, in the face of the recent land grab by the Masvingo governor and his cronies, Roger was less enamoured of the idea of tourism than he had been in June during the Australian safari. What tourist would come to Zimbabwe with shenanigans like that going on? He had a point that was hard to argue with. This area might have had all the right prerequisites for a great tourist destination, but the government wasn't mak-ing it easy for the country to encourage tourists to return.

Other economic prospects to keep the place afloat, like legal-
ising the sale of rhino horn so that they could regularly dehorn the
rhino and sell the horn to Asian markets, had more potential to
an increasing number of ranchers in this part of the world. Roger
wasn't the only person in Zimbabwe to consider this option.
There was a growing coalition of voices coming from southern
Africa who wanted the rhino horn trade legalised. They believed
that the demand for rhino horn would always exist in Asia as
it had always been a part of Traditional Chinese Medicine, so
why not enable the custodians of the rhinos to benefit rather than
the black market criminals? The horn would grow back in three
years, enabling a sustainable resource without injuring or killing
the animal.

Roger told me he had heard of some Chinese investors who
were interested in getting involved in the conservancy and the
prospect interested him. I couldn't help but worry that this
might create a whole load of new problems. If the market was
opened up for legal rhino horn in Asia, this might lead to a drop
in prices, but were there really enough rhinos left to justify the
trade? What would be the effects of immobilising these wild,
heavy creatures to dehorn them every few years? It would be
both stressful and dangerous, for the rhinos and the people doing
the procedure. The trade itself could easily breed corruption on
both the African and Asian sides. How would a legal trade in
rhino horn be regulated? But if trade wasn't legalised, what was
an alternative that gave local people a way to benefit from the
rhinos in places, like Zimbabwe, where political instability was a
direct threat to the tourism industry?

I had a strong feeling that no matter what happened,
Humani's future was going to make it quite a different place from
the one I had known as a young woman. Change was inevitable,
but it was hard to tell whether the conservancy was heading out

of the storm or straight into another one. The country had certainly turned a corner and now it needed to be rebuilt. Only time would tell if the Save Valley Conservancy would continue to be one of Zimbabwe's great jewels of the wildlife industry, a title it had earned through the blood, sweat and tears of those who had sacrificed so much to keep the wildlife alive.

As for me, with the solar power system in place at the school, the next thing on my agenda was to spend some time with Bryce and Lara Clemence, the husband and wife team who had been brought in to get on top of the rhino poaching in April. They lived at Chishakwe, a ranch in the north of the conservancy about half an hour by car from Humani, and it was there I was headed next. Although I was no longer representing Animal Works, it still mattered to me to know personally that the funds we had raised from the dinners in Sydney were being used wisely. The Clemences' rhino anti-poaching operation had received two-thirds of the funding, so I had arranged to go and see how they operated and what progress they were making. I said goodbye to the Whittalls and the teachers at Humani school and prepared myself to go on anti-poaching patrol.

CHAPTER 8

RHINOS OR RANGERS?

Lara Clemence met me with a welcoming smile as I stepped through the gate into the sprawling garden around their enormous old home at Chishakwe. The half dozen old homes on the ranch were the original ones built by the first settlers back when it was still cattle country. This was also the base for the conservancy's wild dog project, run by Dr Rosemary Groom. In her late twenties, Lara handled the communications supplies for the anti-poaching operation from home, while Bryce managed and trained the game scouts in the bush.

In nature's stark surroundings, an array of water sprinklers fed by ground water made the Clemences' vast green lawn an inviting oasis. This time of year in Zimbabwe was hot and dry, the dirt bare or with a light cover of dry grass. It would be another month at least before they saw any decent rainfall. The landscape crackled underfoot with crunchy, dead mopane leaves, their shrivelled husks forming a carpet of fading brown on the sunbaked, red sand. The mopane trees themselves were skeletal anorexics, without a single leaf left on their limbs for modesty.

A light sprinkling of rain a few days earlier had resulted in occasional patches of short green grass in low-lying areas, but the puddles had long ago dried up in the heat of the day and there was little other grass left to speak of that hadn't already been eaten by the animals. For the most part, the conservancy felt like a desert at this time of year, prior to the transformation that the rainy season would bring. The dry heat parched my throat and made it impossible to rehydrate completely during the day. Water was everything here, both the bringer of life and the destroyer of it.

The dry landscape at this time of year had one major benefit, though: it made for excellent game watching. With limited grass and leaves interfering with the view, you could see a long way into the bush as you drove, revealing animals too large to hide with little cover. It also meant that animals congregated near rivers and waterholes, so their patterns were a little more predictable. I had seen more giraffes on the drive from Humani with Anne than I had in years.

The first thing Lara said was, 'Our guys have found some rhinos close by. Do you want to see them?' Her eyes twinkled as she knew what my response would be.

'Hell yes!'

About five minutes later Bryce arrived in a Save Valley Conservancy LandCruiser. I was expecting a macho man who would crunch my fingers as he shook my hand, but that couldn't have been further from the truth.

'It's great to have you here, Tammie. It means a lot to us when people actually come out and see what we're trying to do.'

He was instantly likeable and there was a humility about him that made me warm to him. The Whittalls had told me a little about his background because his father, Pete, who shared the tracking business with him and Lara, was well known in Zimbabwe, having been a chief instructor of the Rhodesian Special Forces during the war for independence and a founding member of its tracking unit. Bryce had been trained by his father, who became a Christian missionary after the war and started a bush skills and conservation camp for children at Kariba. Bryce and his siblings had been home schooled. This was no tattooed, rifle-brandishing tough man with a crushing handshake and macho facade. He was not at all what I expected.

As I drove off with Bryce he seemed delighted to be able to share some of his day-to-day experiences with me. The money that our dinners had raised in Sydney earlier in the year meant a lot to him and with some of it Nicholas Duncan, the founder of SAVE Foundation, a Western Australian organisation that had been supporting rhino conservation in Zimbabwe for decades, had purchased a new spotting scope for Bryce that would enable him to get much better sightings of the poachers using the height advantage of the many rocky outcrops in the conservancy.

'Let me ask you a question, Tammie. What is more important – rangers or rhinos?'

I thought about it for a moment. The rhinos were obviously extremely important, but were they more important than the rangers who were protecting them? Of course they weren't, but I surprised myself by having to think about it for a second.

'Most people say rangers,' Bryce went on, 'some say rhinos. But of course, we are talking about people's lives here. Rangers are more important by a long way, but that's not how we've been operating in this country. This war against poaching will be won with good, reliable men. They have to come first.'

As we chatted a dark green Land Rover rounded the bend towards us. Bryce seemed to recognise the driver, who had a grin on his face for all of Africa. His reaction to Bryce showed that he clearly respected him. The man got out of his vehicle and came over to ours. He was smartly dressed in a dark green uniform, complete with shiny new boots. In this part of the world a smart, well-kept uniform was always an indicator of a sense of pride in one's work. As I stepped out of the Cruiser to shake his hand, I noticed the SAVE logo plastered on the side of the Land Rover. For twenty-five years SAVE had raised millions of dollars, mostly through dinners in Perth that auctioned unique cricket memorabilia, to support rhino conservation in Zimbabwe. With the grave poaching of rhinos in the country's national parks, leaving no more than a handful in places like Hwange, Nicholas Duncan had told me on an earlier phone call that SAVE was stepping up its support in the private conservancies like this where most of the country's rhinos now remained.

'This is Gonas, my chief ranger,' Bryce introduced us, and I reached out to shake the man's hand.

The two men spoke briefly so we could get a location on the rhinos. Two of his guys, one employed by the conservancy, the other working for the Department of National Parks, were apparently close by and watching a herd of three white rhinos, a male, female and a youngster.

Bryce parked the Cruiser in the limited shade of a leafless mopane tree and we walked from there. By now it was late morning, around 11 am, and the sun was scorching. It burned into my head and the side of my face with the ferocity of a laser beam. There was almost no shade at this time of year and walking through the bush in the middle of the day felt a little suicidal.

I took note of the shapes of the rocky outcrops around us. They created navigation points that could be followed back to the vehicle if we got lost. It was an unnecessary action, given that I was with guys who knew the area well, but it was something that I still did subconsciously, out of habit. When the sun is almost directly overhead, as it was now, there are no shadows in the landscape to help tell the way as there are at other times of day, so you need to rely on landmarks.

Dry mopane leaves crackled loudly underfoot, so I did my best to land my feet on bare soil to avoid making a sound. I didn't usually worry about walking up to white rhinos as they were less aggressive than black ones, but I didn't know how nervous these rhinos would be, given how persecuted their species had become since I had last done this in the conservancy. There was also always the chance that we might walk into lions or elephants, both of which had excellent hearing.

After about twenty minutes of weaving through the bush, two young men in uniform materialised. One was leaning against a tree in the meagre shade, the other on a rock. I shook the men's hands as Bryce introduced them as Colin and Tendai. Later he explained that together these two men along with a radio were a management unit that he identified as a 'call sign'. Tendai was a representative of the Department of National Parks and his presence in a call sign was essential because it meant that they could 'shoot to kill' if they came across poachers. Without a National Parks' representative they weren't allowed to shoot as they could end up on manslaughter charges. It didn't matter in court whether it was in self-defence (the poachers could still fire at them, of course).

We walked in almost complete silence towards where the men had left the rhinos. They checked the wind every minute or so, making sure it was in our favour and not carrying our scent to the rhinos.

'Whites have better eyesight than blacks,' Bryce whispered. 'If they come for us . . . which they won't usually, being whites, but the female has a calf with her so we have to be more careful . . . so if she does charge, get behind a tree.'

Bryce was confident in the bush without being arrogant about it. He didn't know my level of experience with rhinos, so he was erring on the safe side. The truth was, although I had done this before, it had been a long time since I had walked up to an African rhino and there didn't look to me to be that many climbable trees around. I felt slightly dazed by the sun, so I hoped I didn't have to make a quick getaway.

The guys spotted them a long time before I did. The three animals were hidden behind bushes about thirty metres from us, our view almost completely obstructed by thick branches. At least one seemed to be sleeping. They were so well camouflaged that in spite of their size (white rhinos can grow up to three and a half tonnes) anyone who wasn't looking out for them probably would have simply thought the dark shapes were boulders.

The mother was the first to detect our presence. She faced our position straight on, as her little one bumbled around beneath her. This competent mother wasn't taking any chances, I was pleased to observe. While she didn't run, she was extremely alert. The male, on the other hand, was sleeping peacefully and didn't even seem to know we were there. Not wanting to bother the little family for too long, we only stayed with them for about ten minutes before leaving them in peace for their midday siesta.

In the Cruiser on the way back, Bryce got a call from one of his team saying that a young female black rhino was nearby, so we decided to go and take a look. At the rate at which we were finding rhinos that day, one would have thought they were as common as flies. But of course, that wasn't the case.

The relentless hunting of rhinos across Africa was particularly severe in Zimbabwe in the 1980s and 1990s. Zimbabwe had been Africa's rhino stronghold until then, with around 75,000 of them, but their numbers dropped from 1,775 in 1987 to just 315 in 1995. The enormous losses in the Zambezi Valley led to a translocation of almost fifty black rhinos to the Save Valley Conservancy and with the intensive protection that the private landholders provided, the population climbed to one hundred and twenty by 2006. That year, thirty white rhinos were also introduced to the Save Valley Conservancy, making it home to the largest rhino population in the country.

In 2012 the conservancy had the second largest rhino population in the country, a title that it would not hold much longer if the poaching continued at current rates. With the land reform program and political instability of the preceding twelve years, including at least a third of the conservancy being settled, poaching had surged, and between 2005 and 2009 Save Valley Conservancy lost almost a third of its breeding stock of female black rhinos. Between 2008 and the middle of 2009, a further twenty-two black and three white rhinos were poached. The situation had reached crisis point but the poaching continued, albeit at a reduced rate, when the conservancy stepped up its anti-poaching measures with the appointment of the Clemences in early 2012.

Given the enormous area of the conservancy, about 3,400 square kilometres, it was reassuring that Bryce's guys seemed to be keeping a close eye on the rhinos and appeared to have a good idea where at least some of them were.

'I always know where this one is,' Bryce said. 'She is only about two years old. Her mother was shot by poachers just five hundred metres from here. She's never left the area.'

This made her vulnerable, Bryce went on to explain, because her choice of territory was only four kilometres from the conservancy boundary from where poachers often invaded. As a female she was a valuable breeder and she was still very young, having lost her mother before she was able to learn about survival. Females tended to be territorial, making them more predictable and, as a consequence, more at risk from poachers.

This female's story was sad, but Bryce went on to tell me one that was even worse. A few weeks earlier a female white rhino was shot and killed at Humani. The poachers took her horn, but they left something behind – her baby. By the time the game scouts found the mother's body, the lions were eating it. Without the mother to protect it, the lions had killed the baby too, leaving not one but two casualties of the one poaching incident.

When poachers attacked rhinos in this part of the world they didn't always kill them. In April 2011 a male white rhino, named Maduma by locals, was confronted by poachers. He had been dehorned by conservationists in an attempt to provide a disincentive to poachers, but that didn't stop them shooting him several times until he was unconscious and then hacking off what was left of both of his horns. Even the horn below the skin was extremely valuable to them and, being at the base, the surface area was larger than the tip. The poachers took off with their booty leaving the rhino for dead, with numerous bullet wounds and a gaping, bleeding hole in his face.

But Maduma didn't die. Game scouts found him some time later, staggering around half concussed and in a serious battle for his life. Vets were flown in to immobilise him and flood his system with antibiotics, and this rhino put up one hell of a gallant fight for his own survival. Against all the odds, over the next week or so skin grew over the wound and Maduma appeared to be able to breathe and eat. Tragically, almost three weeks after the gruesome attack, vets made the decision to euthanase him as his shattered shoulder was unable to support his weight.

Maduma had been killed a year before the Clemences started their anti-poaching operation in the conservancy, and even though the rate of rhino poaching had declined significantly since they started, Bryce knew it was a massive task to stop it completely.

'The big challenge we have here is we just don't have enough men to cover this whole conservancy. At Malilangwe, the game ranch next door, they have seventy scouts for an area a tenth of the size of Save Valley. At best we only ever have twelve men on the ground at any one time, including National Parks staff.'

The image of a rhino staggering through the bush, dazed and in severe pain, with a bloody hole where its horns used to be, was one that would stay with me for a long time. But it wasn't just the rhinos that bore the brunt of the poaching.

'I want you to meet Luxon,' Bryce said, as we drove back to the house. 'Now there's a man with a story. But first, lunch.'

Back at the house Lara and her housekeeper had prepared a feast of home-grown grilled chicken on the bone with crispy skin, mashed butternut pumpkin, steamed broccoli and rice.

'Do you mind if we say grace?' Bryce asked, reaching for his wife's and my hand from the head of the table.

I lowered my eyes slightly awkwardly as Bryce recited the verses. It wasn't that I was uncomfortable. After all, my family had often said grace when we were growing up. After the formal version my dad had often said, 'Two, four, six, eight. Grub's up, don't wait!' or some other version that made us kids laugh. I suppose what felt strange was simply that it had been a very long time since I had done it. Thankfully I wasn't asked to provide the words. I might have been tempted to come out with one of my father's versions.

It was the first of a number of things Bryce and Lara said or did over the next couple of days that demonstrated their Christianity. Their faith was the backbone of their lives and it gave them the confidence to do what they did for a living, a profession in which to kill or be killed was a daily risk.

Over lunch Lara explained that all of her siblings now lived in Australia, where her parents were living after losing their farm near Banket, north of Harare, early in the 2000s during the first lot of political land grabs. With no remaining family in Zimbabwe to support her, they had very much wanted her to consider a future in Australia too. But at nineteen she was in love with Bryce, and they married so that she could stay in Zimbabwe.

'It was the right decision for me,' Lara said. 'I love it here.'

'Do you ever worry about your safety?' I asked her.

She smiled. 'Sometimes. It can get a bit lonely when Bryce is out all day. But it's beautiful, this place, and I have a job to do.'

I suddenly realised how funny it was for me – of all people – to be asking someone about their safety. When had I started caring about safety? The answer was clearly only recently. If someone had asked me to do the Clemences' job now with a two year old to care for, I would have said definitely not. Before kids? Yes. But now it was a different story. It was one thing to risk your own life in a war zone in which rhinos were like diamonds to criminals who wouldn't hesitate to slit your throat if you stood in their way, but another to risk your child's. I wondered whether Bryce and Lara would still be doing this kind of work when their children came along.

After lunch, Bryce and I drove across to the ranch next door, Sango, where Luxon lived. I knew there was something not quite right about the man as soon as I saw him. He walked with a serious limp, as if one leg was being dragged by the other. He seemed shy and a little nervous about meeting me, avoiding eye contact until Bryce explained that I was there to hear his story. My interest seemed to give him a boost of confidence.

I listened as Luxon told me in harrowing detail about the day a poacher tried to kill him, leaving him bleeding and paralysed from the waist down, the day he lost the use of his legs. He and a fellow scout had been tracking poachers hunting for meat with dogs and spears when the situation suddenly turned. They made contact with the poachers at a water pan, but couldn't shoot at them, despite having a rifle, because of the risk that they would be thrown in jail by the police.

Luxon had almost caught one of them, but then at the worst possible moment he tripped and fell into a deep elephant footprint, a hole in the dried mud. The poacher took the opportunity to attack him while he was down, viciously stabbing him once in the back. Immediately Luxon lost all feeling in his legs and couldn't move. The poachers took his rifle and his radio, and chased after the other scout, who had run away when Luxon was attacked. They left Luxon for dead in the bush, paralysed by the strike to his spine, able only to drag himself along with his arms, and gushing blood into the sand.

'I was down. I couldn't feel my legs. Ahhh nothing!' Luxon said, his eyes wide as the painful memories flooded back.

Night was coming and he knew that predators would follow, drawn by the smell of his blood, if his injuries didn't kill him first. Terrified, Luxon thought his number was up. He must also have been in enormous pain, although not once did he mention this as he relayed his story to me. As night fell, he was completely alone.

'I was shivering! And I couldn't move!'

Incredibly, by chance, the game scout who had run away during the attack came upon a safari vehicle on the road. He told them what had happened and they immediately sent out a search party for Luxon. By this time it was dark.

Extraordinarily, the men found Luxon before he succumbed either to his wounds or to predators and he was hospitalised in time for doctors to work on the spinal damage. It was now six years down the track and Luxon could walk again, albeit with a severe limp. Walking, something he had always taken for granted, was no longer an easy task for him. When I asked whether all this time later he was suffering continued health problems as a result of the injury, he explained how he still had a lot of pain in one leg and a complete lack of feeling in one part of the other.

It amazed me that he had a sense of humour about the incident. He laughed as he told me how, the next morning, the game scouts had returned to where they found him and discovered fresh lion prints in the sand next to his bloodstains.

'Lions came there and they saw the blood!' he explained, chuckling, his eyes wide. 'They licked my blood!'

Talking to Luxon really brought home the reality of the courage of these men who went to war every day to protect Africa's last rhinos. The poachers who had attacked him had been meat poachers, not even rhino poachers, who were known for being much more ruthless. It wasn't like the game scouts were receiving danger pay or any kind of monetary incentives other than a basic wage and rations. They all had to provide for families who they didn't see for months at a time. What Bryce had been saying when he'd raised the question about who was more important – rhinos or rangers – really sank in now that I had heard Luxon's story.

Later that afternoon, Lara joined us to drop off a couple of the game scouts who were going out on patrol. On their backs they carried everything they needed to survive for the next four days and nights, from rolled-up camping mattresses and small tents to water bottles and food. They would live on *sadza*, the staple diet of most people in this part of Africa, which was made from ground white corn, plus dried meat and cabbage. In this case, both men carried automatic weapons.

'Not all of our men carry guns,' Bryce said. 'They have to earn it. The last thing I want is to train up a guy and have him turn . . . with a gun on him. It takes time, training and trust.'

I watched a herd of plains zebra pelt through the bush, dizzying in their stripes against the barren landscape as we drove past. Dust flew up around them in the late afternoon light, bathing them in a peachy glow.

Bryce stopped the car in the bush at a ranch called Mkondo where the scouts would start their patrol at first light the next day. I shook their hands and tried to convey my respect for their work with my eyes. Bryce had made a special effort to ensure that as many of his men as possible met me while I was there because he felt it gave them a boost to know that someone who had helped raise funds for them was making the effort to see their work. The endless business of tracking rhinos hour after hour could become a bit of a grind when you did it every day, apparently!

As the sun set Lara poured steaming cups of *rooibos* tea for us. Neither she nor Bryce touched alcohol. I was hankering for a beer, but their decision not to drink was one I respected. Bryce wasn't one of those guys who needed a drink to loosen his tongue. He was open and honest and wanted to talk about the challenges they faced in their work. He wanted people to know that building the capacity of scouts on the ground was the backbone of a successful anti-poaching operation and essential to save the rhinos. His guys needed better pay, bonuses so that they could build houses for their families and pay their kids' school fees. He wanted them to feel more valuable than the rhinos, so that the job of a game scout became one of such pride to be protecting their national heritage that every kid in the country would want to do it, so the children of those who protected Zimbabwe's rhinos were proud of their dads and wanted to be just like them when they grew up. So the money that enticed people to kill rhinos wasn't worth the shame of being a poacher.

What he was saying totally made sense, but there was a burning question that I just had to ask. One of the things I found contradictory was Bryce's attitude to killing – he was obviously a devoted Christian but I knew that he had killed poachers in the course of fulfilling his duty and that he was prepared to do it again if he had to. Clearly, killing and the Christian faith did not seem to sit well together.

Bryce had told me a story about how at Sinamatela in northern Zimbabwe he and his anti-poaching team, including National Parks staff, had opened fire on poachers who were refilling their water bottles in a river. He and his men had danced around avoiding the return fire aimed at them and, amazingly, none of them was shot. However, a poacher was shot that day. Bryce and his men slept with the body that night as they were on foot and it was a long way back to the vehicles.

'My guys had mixed feelings about it, I could tell. They were happy that God had helped them. They were saying to him – to the dead body – things like "your day has come". There was some remorse. Certainly no pleasure in it.' Bryce paused pensively, recalling the memory before continuing: 'One of my guys was asking him, "My friend, why did you do this?" They looked at his face, and there was a mixture of remorse and relief. A man had died but the rhino had survived. That was our job, to protect the rhinos. We knew this guy [the poacher]. He'd killed up to fifteen rhinos.'

'And what about you, Bryce? How do you rationalise your belief in God, your Christian values, with the fact that every day you go out to work you might have to kill someone?'

'It's because of my faith that I do this . . . I believe that God protects us in the work that we do . . . and protects my guys, like that day in Sinamatela. That morning we were thanking the Lord for breakfast. That day . . . I had an unusual feeling that we'd be protected. I had it there in the back of my mind that if we find these poachers today, would we have the courage to tackle them? When we went out, I felt unusually calm.'

In the car later, I asked him, 'Is it worth it? The danger?'

'Tammie, this is a worthy cause. You get used to the fact that you could get killed every day. You can't get complacent, but you learn to live with it. It's my job to keep my guys motivated. That's why I put rangers before rhinos. They constantly run the risk of being shot or attacked by dangerous animals.'

I wasn't sure he had answered my question exactly, but he had raised some interesting points. Even if Bryce's scouts were relatively well paid, most received salaries well below the poverty line. And yet these men were at the forefront of the battle to save Zimbabwe's last rhinos. If a poacher offered them a thousand dollars to give them some information on the location of a rhino, that would have been very hard to turn down. He was relying on loyalty and pride to keep them straight.

'The challenge we have here is the internal corruption,' Bryce went on.

He wasn't talking about his own game scouts, but others who worked in the conservancy at some of the ranches. His sources told him that the poaching syndicates were being given information by men working for the conservancy itself, some of them high ranking and, ironically, receiving salaries to *protect* the rhinos. He had suspicions that some of the game scouts employed to catch poachers on some of the ranches were involved too.

'How do you work it out? I mean, how do you know that someone's working for the other side?' I didn't want to believe what he had just told me, but it didn't surprise me that much. The rewards for poaching rhinos were just so high. How could the opposition compete with that?

'It's a game of patience and intuition,' he said, unable to elaborate too much and being more careful with his words now. 'I gather intelligence using military strategy. It's about discernment of character. When I meet someone I ask myself, "Is he decent or conniving? Does he drink a lot? Does he tell small lies? Does he show loyalty to his employer? How does he conduct his work? Does he avoid looking me in the eye?" All of these things tell me something about a guy's character. You learn to ask the pertinent questions.'

This was a world of double agents, men working for both sides, all of them driven by money and corruption over a resource that was becoming more valuable as it became scarce. Every little man was getting a cut along the way of the treasure chest that was the last of Zimbabwe's rhinos.

I recalled the story that TRAFFIC's Chris Shepherd had told me a couple of months earlier about a guy in Thailand who had stockpiled about six rhino horns at his house. He was holding on to them and looking forward to the species becoming extinct. On that day he would make a fortune. Those horns were his investment strategy. The rarer the species, the more his horns were worth.

'Operating undercover is essential,' Bryce said. 'Proving the internal involvement takes a lot of work. And it is dangerous. These guys are making a lot of money out of this and with every month we prevent them taking horns out, that's money they're losing. What's stopping them knocking me off?'

Lara was standing on the back of the LandCruiser, not listening to the conversation. That was probably a good thing, I thought to myself. Bryce's words were making me nervous about my own safety and I was only sleeping in their guest room for a short time.

'What about Lara? Does it worry you? She's there on her own the whole time.'

'*Ja*,' Bryce paused, thinking. This was a man who clearly loved his wife and was very protective of her.

'I sleep with a gun by my bed and I do lock the house when we go to sleep. We have dogs . . . and I take precautions, like changing my habits, not becoming too predictable in the time I come home and things like that, how I get out of my car. I make sure I do things differently all the time. But there's nothing stopping someone coming over the fence and firing a round of automatic fire into our bedroom while we're asleep.'

My stomach churned. I wouldn't sleep well that night.

'Wild dogs!'

Lara had spotted two dogs by the road on a fresh impala kill. It was a welcome distraction from what had become a deeply serious conversation.

In all my years in Africa this was the first fresh kill I had seen by these rare but formidable predators and there was just enough light left in the day to catch it on film. The dogs' black faces were smothered in blood as they yanked out the liver and the heart, devouring as much meat as they could before another predator came and took over. In just a few minutes they had finished feeding and moved on with their bellies full. They were probably heading back to the den to regurgitate the meat for the pack's litter of pups and the alpha female whose teats would still be full of milk.

I marvelled at the wild dogs' beautiful blotchy coats of blonde, black and white, which allowed them to blend seamlessly into their environment, the fluffy white tips of their tails one of the few things that might give them away. It was the perfect ending to what had been an enlightening day with the Save Valley Conservancy's rhino anti-poaching squad.

After a restless night, I joined Bryce the next morning while he collected two more of his scouts at a ranch called Savuli that had recently been taken over by politically connected people. The two guys had just finished a four-day patrol and were due to have a couple of days off. We drove to a meeting spot at the base of several *kopjes* and waited for them to join us. As we waited, Bryce pulled out his iPhone and showed me his favourite app – one that identified birds by their call. It was a sign of the times that even out here in the middle of a remote part of Africa this kind of technology had taken hold.

'This is even better,' Bryce said excitedly, pulling up a different app. 'You don't even have to be online to use this. It's a version of Google maps that works like a GPS even when you're not in internet range.'

While Bryce tinkered with his iPhone, two men in dark green overalls emerged from the hills, one of them carrying over his shoulder about twenty wire snares that they had collected nearby. The mass snaring for bush meat that had occurred in the conservancy in the early 2000s, using wire stolen from the conservancy fence, was not happening as much anymore as the hardline criminal syndicates' pursuit of rhinos took over wildlife killing from the meat poachers. But that didn't mean that the small-scale poaching had stopped completely. There were now lots of settlers in the conservancy and people were always after a cheap meal.

After the cornucopia of rhinos the scouts had spotted the day before, no one radioed in for the rest of the day with news of fresh spoor or a sighting. It was starting to look like I had seen my quota of rhinos for this trip. But very late in the afternoon one of the scouts called in a location. It was hard to make out what the scout was saying – he was breaking up and there was a lot of static.

I deciphered the words 'black rhino' followed by 'near a road' and then 'by a *gomo* [*kopje*]'. We all cracked up laughing.

The scout's description – or at least as much of it as we could understand – meant the rhino could have been almost anywhere there was a road or *kopje*. It was a bit like telling a friend to meet you at the house on the corner in a city the size of Sydney. Finally Bryce seemed to work out where to go and as we got closer we were able to home in on the scout's position as the radio signal improved.

The scout was standing on the dirt track on Sango, indicating the place they had last seen the rhino. He was very close by, the scout said, so we had to be quiet. The rhino had only recently woken from a long siesta during the heat of the day. Again Bryce reminded me of the seriousness of this situation and the danger of walking up to a black rhino. I appreciated his concern, but I didn't need to be reminded to keep looking out for a climbable tree. I knew how dangerous black rhinos could be. This species was notoriously more unpredictable and nervous than the white rhino. They couldn't see very well, but one would flatten you if it saw or smelt you inside its comfort zone.

The sun had turned auburn as it sank below the thorn trees, creating a rosy glow across the bush. I loved being in Africa at that time of day. It was the shift swap between day and night, when predators came to the fore and prey became nervous. There was a buzz in the air that made baby animals frolic and leap. The beauty of nature at this time was breathtaking, the colours of the bush changing every few minutes as the sun dropped. A photo couldn't capture the energy; you had to *feel* it. No matter what I was doing, sunset in Africa always made me want to pause and just breathe it in.

I trod carefully behind Bryce and two of the scouts, stepping as quietly as I could through the sickle bush and acacia thornbushes. We stopped frequently, checking the wind, listening for sounds that might indicate a rhino nearby. Adrenaline fizzed through my veins, heightening my senses of sight, smell and hearing. And then I heard him. The sound of crunching was surprisingly loud in the bush, like when someone starts eating popcorn in a hushed movie theatre. This rhino was munching for Africa. After a long sleep he was hungry and the dried twigs and leaves that he was devouring made as much noise in his mouth as a hundred Maltesers being chewed simultaneously.

My heart sped up when I finally made out his boulder-like form ahead of us. At close range and on foot, an African black rhino is a formidable, prehistoric machine. They never cease to impress me. Only the humble stumps remained of his horns from where he had had them purposefully removed by conservationists. I could never get used to seeing rhinos without their horns. It just wasn't natural. Although I understood the rationale behind the conservationists' intensive and expensive dehorning programs, in their view to provide a disincentive to poachers, I wasn't a big fan. Studies had shown that dehorned rhinos were less likely to be poached than those with intact horns, but dehorning certainly wasn't a guarantee that they were safe. The stump of the horn was still valuable to poachers. Maduma was the prime example of how dehorning wasn't a foolproof protection method.

But no matter what my personal views were, as we crept closer towards the bull, I began to think that perhaps this was how we would see rhinos in future – at least in the wild if not in zoos – if dehorning becomes a regular part of rhino management. The growing voice in southern Africa supporting legalisation of the trade in horn argued that dehorning rhinos was no different from taking wool from sheep or milk from cows. It wasn't going to happen straight away, but I wouldn't be surprised to see it happen at some point if the industry and the trade chain can be controlled.

Bryce looked back at me and pointed at a solid tree with a trunk that looked climbable. The unspoken message was clear: we were very close to this rhino now, perhaps twenty metres away, a distance he could cross in seconds. A charge could flatten one of us in moments if he decided that was what he felt like doing. But at this stage, the rhino either wasn't aware of us or he wasn't bothered. I hoped that it was the latter, as our proximity to him showed just how close you could get to a rhino, well within the shooting range of a poacher. No wonder his species was being eliminated at such a rate of knots. This two-tonne beast may have had the potential of a steam train in him, but he rarely used it. Most of the time, he couldn't see well enough to detect a threat. The rhino's ears flickered as ox peckers leapt around his back, feasting on the insects on his thick skin. He was listening, alert but not alarmed.

We followed him at a distance as he continued to forage on bushes, crunching loudly as he consumed his evening meal. The strong smell of rhino was thick in the air. In between mouthfuls, he was marking his territory, pointing his rear end at a tree and releasing a torrent of urine. I kept my eye out for appropriately sized trees that didn't have thorns the length of a match. There weren't many around. There never were when you needed one. When the rhino stopped to look and listen, we did too.

Hanging out with a wild black rhino going about his business in his natural environment was a special experience. In my head I had been doing the maths and it occurred to me that at the rate rhinos in Africa were being poached, the future for the species was so grave now that my son might never get to experience this. In 2012, 668 rhinos were poached in South Africa, up from 448 the year before. There were only about 5000 black rhinos and 20,000 white rhinos left. If South Africa continued to lose almost two a day to poachers, and with Zimbabwe's population already decimated, by the time Solo was grown up there was a very real possibility that wild African rhinos with intact horns would no longer roam Africa's woodlands. It was a sobering thought and one that made me appreciate this moment all the more.

I had walked up to rhinos dozens of times in different parts of southern Africa, including at night during Etosha National Park's black rhino census, a heart-stopping experience in the name of data collection for population monitoring. But not since becoming a mother had I been this close to a wild black rhino on foot. My adrenal glands felt the difference. The self-preservation gene that had malfunctioned in me for so long had finally kicked into gear. However, having a child had given me even greater focus when it came to wildlife conservation. I couldn't imagine a world in which Solo wouldn't be able to share the pleasures of watching animals like African wild dogs, elephants and rhinos in the wild, let alone the myriad smaller endangered creatures that so often go unnoticed. I worried greatly that this was where we were headed. The thought both saddened me and motivated me to do all I could to stop that happening. Motherhood had made me more vulnerable in some ways, but in others it had made me stronger and more determined.

Back in Singapore a few days later, Solo, then a couple of months shy of his third birthday, asked me, 'Did you find the elephants, Mama?'

'I did, darling,' I said. 'Elephants and rhinos and lions too.'

As I hugged my small son, I knew in my heart that this was a battle that Africa could not win on its own. The root of the problem was a world away in Asian lands already depleted of pachyderms, a place I was only just beginning to get to know, my new home. The question was, what had happened to Asia's elephants and rhinos? If I could understand that side of the story a little more, perhaps there was something to be learned that would help save Africa's.

CHAPTER 9

WHERE DID ASIA'S PACHYDERMS GO?

Across Asia, people and elephants have had a special relationship for thousands of years. In India, Nepal and beyond, people worship the Hindu elephant-headed deity Ganesh, both the protector and the remover of obstacles. Airavata, the giant white elephant god who carried the Hindu deity Indra across the heavens and earth, is linked to the coming of rains, and features in the national flags of a number of countries including Thailand and Laos. In Sri Lanka, elephants are central to the most important of the Buddhist religious processions, with tusker bulls having been used to carry the sacred tooth relic, believed to be the ancient tooth of Lord Buddha himself, during the annual festival of the tooth. Elephants and rhinos both also feature in ancient Asian art. In China, there are examples of rhino 'wine vessels' dating as far back as the eleventh century BC, and there is evidence of a flourishing ivory carving tradition there during the late Ming and early Qing dynasties (1644–1911) which focused on the carving of primarily Buddhist and Tao divinities.

Elephants and rhinos hold functional roles in Asia as well as having religious and artistic significance. Traditional Chinese Medicine has long held that rhino horn has special medicinal properties, and ivory is used to treat a range of conditions, including epilepsy and smallpox. People once used Asian elephants to fight wars and, more recently, to log forests that were much more accessible to elephants than to heavy machinery. Today elephants are also used to carry tourists on safari in the national parks of places like India, as well as being used to transport rangers on anti-poaching patrols.

You would expect that an animal so revered in Asia would be thriving in the wild, but that is a far cry from the reality. In 2008 the International Union for Conservation of Nature (IUCN) Red List classified Asian elephants as endangered, with at best 52,000 remaining, about a tenth of Africa's elephant population. The only country in which they live in reasonable numbers is India, where the population is thought to be in the realm of 26,000 to 31,000. Sri Lanka has the second largest population of Asian elephants, between 5000 and 6000, followed by Myanmar (4000–5000), Indonesia (2,400–3,400) and Malaysia (2000–3000). The remaining seven Asian countries that still had elephants at that time all had fewer than a thousand, and some, like China and Vietnam, had only a hundred or so, barely clinging on to existence.

And, of course, there were those countries where elephants had become extinct a long time ago, like Singapore, where I now lived, and Flores, the Indonesian island I had recently visited with my family. There, a ranger on Rinca Island had told me that in one part of Flores local men in search of a wife had at one time been required to find an elephant bone to give to the family of the woman they wanted to marry. Unsurprisingly, there were no elephants left on Flores.

The situation for Asia's rhinos was even worse. The two southeast Asian species, the Javan and Sumatran rhinos, were almost extinct. Once widespread across Asia, only a tiny population of about forty Javan rhinos were left on the Indonesian island of Java, making them possibly the most endangered species on the planet. The smaller, hairier Sumatran rhino had fared only slightly better, with two populations left, one on the Indonesian island of Sumatra and the other on the Malaysian island of Borneo, together numbering fewer than a hundred animals. The Indian greater one-horned rhino population, with its large size (comparable to Africa's white rhinos) and impressive armour-like plates, was confined to a small population of a few hundred in Nepal and a larger one numbering a couple of thousand in Assam, in north-eastern India. Their population was increasing, but remained critically low overall and vulnerable to poachers.

Considering the close relationship that people have always had with Asian elephants, the declining status of Asia's wild elephant population didn't make sense to me. People I had met so far in my Asian travels in places like India and Indonesia loved elephants. Surely if you loved something, you did all you could to conserve it, right? In theory, the Asian species should have been less attractive to poachers than the African one because only the males have tusks. So why were all the Asian elephants disappearing? Were the same factors at play for Asia's rhinos, and could anything be done to turn things around?

I knew that these species lived in the places with the highest human densities in the world and elephants in particular constantly came into conflict with people. I had seen this for myself in Assam, where people and elephants went to war with each other every night during the rice harvest. But was this also the case in other Asian countries that still had elephants and rhinos, even those with smaller populations? I had my first chance to find out when WWF invited me to teach a conservation communication course to their field staff in Sabah on the Malaysian island of Borneo in September 2012. Borneo is one of the few parts of Asia that still has both elephants and rhinos living in the wild, although both in very low numbers.

After my two-day course, Andy and Solo met me in Kota Kinabalu and together we flew east across the island to the small town of Sandakan. It was another two hours of driving through endless palm oil plantations before we made it to the village of Sukau, where we caught a boat to our lodge on the latte-coloured Kinabatangan River.

Some time earlier I had been in contact with New Zealand PhD student Megan English, who had been studying Borneo's pygmy elephants in this area for the preceding couple of years. Although she had now left to write her thesis, she helped me plan our trip to find one of Asia's more elusive elephant subspecies and suggested we see if her former research assistant, Sulaiman Ismael, would be available to guide us. I was delighted when he agreed as there was no one better to take me in search of elephants than someone who had worked closely with them in the wild.

I was intrigued to meet Borneo's pygmy elephants. Recent DNA evidence suggested *Elephas maximus borneensis*, known as pygmy elephants because of their small size, were a separate subspecies of the Asian elephant, having separated from those in mainland Asia 300,000 years ago. The other three subspecies of Asian elephants were the Indian or mainland Asian subspecies, *Elephas maximus indicus*, the Sri Lankan subspecies, *Elephas maximus maximus*, and the Sumatran subspecies, *Elephas maximus summatranus*. While there was some debate among scientists as to their origins, the genetic uniqueness of Borneo's pygmy elephants meant that conserving their small population of about two thousand animals was essential.

There were a couple of things that hit me as soon as we arrived on the slow-flowing Kinabatangan River. The first thing was the weather. It was the most overwhelming combination of heat and humidity that I had ever experienced, way beyond what I was only just beginning to acclimatise to in Singapore. The whole world was a sauna there and even the air conditioners failed to work under that much pressure.

The second thing, which we discovered on our first boat ride along a tributary of the main river that afternoon, was how much harder it was to find the animals in this part of the world. Sulaiman, a man in his late twenties with a broad smile and kind eyes, had arrived in his father's eighteen-foot fibreglass fishing boat around 3 pm. He brought disappointing news. The elephants had been nearby the week before, but now they were a long way away from where we were staying. It would take at least two hours to get to them by boat and he believed they would be in the swamp, an area that was very hard to get to. We decided to take a leisurely afternoon boat ride to look at some local fauna that wasn't elephantine and just take in our surroundings.

We weren't disappointed. This area was known for its impressive proboscis monkeys and we soon found a troop of these unusual primates in the secondary forest that lined the river. The males were the most impressive looking of the sexes, with bright orange heads and faces topped off with long, wobbly noses that made them almost comical in appearance. When you see a species like this you can't help thinking that someone up there has a sense of humour. Endangered and endemic to Borneo, it was a rare treat to watch the troop as its members foraged on fruit and leaves, their long grey tails dangling from the treetops. Solo, who at three years old considered himself to be a little bit monkey himself, was riveted.

Hoping that the elephants would return to where we could see them, over the next couple of days we explored the river in the early morning and late afternoon, the only times of day when it was cool enough to be out on a small boat with no roof. It was wonderful being in the forest, despite our necks kinking as we scanned the massive trees by the river bank for animals. The river teemed with birds, from the regal stork-billed kingfishers with their striking orange beaks, golden bellies and bright blue wings to the petite blue-eared kingfishers that darted across the river in flashes of royal blue. This area had once been commercially logged, so many of the ancient trees were long gone, but the secondary forest was growing back as the area was now used for nature-based tourism.

Sulaiman told us that this part of the Kinabatangan River also was home to wild orang utans and clouded leopards, although you had to be lucky to see them. Sumatran rhinos probably once used these forests, but WWF colleagues had told me that these days there were so few remaining in Borneo that they couldn't even find each other to be able to mate. The destruction of their habitat for commercial logging and then agriculture, particularly the palm plantations which now dominated the landscape, had decimated them. Combined with the effect of poaching for their horns, human development had almost exterminated the species, which was now relying on captive breeding to reproduce, a strategy that hadn't been very successful to date. Our chance of seeing one in the wild was virtually nil.

On the third day we still hadn't found the pygmy elephants that I had my heart set on seeing, so Sulaiman suggested that he and I make the trek downriver, leaving Solo behind with Andy. It would be too hot in the boat for Solo if we were still looking by midday as there was no shade on the river. There was no guarantee we would find any animals, but I figured it was worth a shot.

By 8 am it was already boiling hot and the only thing that stopped us being baked alive was the fact that the boat was moving, creating some wind on sweaty skin. As we sped along Sulaiman watched the river carefully, dodging randomly scattered logs and other debris, some of which were big enough to flip the small boat if we hit them. Several times he pulled in to the river bank to check openings in the long grass where he knew that elephants came down to drink. He was looking for fresh tracks and also fresh green grass growth to judge whether any had been there recently. Each time he shook his head, wiped his brow and refocused on the river with renewed vigour. But after an hour and a half there was still no sign of any fresh elephant activity.

When we came upon a local fisherman checking his prawn traps in a canoe by the river bank, Sulaiman asked him if he had seen any. He shook his head and advised Sulaiman to keep looking for tracks. There wasn't much boat activity on this river, other than the occasional local fisherman and the speedboat of a local palm plantation owner, so I wasn't sure if I was seeing things when a large yacht materialised in the distance. Maybe the heat was getting to me. But no – Sulaiman had noticed it too. As it drifted slowly towards us I could see two Europeans, a middle-aged man and woman, perched on top. They were tourists. The yacht slowed down a little as Sulaiman turned our small speedboat in their direction.

'Excuse me,' Sulaiman said politely, 'can I ask if you have seen any elephants today?'

The woman's face, which a moment before had looked sceptical, broke into a wide grin.

'Yes!' she exclaimed excitedly with what sounded to me like a Belgian accent. 'About an hour ago . . . That way!'

'Yes!' Sulaiman cheered. 'Which side of the river?'

The man pointed and waved us on, leaving us feeling significantly more hopeful than we had all morning. Maybe – just maybe – I might get to see a wild pygmy elephant after all!

'I think I know where they will be,' Sulaiman yelled over the roar of the engine, with the sixth sense of someone who has been working on elephants for years.

We followed a bend in the river, but Sulaiman's face dropped when he saw that there was a boat already there with about six people disembarking onto the bank.

'Who are they?' I asked. 'Are they looking for elephants?'

'Yes, they will be. Sabah Wildlife Department.'

Oddly, Sulaiman didn't seem happy to see them.

'Can't we follow them? Maybe they know where the elephants are,' I suggested.

Sulaiman shook his head, looking decidedly uncomfortable. That was when he told me that his research permit had expired, so while he could guide me in the boat he wasn't legally able to take me on foot into the forest. He planned to bend the rules if there was no other way, he said, but it was clear he couldn't in the presence of officials like these.

My heart sank. The Sabah Wildlife Department staff obviously knew where there were elephants as they would have been following tracks. What if these were the only elephants in the area? Had we come all this way only to have to go back now?

'I have an idea,' Sulaiman said, as he reversed the boat and continued upstream. 'They might be around the corner. It is worth looking.'

We drove on for another few minutes before Sulaiman slowed down and turned sharply into a narrow tributary off the main river.

Above us, a ceiling of overhanging trees provided welcome relief from the mid-morning sun. I dodged the long vines that dangled from the trees. With the dense jungle on both sides it was like going through a tunnel. A field of lily pads floated on the surface of the river on one side as the tributary opened up into an oxbow lake (a U-shaped body of water lying alongside the river).

Sulaiman seemed to know exactly where he was going. A few minutes later he pulled the boat over to the river bank, telling me to stay put while he did a quick check for elephant signs.

'Would you like to take my knife?' he said, removing it from a holder on his belt.

'What for?' I asked innocently.

'Oh, just snakes . . . and crocodiles.'

I chuckled, but my laugh caught in my throat as I recalled the deadly green Wagler's viper I had seen hanging from a tree the morning before. Being identical in colour to the fluorescent green leaves of the tree in which it hung, it had been invisible to me until the lodge guide pointed it out.

'Don't get too close,' he had said. 'If he bites you it only takes a few hours until you are dead.'

'Oh . . . Where is the nearest hospital?'

'A couple of hours away, but they don't always have antivenene.'

Sulaiman hadn't been gone more than three seconds when I heard a massive crash that sounded like a very large animal about ten metres from the boat.

Sulaiman ran back to the boat and with a huge grin on his face exclaimed, 'Come! It is an elephant! Right here!'

As I stepped onto the mushy jungle mud I had no idea that I was about to walk into a situation from which I might not return alive. The thought never occurred to me. I just wanted to see a pygmy elephant. My excitement mounted as I stepped over fresh piles of elephant dung; their boluses were smaller than those I was used to seeing in Africa, but the smell was familiar. Hundreds of tiny flies hovered around them, swarming up to surround us as we plodded along. I was looking forward to seeing this elephant.

But not all elephants like to be seen. Some just like to be left alone sometimes. Some pygmy elephants aren't so keen on the idea of being considered little, and have a serious case of small man syndrome. Whatever you do, don't call them *pygmy*. Unbeknown to Sulaiman and me, this was one of those elephants and one of those times.

I had walked up to wild elephants across southern Africa and in India, always cautiously of course, but this was different. What I wasn't prepared for was the density of Borneo's jungle and how utterly invisible pygmy elephants were in it until you were just a few metres away from them. Perhaps the heat had befuddled my brain and robbed it of common sense. Maybe there is an annoying part of my make-up which clouds my better judgment when I want something *a lot* and can see nothing but the goal. Whatever it was that led to that moment, a few minutes later I achieved my mission to see a pygmy elephant, but he was a lot closer – and angrier – than I had envisaged. And he certainly wasn't as pleased to see me as I was to see him!

As he charged, I ran for my life, the terrifying scream of the bull seemingly right behind me. I was unaware of Sulaiman's movements, only that he was still standing there when I started to run. As tangling vines and hollow, fallen tree trunks threatened to trip me over, I tried to stay on my feet. It was pure instinct that was powering my legs, and pure adrenaline that was driving my body forward.

Surprising things pass through your mind when you think you might be about to die. You're not thinking about how much it's going to hurt when the elephant crushes you. You're thinking about the people you're going to leave behind. You're thinking, has it all come to this? You're thinking, you're not done yet.

Let me go, elephant. Please let me go.

And, thankfully, the elephant gods must have been smiling on me that day because he did.

By the time Sulaiman caught up to me about ten seconds later, I was almost back at the boat, although I didn't know it as all of the rainforest looked the same to me.

'Are you alright?' he asked, genuinely concerned. 'Did you get the shot?'

We were both panting like hunting dogs.

I shook my head. 'I'm fine. I didn't get a shot.'

I couldn't have cared less about the photo at that stage. I had completely forgotten about the camera around my neck. I looked down at it then and realised I was still filming. When I tried to turn it off, my hands were shaking so much that I couldn't press the button. Sulaiman reached over to help me.

'That was close,' I said, looking around frequently to check that the bull wasn't still in the vicinity. 'We were too near him.'

I was sorry to have disturbed the elephant, but I was amazed at Sulaiman's bravery during the charge. The bull had to have been just a few metres away from him when he stood his ground and clapped and shouted, the point at which I had bolted. He had saved my life. There was every chance the bull would have kept running if Sulaiman hadn't stood up to him and stopped him following through. I now knew there was no way to outrun an elephant in that habitat.

As I caught my breath, Sulaiman smiled and said, 'The first time one ran at me like that, I ran too. Soon you learn to understand them. You know how far they will go.'

I nodded, feeling humbled – and a little embarrassed – by the whole experience.

I believed this young Malaysian man, with his big heart and open smile. He knew these elephants and he loved them. He had grown up with them on the Kinabatangan River and now he worked towards their conservation.

'But he had a temper, that one,' Sulaiman went on. 'I don't know why he charged.'

'Do you normally get that close?' I asked, sure that it was our proximity that had provoked the bull's response.

'Yes. Always. Sometimes we just sit there and usually they just carry on feeding.'

We would never know why the bull had charged. He had his reasons and that was okay. I was in no rush to go back and try to get another photo of him. After many years of close calls in the wilds of Africa, I wasn't willing to risk another of my nine lives (I figured by now I was running pretty low). I had seen a pygmy elephant at much closer range than I needed to.

Amidst the heady sense of relief that I was still in one piece, a small part of me felt a little bit annoyed at myself for taking off so fast. I had been out of my element, in a foreign environment, and far too close to a wild elephant – all good reasons to make the impulsive decision to run. But I knew there was more to that unthinking, split-second instinct that had powered my legs into exit mode. As the mother of a small child, I knew it hadn't really been a choice but an inevitable course of action – less decision, more automatic response. Mums can have adventures, but they can't afford to get killed having them.

Back at the lodge a few hours later, we decided to return to the area in the afternoon to give Andy and Solo a chance to see the elephants too. We wouldn't go on foot, of course, after Sulaiman's and my close call that morning, but if there were bulls in that part of the river there were possibly larger herds of females too, and Sulaiman hoped we might be able to see some from the boat.

For Solo, the boat ride was half the adventure. With his small life jacket on and the wind in his hair, he shrieked excitedly every time he saw a monkey or a bird, so when we saw the distant bodies of not just a few but dozens of pygmy elephants on the river bank after about two hours on the boat at top speed, he, like his parents, was ecstatic.

'They're el-fants,' he told me. 'Look, Mumma, el-fants!'

It was a special moment for the whole family to sit on the boat and watch this large herd of about forty elephants, mostly females with young, foraging on the long grass by the river. They were completely relaxed, even as boatloads of other tourists turned up to take photographs. With their baby faces and heart-shaped heads, they were undoubtedly the cutest elephants I had ever seen. They were mesmerising.

Two bulls jostled in the river to one side, pushing each other head on, their trunks tangling like mating serpents as the water splashed around them. Their antics were playful rather than aggressive, like young boys wrestling and testing each other's strength.

'That one is the one that charged us,' Sulaiman observed, pointing out the smaller of the two males.

There was no sign of the grumpy character whose personal space we had invaded that morning, just a chilled-out bull relaxing with his mate in a nice cool bath.

'He seems in a better mood,' I commented, and Sulaiman chuckled.

So I had seen a wild pygmy elephant, not just one but lots of them, in what remained of their natural forest habitat. It was an experience my whole family would never forget (and even if Solo was too young to remember, we'd still have the photographs). Unfortunately I had also seen the vast monocultures of palm trees that had replaced most of their original range.

These plantations produce one of the world's most wanted commodities – palm oil. Malaysia is the world's second largest exporter of palm oil after Indonesia, and Sabah, home to rare pygmy elephants, orang utans and Sumatran rhinos, produces more than any other Malaysian state.

In Australia, there is no mandatory labelling on products containing palm oil, so it's hard for consumers to make smart decisions. Palm oil is in many everyday domestic items, from potato chips and biscuits to soaps and pharmaceuticals. Chances are it's in your pantry right now. Vegetable oil is often palm oil, so one of the best things that consumers can do is to buy alternative cooking oils, like olive or sunflower oil.

It didn't take a genius to work out why elephants and rhinos were disappearing in Borneo. Tourism was increasing but its economic impact was insignificant compared to the windfall that the palm oil industry was providing to this rapidly growing human population. While the global demand for palm oil was increasing exponentially, thankfully this industry's expansion in Malaysia has been capped by the government, and most of the available land in Sabah has already been cultivated. However, the conversion of reserve forests to industrial plantations like rubber and timber continues.

A couple of months later in December 2012, in a very different part of Asia, Sri Lanka, the same issue of expanding human development pushing elephants into smaller and smaller spaces was evident. Sri Lanka is a great place to see wild Asian elephants. After a long and bitter civil war, in 2009 the country emerged with somewhere in the realm of six thousand elephants, the second largest wild Asian population after India's, and about ten per cent of the global population. There would have been at least double those numbers prior to colonial times when the island was covered in forest, but commercial agriculture in the last few hundred years, especially coffee, tea, rubber and coconut, led to elephants being declared vermin. British trophy hunters shot thousands of elephants in the nineteenth and twentieth centuries, among them a major by the name of Thomas Rogers, who single-handedly killed more than fifteen hundred.

Andy, Solo and I were in the country on holiday, visiting historic World Heritage listed relics like the ancient cities of Sigiriya and Polonnoruwa in Sri Lanka's cultural triangle in the centre of the island, as well as looking for elephants in nearby national parks. Sri Lanka is famous for 'the gathering' of elephants in Minneriya National Park, where hundreds of elephants come together in the dry months of July and August, providing tourists with an incredible spectacle. Unfortunately, we were there in the wet season – December – and had been cautioned that our chances of seeing elephants weren't great as the national parks became largely inaccessible after rain.

However, as if they had got wind that we were on our way, we didn't have to look for the elephants; they found us. In Hurulu biosphere reserve, near the town of Habarana, our jeep barged through deep mud and water on the dirt tracks in search of elephants in the long green grass. We saw several breeding herds there, and the following day in Minneriya National Park, a large bull in the early stages of musth let us watch him feasting on bamboo for about half an hour.

But the elephants weren't just in the reserves and national parks. As we passed through a town near Minneriya National Park, two wild elephant bulls were holding up traffic on the main road. Tuk tuks, motorbikes and buses simply swerved around them as they took up half of one side of the road. Local people stood nearby watching them with a kind of awe, some of them throwing the bulls pieces of mango. They stopped to pick the fruit up, then ambled onwards, ignoring the trucks that passed by close enough for someone to reach out and touch them.

Our driver asked a man by the road if he had seen this before. He said that these two bulls often came through town. They weren't bothered by traffic and people and they didn't usually cause any trouble. They were wild though, not domestic, and had probably come in from the national park. I loved watching them plod down the road as if they owned the place, without a trace of malice or fear.

As we followed the bulls along the road in our Nissan van, the tops of their heads almost touching the low-hanging power lines, we watched them make a sharp turn into a military base and walk up the road. These two big boys knew exactly where they were going and what they wanted. At the entrance, two army guards wearing black berets and carrying automatic weapons simply watched the bulls walk by before lowering the boom behind them. It was as if this happened every day, and perhaps it did.

The local man told us they were going to raid the rubbish bins at the back of the base. It was the wet season and there was plenty of food for elephants in the forests. The only problem was that there was a lot less forest than there had been before and so as Sri Lanka's elephant population continued to increase, elephants like these would roam outside the parks and reserves to find extra food. As we got closer to them I could see that both bulls had numerous wounds on their bodies, some of them swollen up into what looked like hard, round balls under the skin. Later I would discover that these were shotgun pellet wounds, probably the result of communities fighting back as they raided their crops. In 2011, human-elephant conflict accounted for 255 elephant and 60 human deaths in Sri Lanka, and the problem was increasing.

The previous day I had visited Professor Missaka Wijayagunawardane and his colleague Thusith Samakone of the Department of Animal Science at the University of Peradeniya in Kandy to find out more about an interesting project they had been working on to help reduce the growing problem of human-elephant conflict. Their study of twenty-two wild Sri Lankan elephant bulls had looked at how they responded to pre-recorded playbacks of a variety of sounds in search of one that might be effective to use as a tool to keep elephants away from crops.

The researchers found that the sounds of African honeybees and African elephants produced no responses, but the sound of wild Asian elephant cows and calves, and to a much lesser extent the sound of Sri Lankan hornets, did produce strong responses. Most interestingly, in seventy-two per cent of playbacks, the sound of a distressed breeding herd from India caused the bulls to flee. I watched video footage of one bull and was surprised to see how immediate the response was. As soon as the sound of the distressed Indian breeding herd started, the bull in question stopped and stood still, clearly listening, then a few seconds later turned and fled into the bush with his tail in the air. How I wished I could understand the language of elephants! No one knew what the herd was saying in the playback, but whatever it was, they weren't happy and the bulls responded accordingly. I could only guess it might have been anger or a warning in elephant-talk.

These scientists' results were only part of a preliminary study, but I thought they had real potential, because of their possible application to reduce human-elephant conflict. I imagined a low-cost speaker that villagers in the vicinity of national parks could use to broadcast the sound of distressed elephants, a much less intrusive defence strategy than shooting pellets at them. Of course, there was always the possibility that such intelligent creatures as elephants would become accustomed to the play-backs and it might not work forever. Still, like everything in the battle between people and elephants, it could be a useful tool that helped reduce the impact a little for a while, even if it wasn't *the* solution.

The bigger picture for Sri Lanka's elephants, according to Sri Lankan wildlife biologist Dr Manori Gunawardena, was that in the context of the increasing human development taking place post-war, there were already almost too many elephants. Conservationists weren't concerned about the impact of poaching as only about three per cent of Sri Lanka's bulls bore tusks, which made them less attractive to ivory poachers.

'It's tough,' Manori said. 'This last couple of years have been the toughest due to these development issues. We have a lot of excellent information on the elephant picture, but the government doesn't see the value of their natural assets. Conservation is the last thing on this president's plate.'

Manori explained how there was increasing public pressure to move the elephants away from where people lived, but in her view moving the elephants wasn't going to work. It was a space issue.

'We need to work around development and not move the elephants. We can fence people in but not elephants. I mean, where do you put them?'

Manori had a very good point. There was only so much land on this 65,000 square kilometre island. There were more than twenty million people, almost the population of Australia, in an area smaller than Tasmania.

'This is not a problem that's going to go away,' she continued, then switched topic: 'But have you heard about the three hundred tusks that were seized here? The president has gifted them to Buddhist temples.'

Now there was a contradiction in terms if ever I had heard one. Blood ivory from illegal killings in Africa held in temples designed to represent a religion that said you shouldn't harm a leaf? Sri Lanka was a predominantly Buddhist country and protecting elephants and all living creatures from harm was central to Buddhist philosophy. It is said that Buddha's mother, Queen Mahamaya, dreamt that a heavenly white elephant holding a lotus blossom in its trunk circled her three times and then entered her womb as the Buddha. Even today, it is believed that a child who walks or is carried under the belly of an elephant three times will grow up to be strong and brave.

A few days earlier when we visited Kandy's Temple of the Tooth, which holds the sacred tooth of the Buddha, elephants were everywhere. From the manifold intricate ancient elephant carvings in the walls to the genuine ivory tusks that guard the altars, we were left with the very strong feeling that Buddhism and elephants were very much interconnected. It was fine if a local elephant had died naturally of old age and its tusks were kept by the temple that had owned it, but it was another thing altogether to display the tusks of illegally killed elephants from Africa as if they were religious relics.

'What do you think they should do?' I asked Manori. 'They came from Africa so maybe they should be returned.'

She was adamant: 'Either destroy them or put them into storage.'

Both of us knew that there was every chance that if these tusks were displayed in Sri Lankan temples it wouldn't be long before they ended up on the black market fuelling the ivory trade.

I didn't know how to feel about the president of Sri Lanka, a man who had been accused of human rights abuses by the United Nations, for the way he had concluded the war against the Tamil

Tigers, a terrorist organisation representing the minority Tamil people, who were originally from India. Western media reports on him were damning, but talking to average Sri Lankans there led us to believe that there was another side to the story. The Tamil Tigers had done a lot of damage in their quest to have the northern part of the country declared a separate Tamil state, including bombing sacred Buddhist sites like the Temple of the Tooth, and people were generally glad that the war was over. On both sides, crimes were committed and tens of thousands of innocent people were killed. Even elephants had been killed and maimed by landmines during those years.

But no matter what I had heard and read, Andy and I were going to be able to judge for ourselves as we would be talking with the man in person at the end of our holiday. Andy had received a special invitation to meet both President Mahinda Rajapaksa and some of his top ministers to talk about Earth Hour in Sri Lanka, and Solo and I had been invited too.

After drinking tea with Minister for the Environment (western province) Udaya Gammanpila in his office, and hearing his views on Earth Hour and what his government was trying to do to achieve sustainable development, we travelled with him in the back seat of his jeep to the president's quarters in Colombo. Udaya was staunchly Buddhist and even resembled a priest in the white robes he wore. Several of the president's people, including multiple security personnel, greeted us as we got out of the minister's jeep, checked us over and asked us to leave all bags, cameras and phones in the car. We were then led through the old colonial building to a large office where the president worked – the equivalent of America's Oval Office, we were told.

We were seated in a sitting room which opened into the office itself, where wooden chairs with opulent golden covers that made them look more like thrones were arranged in two rows facing each other with the president's at the centre. To one side was a large tank full of colourful reef fish. I could see right into the president's office as there was no door separating it from the sitting room. On his desk a model of a 777 airplane and some kind of pirate ship captured Solo's attention and it took a lot of convincing for him to understand that these toys belonged to the president and weren't his to play with. Behind the desk was a shelf with lots of different Buddhist artifacts and a picture of his parents in black and white.

After a short time we were led to another room full of thrones in another part of the building where we were told the president would soon join us. We all took seats on both sides of the president's chair and waited for him to arrive. Solo was on his best behaviour, his little legs dangling off the enormous chair. He was aware that someone special was coming, but he didn't really understand the concept of a president. Earlier I had tried to explain that the president was the big boss of Sri Lanka. Now as we waited quietly for his arrival, Solo asked me hopefully, 'Is Santa coming, Mama?'

When the president entered the room, we all stood up and greeted him. He had been ill recently and didn't look particularly well although, strangely, on the TV news clip of the meeting we saw later, perhaps due to some impressive photo-shopping, he looked remarkably healthy! Andy listened as he explained some of the challenges his country was facing. It was clear that he and the entire Sri Lankan government needed some good publicity. The conversation lasted all of ten minutes, during which time Solo crawled down off his throne onto the floor to play with his cars at the president's feet. It turned out that Santa was coming after all, as one of the president's people entered with a bag of toys, which he gave to Solo. It included a drumming Santa. Solo was delighted.

As we left the building I spotted a large ivory tusk perched on a golden holder by the door, similar to those I had seen in Kandy's Temple of the Tooth. I thought about the seized tusks that the Sri Lankan government had gifted to Buddhist temples. Ivory was a symbol of power and strength in Sri Lanka, just as it was in other countries around the world, linked to the characteristics of the elephant itself. Everyone, it seemed, wanted a piece of it.

But it wasn't only the demand for cultural artifacts in these developing nations that was causing the trouble. It was also the increasingly high human populations, and what they were doing to provide for global consumers of products like palm oil, timber, rubber, tea and rice, many of whom lived a world away in lands like Australia and the United States, places where *over*consumption had led to massive problems with obesity and heart disease. It was all interconnected. People in countries like Malaysia and Sri Lanka were just trying to reach the same privileged level of development that we in the west have. They weren't to blame. We *all* were, because we were buying those products. We were all part of one big, interconnected global community that was turning a blind eye to what was happening to the natural world because of the desire for profit.

The solution was there. Development could be truly sustainable, taking the needs of the environment on which it depended into consideration while also providing for people. When that happens, as it has in places like Namibia, then species like elephants and rhinos might stand a chance of existing in the future. It wasn't too late for countries like Sri Lanka to start imagining a truly sustainable future in which people and animals lived in harmony with each other, leading the way for other countries to follow. One of the first things they could do was enact a public ceremonial burning of the seized tusks from Africa, declaring their zero tolerance of illegal elephant killing.

While in Asia it was mainly human-elephant conflict linked to decreasing habitat that was the problem for elephants and rhinos, in Africa the greater problem was now poaching. Pachyderms were cursed with appendages that unfortunately fell into the same category that was causing the loss of habitat – the pursuit and acquisition of money. Ivory and rhino horn were now in greater demand than they had been in decades. Both were luxury items for which people would pay a premium. This wasn't a problem that was going to go away by itself. But how much ivory was really for sale today? Who was buying it and what was driving demand for both substances?

I had been pestering Bill Schaedla, head of TRAFFIC's south-east Asian office based in Kuala Lumpur, Malaysia, for answers to these questions ever since moving to Singapore and beginning to learn about Asia's role in the illegal ivory and rhino horn trade. I decided it was time to go and see for myself what was happening in two of the main consumer countries. First, I convinced him to let me join an ivory survey in Thailand.

CHAPTER 10

BANGKOK'S BLOOD IVORY

Bangkok, Thailand, December 2012

'See here, you've got to look for the cross-hatching. That's ivory.'

It was mid-morning on a Saturday in one of Bangkok's bustling marketplaces and Tom Milliken, one of the world's top wildlife trade experts, was giving me a crash course in elephant ivory identification.

'See that?' he asked me, rubbing his finger over the characteristic mesh-like grain in the polished curves of a small, carved elephant amulet. This harmless-looking piece of jewellery would one day end up strung around someone's neck. A necklace for one, noose for another.

I peered at the gleaming, creamy object through the cheap magnifying glass bought a few minutes earlier at a stall down the road. Tiny fine lines crossing over each other were clearly visible in this piece, a definite indication that this was the real deal: elephant ivory. Probably from poached forest elephants in central Africa, the most persecuted of all Africa's elephants today, Tom observed.

With my camera over my shoulder and sporting a plain T-shirt, I was trying to blend in to the crowd like any old tourist. Dressed in appropriate 'holiday' clothes and wearing light backpacks like many of the foreign visitors hitting Thailand's market on the weekend, my male colleagues just looked like ordinary guys. But they were anything but ordinary.

Bill Schaedla and Tom Milliken both worked for TRAFFIC, the global wildlife trade monitoring network. They had been in the game for a long time and, as a result, their brains were a veritable treasure trove of filed information on the illegal trade in elephant ivory, rhino horn, reptiles, pangolins and more. The information they obtained through undercover operations like this was often used by police and other officials to prosecute those who illegally trafficked wildlife. Sometimes – although not often enough – it led to large fines and jail time for those involved in smuggling. CITES – the primary international agreement between governments to ensure that trade did not threaten species' survival – relied on guys like these to make decisions about the future of species such as elephants and rhinos. The greatest demand for illegal ivory was now coming from China, which was the end point for at least half of the seized large consignments of illegal African ivory globally (a large consignment being one weighing more than eight hundred kilograms). But unlike Thailand, China was at least trying to clamp down on the illegal trade. The demand for ivory in China was still increasing at a steady rate, as it had been for the last decade, but if you were caught smuggling ivory there you could be severely penalised – including, under current laws, the possibility of being sentenced to life imprisonment.

Since 2007, China had operated an internal ivory control system, which it had set up in order to become a CITES-approved legal buyer of ivory from southern African stockpiles. In 2002,

CITES approved a one-off sale of sixty tonnes of legal ivory to China and Japan from legitimate stockpiles of African tusks in Botswana, Namibia, South Africa and Zimbabwe under strict conditions that it would take another six years for China to meet before the ivory was allowed to actually arrive in the Chinese markets. There had already been an earlier CITES-approved one-off sale of forty-nine tonnes of ivory to Japan in 1999 from Botswana's, Zimbabwe's and Namibia's stockpiles. These were decisions supported at the time by WWF and TRAFFIC. No elephants were killed for this legal ivory, which had resulted from natural mortalities of elephants from four approved southern African countries that had been seen to be demonstrating a positive effort towards conserving their growing populations of elephants.

It wasn't a perfect system by a long way, with some saying that the legal trade of ivory in China just provided a cover for what continued to be a rampant illegal trade. But there had been numerous seizures of illegal ivory in China in 2012 alone, including one in which nearly one tonne of tusks was seized coming from Tanzania. Assuming that these tusks came from mature African elephants and weighed, for argument's sake, about fifty kilograms each, that single seizure represented at least ten slaughtered elephants. A herd. It was too late for those elephants, but the seizure in China meant that at least their ivory wasn't in the hands of criminals anymore and it couldn't be used to keep driving the trade that would lead to other elephants being killed.

Thailand, on the other hand, had a long way to go to prove that it was in any way serious about protecting wild elephants. According to TRAFFIC and WWF, it was the largest unregulated ivory market in the world. Via Skype from Singapore a week earlier, Bill had told me that there was still plenty of ivory for sale on the streets of Thailand. With the recent mass slaughter of three hundred elephants in Cameroon by Sudanese horsemen, and the number of illegal killings of African elephants higher than it had been in a decade, it was very likely that this ivory was from poached African elephants.

How was this possible? I had never been to Thailand, but if I knew anything about the place it was that the people loved elephants. Elephants were an important part of Thai spirituality, featuring strongly in Buddhist and Hindu beliefs. Thailand's own population of Asian elephants had remained largely stable at around 1650 animals from the late 1980s. On the phone Bill had tried to explain to me that it came down to the law: 'There are eighteen laws in Thailand that relate to elephants. Some conflict, but that doesn't matter. Each one of them has been royally promulgated. Because they come down from the king, they can only be amended, not revoked. The situation makes for lots of legal loopholes.'

I'm no lawyer and none of this made a lot of sense to me. I needed to see what was going on in person.

Bangkok is an easy two-hour flight from Singapore and my trip would coincide with TRAFFIC's ivory survey. I figured there were probably no better people than Bill and Tom to go with to introduce me to the world of illegal ivory, and this way I would also get an insight into how to identify ivory, a skill which I could apply in other parts of Asia too.

I had met Bill once before on a work trip to Kuala Lumpur. His laidback, friendly manner and American accent gave the impression of someone who wasn't fazed by much. In his early twenties he had moved to Thailand as a Peace Corps volunteer, won a Fulbright scholarship to do a PhD on harvesting termite behaviour, sidelining a passion for reptiles, especially snakes, and later joined WWF. Bill had been in charge of TRAFFIC's southeast Asian operations for the last two years and, having lived in

Thailand for so many years, he spoke fluent Thai – with a Thai accent, or so it sounded to me.

Tom Milliken was an enigma I had yet to meet. At the last CITES meeting, he had been the only NGO representative allowed into the room to present his findings on ivory on behalf of TRAFFIC. CITES trusted him, which meant that the government representatives of those countries heavily involved in the illegal wildlife trade listened to him. Tom had been in the wildlife trade business for decades, based first in Japan, and then in Harare, Zimbabwe, where he was head of TRAFFIC. He was responsible for ETIS, the Elephant Trade Information System, which has been tracking illegal trading in ivory for CITES since 1989, when the ivory ban took effect. Back in September I had written him an email, trying to meet him on my last trip to Harare, but had never heard a peep in reply. Feeling slightly peeved at being ignored, I was expecting a typical macho Zimbabwean man with a big ego. I figured I had met his type before.

I had left Andy and Solo still asleep at 5 am that day, sneaking out the door of our apartment on the fourteenth floor with just a light backpack over my shoulder. Inside was my passport, another set of clothes, my laptop and phone, plus a copy of John Walker's *Ivory's Ghosts*. At times like this, I felt like a double agent: half mum, half conservationist. The last two weeks I had been fighting another war – toilet training Solo, now three years old. My strong-willed son was refusing to use the potty for anything other than number ones, and we were locked in a battle of wills. It was him versus me and the potty, and my pint-sized opponent was winning. Leaving Andy to continue the battle of the bum, it was something of a relief to turn my attention to a different kind of conflict.

I didn't stop being a mum when I travelled away from Solo for my conservation work, but, when I had to, I had learned to switch that part of me off to some extent. Living in Singapore for the preceding six months had made life immeasurably easier with the employment of a wonderful live-in Filipina nanny, Julie, and with Solo attending preschool three mornings a week. Solo still clung to me as if I was never coming back when I left on work trips, but we were both getting better at saying goodbye. By now, with him talking fluently and understanding things more, he knew that I would always return. I knew that I could trust Julie and Andy to look after him when I was away.

Besides, for both Andy and me, work trips were shorter now that we lived in Singapore, which was closer to the rest of Asia, Africa and Europe than Sydney was. We had a rule that one of us was always home with Solo, even if that meant, as it did this time, that we would cross over at home in Singapore for all of seven minutes between my return from Bangkok and Andy's departure for Switzerland. It was worth it though. I felt more fulfilled in my career and family life than I had in years, closer to that elusive balance that I had thought was impossible a couple of years earlier. Now I was able to be in the conservation action while still relishing quality time with my family. And the truth be told, I knew how lucky I was to be able to have the greatest of all perks for expats living in Singapore – a household helper. I didn't miss the daily cleaning up after a toddler one little bit.

After landing at Bangkok airport I made my way to Siam Square, where I grabbed myself a cup of tea and a custard pastry and settled in to wait for a text from Bill. A polluted sky had greeted me as I flew in that morning. Bangkok was certainly far from the famous Thai beach locations sold in tourist brochures, at least environmentally if not geographically. As I had driven into town in a hot-pink taxi, grey pollution had obscured the high rises in the city, wrapping around them like ghostly clouds. I coughed subconsciously.

Inside the taxi, trios of marigolds graced the dash like splashes of sunshine, and beside them gleamed a fake gold statue of two men riding an elephant with huge tusks. Perched on top of the radio was a miniature statue of Ganesh. It was the creamy colour of ivory, the colour of my wedding dress. We passed a massive billboard with a huge, pink picture of Ganesh lying in a reclining, suggestive posture.

The driver, who I had already discovered spoke no English when my attempt at small talk had been received with an embarrassed shake of the head, withdrew a small brown bottle from his pocket when we stopped at the lights. He then rubbed a generous portion of the liquid in it under his nose and on his neck. It smelt like some kind of natural cough remedy.

An hour later, as I texted Bill to let him know where I was, I was grateful for some breakfast in an air-conditioned bakery. By nine o'clock it was already warming up to the thirty-degree mark outside. If this was Bangkok in the morning, I didn't want to imagine what the markets were going to be like in a few hours.

'Tammie!' said a booming male voice.

Bill greeted me with a friendly hug and introduced me to the elusive Tom Milliken. He was not at all what I expected. With white hair, glasses and a goatee beard and moustache, he looked to be part hippie and part yogi. The handshake was firm but not overbearing, the smile genuine and warm. He was probably close to my dad's age, I estimated. Enthusiasm oozed from him like a contagious energy and he was immediately engaging and conversational.

After we had had a coffee, Bill flagged down a taxi and we were on our way to Tha Pra Chan market. 'Tha' meant 'dock' or 'pier' and 'pra' meant 'monk', Bill explained. Few international tourists came to this market, which was largely frequented by locals. No one spoke English, which made Bill's language skills invaluable.

Within five minutes we were in the thick of ivory bracelets, necklaces, amulets and carvings. They were being sold alongside the stingray jawbones, fake tiger skins, brass bowls with elephant engravings and amulets of every possible description, from small wooden penises and claw-shaped bone carvings to ivory elephant heads crowned in gold and colourful jewels. A collection of bracelets I immediately recognised as being made of elephant tail hairs sat beside several ivory tusk tips destined for people's altars. The ivory tips were real, Tom said. Although it wasn't obvious on all surfaces of the object, you could see areas of cross-hatching in the grain where it hadn't been polished as much.

I followed the guys closely, pretending, like them, to be an ignorant tourist interested in buying goods. Two bald monks in orange, off-the-shoulder robes floated past, eyeing a display of what Bill informed me were monks' gums complete with their human teeth in various states of decay inside a glass display counter.

'See this one,' Tom said, standing next to a crocodile head carving for sale. 'It's probably not ivory. You can't see the cross-hatching in the grain.'

I looked at it under the magnifying glass and immediately saw what he meant. You didn't need to be an expert to be able to tell real ivory from plastic or bone. It was often the same creamy colour, but only ivory had the mesh-style hatching.

'This one, on the other hand . . . ' He trailed off, picking up a thick bracelet made of gold and ivory and peering at it closely. 'This is ivory.'

He turned to the salesperson, a young Thai woman, and asked, 'How much is this?'

She pulled out a calculator, unable or unwilling to speak English, and the figure 175,000 was shown to us. That was roughly $5,500.

'It's beautiful,' Tom said, playing the tourist. 'Try it on, Tammie. Does it fit you?'

I squeezed the solid, chunky piece onto my wrist with some difficulty. Once I managed to get it on, it sat there nicely, shining like pearl in the sun. I couldn't help but admire it, both the look and feel of it. That is the thing about ivory. It *is* beautiful. There's a reason why humans have been trading in it for thousands of years. Human history and ivory, which hails from the sixth millennium BC, are irrevocably connected. In prehistoric times early humans used flakes of mammoth tusks to create Paleolithic art. Egypt's King Tutankhamun was buried with an exquisitely carved ivory neck rest, and thousands of ivory objects decorated the royal Egyptian tombs. In China, a plaque with sun and bird imagery is the oldest example of worked ivory in that culture. The ancient Romans loved it, making lavish use of it in things like furniture and art. King Solomon's throne was made of it. Every culture across every age has found a use for the magnificent treasure that derives from the teeth of elephants.

In the 1800s, the West became a major consumer of ivory for piano keys, combs and billiard balls, with Britain importing five hundred tonnes of raw ivory a year between 1850 and 1910. Ivory was tied to the slave trade, with brutal long marches of African slaves – men, women and children – used to carry ivory to the trading coasts. Some said every tusk that made it to the coast cost a human life. Big game hunters like Frederick Courteney Selous and R G Gordon Cumming hunted thousands of elephants during this time, as if there was no end to the bounty of ivory that elephants could provide.

In the 1960s, Japan was importing almost a hundred tonnes of ivory a year, largely to make *hankos* or signature seals. In the late 1970s it became the largest importer of ivory in the world, with more than double that quantity. Large-scale poaching in the

1900s threatened the very existence of the elephants until a global outcry led to the worldwide ban on the international trade in ivory in 1989. Once numbering millions across the African continent, elephant populations had been devastated, with fewer than half a million individuals remaining at the time of the ban. The ivory trade and price of ivory diminished significantly as a result of the ban, though it didn't stop altogether, but in the last few years, seizures of illegal ivory and records of illegal killings of elephants in Africa have shown worrying increasing trends, suggesting a resurgence of the killing fields of last century. I wanted to know why, which was the reason I was now sweating in a Bangkok market with a piece of ivory around my wrist.

I had never worn a bracelet of such financial value before, quite aside from its cost of an elephant's life. It felt cool and smooth, like the sensation of wearing a silk dress on bare skin. But no matter how nice it felt to wear, I couldn't ignore the fact that this was blood ivory, tainted by its terrible history. An elephant had died to create it. I was wearing one of the most beautiful things that nature produces and it just felt dirty. I yanked at the bracelet to get it off my wrist.

I had only recently learned that ivory is like teeth, primarily composed of dentine. Unlike rhino horn, which is more like hair and can grow back if removed, ivory doesn't regrow. An elephant gets one set in its lifetime and when it's gone, it's gone. Either elephants have to die naturally to provide their ivory as a gift back to the earth, or people have to kill them for it. There is nothing else like ivory on the planet, which is why people will pay an arm and a leg to get it.

Tom asked the saleswoman if he could see another piece, an elephant head that looked to weigh about a hundred grams. The head was intricately carved with a headdress of gold and a ruby at the centre.

'How much for this one?'

316,000 the calculator displayed. Almost ten thousand dollars – the price of a very comfortable second-hand car. That was just the starting price, Bill explained. The buyer would be able to work it down. But still, ivory didn't come cheap, especially when coupled with gold and jewels.

As we worked our way through the market, I made notes on the prices of the various ivory items we found. I could have bought an ivory ring for 6,000 Thai baht or about $200. A small, crescent-shaped piece of ivory set in gold and with a ruby at the centre was offered to me for 18,500 baht or $575.

Off the street, inside the undercover market beside the Chao Phraya River, there was an endless maze of trinkets and amulets for sale.

'This market always has ivory,' Bill observed, 'but we're here at the wrong time. At the end of the month the sellers are down on money and inclined to have debts. That's when you tend to see a lot more stuff for sale.'

We had seen a lot of ivory in just an hour, mostly jewellery (bracelets, necklaces and amulets) and varied carvings of elephants and Buddha. But we had also seen a lot of stuff that, while it appeared to be ivory, was actually plastic or bone, probably cow bone. Bill pointed out several fake ivory tusks. They were made of plastic, but they looked real enough to me.

'People use them on their altars for worship,' he explained, sipping on a strange green drink that he claimed was full of chlorophyll.

If people were buying items that looked like ivory even when it wasn't, that showed there was a market for alternatives, which was a good thing.

'Shoo me! Shoo me!' a lady carrying a tray of coffees called out as she ploughed through the increasingly crowded aisle.

I moved aside to let her pass, almost falling over a table full of what looked like tiger claws set in fake fur.

'Are they real?' I asked Bill.

'Could be. They're the right size and they don't look like carved boar tusks or other substitutes. Hard to tell. She's probably got a contact at a tiger farm.'

'Are there tiger farms here?' I asked, shocked.

There could be few worse fates for a tiger than living in a cage being bred for your body parts to supply Traditional Chinese Medicine. Later I learned that Thailand had twenty-seven registered captive breeding facilities for tigers. On paper, these are not farms, but zoos. They are not supposed to be supplying tiger parts for trade. Such facilities are common across China, Vietnam and Laos. There are now more of these regal big cats in captivity than there are in the wild.

People were bringing the sellers plates of noodles and fried food. The smell of sweet barbecuing meat filtered through the air, making my stomach rumble.

'Shall we eat?' Tom asked, his words mirroring my thoughts.

We squeezed through the crowds, past stalls selling sizzling prawns and fish, cold bottles of water on ice and fresh fruit, looking for a good place to eat. For a second Tom and I lost sight of Bill, who had been behind us.

'Where'd Bill go?' I said aloud.

'Do you think he's in the gutter throwing up that green drink?' Tom joked.

He turned up a minute later, still sipping the last of his chlorophyll drink through a straw.

'Found a leatherback turtle shell bracelet back there,' he said bluntly, tossing the plastic bottle into a bin by the road. Then he fished two small bronze elephant amulets from his pocket and gave one each to Tom and me.

'Something to remember the day,' he said, then walked on.

Eventually we came upon a small café selling cold drinks and advertising cashew chicken on a blackboard outside. It was air conditioned, which none of us objected to. I ordered a Coke, Bill a Singha beer and Tom a carrot juice.

'This is my detox,' Tom said, grinning with a hint of mischief in his eyes.

Over chicken Pad Thais, Tom told me that he had grown up near Los Angeles. A self-described 'former hippie', he had been called up to serve in the Vietnam War, a conflict that he strongly objected to. He had been ready to flee to Canada to avoid the call-up when President Richard Nixon let him and many of his peers off the hook. A few months after this, his father died, and his whole world changed. Years later he had met his wife, a Japanese woman, while travelling in India on holiday with his mother, and they had raised two kids together, both of them now at university (one at the University of Queensland in Brisbane, where I had studied). We had much in common and knew a lot of the same people in Zimbabwe, where he had lived for the best part of twelve years.

Living in Zimbabwe Tom had witnessed one of the most significant shifts in the demographics of this and other African countries in recent years – the increase in the number of Asian, especially Chinese, residents. That led me to my next question. I wanted to know whether Tom saw any potential for a solution to the underground trade in ivory, with the growing demand for ivory – and access to Africa – in China.

'China has an internal control policy for ivory and they've taken extreme measures when they've found problems. They know exactly what they have to do and they're doing it.'

'But the demand is still growing, ' I pointed out.

'There are huge issues in China,' Tom admitted. 'We're in for the long term with them, but my experience in Japan shows that you can do it [reduce demand]. Japan was more than half of the ivory market when I started and now it's hardly there at all. But you have to be seen as an honest broker. If you want to influence people in China you have to learn not to say no all of the time. You have to work with people.'

'Do you think the one-off sales from southern Africa have contributed to the surge in elephant poaching and seizures of illegal ivory that we're now seeing?'

'I would be the first to tell you if it did, but the data doesn't correlate. In the year that the ivory hit China and Japan in early 2008, there was a drop in illegal sales.'

'Why is poaching increasing now then?'

'Chinese demand. In the eighties you never had Asian buyers in Africa sourcing ivory directly. Permanent communities put out webs and they're successfully connecting to key end user markets in China and Thailand . . . Elephants are a very complicated story.'

If I was hearing Tom correctly, he was saying that it was just so much easier to get ivory out of Africa and back to Asia now that so many more Asian people were actually living in Africa.

'And what about Thailand? There's obviously a domestic market here, and an international one.'

In the first half of 2012, the number of tourists visiting Thailand increased by almost 20 per cent from the previous year, and there were no prizes for guessing which nations were most heavily represented in terms of tourist numbers: 10.7 per cent of foreign visitors were Chinese and about the same number were Malaysians (10.6 per cent). About 430,000 Australians visited Thailand in the first half of 2012, constituting about 4 per cent of the foreign tourist trade during that period. I wondered how many Aussies went to marketplaces and bought ivory, only to discover at the border that they couldn't legally take it out of

Thailand, nor could they bring it into Australia. It is illegal to bring ivory into Australia unless it has a pre-CITES certificate (showing that it was ivory obtained before the worldwide ban came into effect in 1989).

Tom sipped on his carrot juice before answering my question. 'Thailand has to come to terms with the fact that they have a loophole in their legislation that allows illegal ivory to be sold. Today we found thousands of ivory products for sale. You saw it yourself. That can't all be from captive Thai elephants. We're seeing seizures from hundreds and hundreds of African elephants. It's pretty clear what's going on. This ivory is from poached African elephants. Thailand's improved border points, but they're not taking action in marketplaces.'

I recalled that no one had seemed to mind when I took photographs of ivory. No one was hiding this stuff. The sellers weren't worried about being arrested or prosecuted. There was an easy exit route they could take if they were questioned. All they had to do was say that the ivory came either from a captive Thai elephant or was pre-1989 stock. Like Bill had said, the issue was the law. Because the laws of Thailand pertaining to elephants were different for captive elephants compared to those in the wild, and you could legally sell the ivory from captive elephants, strictly speaking these sellers weren't doing anything illegal. If they were, it was virtually impossible to prove because of this legal loophole.

Another thing that was applicable not just in Thailand but across Asia was the pre-ban loophole. Any ivory that was bought before 1989 when the international ivory ban came into effect wasn't illegal and this situation continued after the ban: if you had ivory in your house, you could always just say it was pre-1989 and therefore legal. But without rigorous and expensive age-testing, which no one bothered to do in Asia, there was no quick, easy way to tell the difference between pre- or post-1989 ivory, or between the ivory from captive versus wild elephants.

There was now a DNA test to differentiate between African and Asian elephants, however, which could be useful, as any African ivory was more than likely from a wild population. But Thailand's legislation made it extremely difficult to keep ivory off the streets, and because it was weak, it was extremely difficult to penalise smugglers.

'The massive slaughter that happened in Cameroon recently – the three hundred elephants that were poached by Sudanese horsemen – could some of that ivory have ended up here?' I asked.

'You've got to understand that what's happening there is tradition,' Tom replied. 'Traditionally people in Sudan go on walkabout with their camels and move into central Africa. They've always killed elephants for meat and ivory. There used to be rhinos all over the Sahel. They've completely wiped them out. Now they've got more powerful weaponry and they're going on horses, further afield.

'Where did the ivory go?' he went on. 'One of two places, probably. From the Chad–Sudan border to Cairo's domestic markets. There are plenty of tourists visiting Egypt who will buy carvings of Cleopatra and Nefertiti. It just goes straight up the Nile.'

'Or, you've also got a big Chinese population now living in Khartoum. It could have ended up there.'

I twisted a forkful of flat noodles around on my plate, my appetite now diminished as I thought about the elephants being slaughtered across Africa to feed the human desire for ivory. Tom gave me a moment to let his words sink in.

'We've got a lot of work to do. I believe the Chinese government is engaged. Thailand is not engaged. They're playing a shell game, just moving the pieces around. Malaysia, the Philippines, Vietnam too . . . They're players in this because these criminal syndicates are adapting to tougher controls on importing to China. If they can't get it into China direct, they use side routes. They get the ivory to places like Vietnam, then send it by truck to China.'

Listening to Tom talk, I was growing increasingly despondent.

'China's growing economy is a big part of the equation. Over time if demand exists then you'll get new dynamics. New players will fill voids left open. It used to be Europeans like the French and Belgians creating the demand for ivory. Then it was Japan. They've all dropped off. Now it's China and Thailand.'

If what Tom was suggesting was true, then demand for natural products like ivory – and perhaps also rhino horn – reflected booms and busts in economic wealth to some extent. China's economy, though still growing, would eventually plateau according to standard economic models, although there was no sign of that happening any time soon. The demand for rhino horn in Vietnam was tightly linked to the recent increase in that country's available wealth. What I think he was suggesting, with the benefit of a historical perspective, was that the high demand would pass in time. I hoped this was true, but I couldn't help wondering, would there be enough African rhinos and elephants left for the species to survive when it did? Or would they, like the Javan and Sumatran rhinos, be left with barely viable populations of fewer than a hundred?

After lunch, Bill led us through the crowds to catch a local boat to the Riverside Markets, a more up-market shopping destination for wealthy tourists. I followed the two men onto the crowded, open boat, leaping over the rubber tyres separating the jetty from the boat, and grabbed a railing by the side where I could get some air.

'This is what it feels like to be a sardine,' I commented to Tom as we squeezed in with tourists, locals and monks.

A big man with a German-sounding accent was on the other side of me.

'Very full!' he said, grinning at me as sweat poured down his face.

The minimal breeze did little to diminish the stench of sweating human bodies as the only place to hold on and avoid falling out of the boat when it crashed into each jetty was a railing along the roof. This meant that everyone had to hold one arm above their head, allowing the less than pleasant smell of multiple underarms to putrefy the air. Each time the boat stopped at a jetty, ramming into it with a bone-jarring thump, a few people got off and even more got on, squeezing us all in a little more.

On the water, other boats whizzed by, most of them colourfully painted wooden longboats with small engines at the back. Ramshackle tin huts on the river bank contrasted with the glitzy, mirror-windowed high rise buildings beside them. Earlier, on the road, it had been motorised tuk tuks competing for space with hot-pink taxis, motorbikes, pushbikes, buses and cars. Everyone seemed to be going someplace in Bangkok.

The river water didn't look all that clean, but I had seen more polluted rivers in big cities in India.

'It used to be worse,' Tom told me. 'There used to be loads of rubbish in there.'

At the Riverside Markets, there were proper shops rather than market stalls, with lots of more expensive pieces of ivory carved into artworks, large and small, and exquisite jewellery. Some of it, like the intricate Chinese Buddha and ancient mythology figurines, appeared to be directly aimed at the Chinese market. There was also vegetable ivory, as Bill pointed out, which came from the Amazon. It looked like the small, carved ilalla palm nuts I knew from Namibia.

'This all went behind closed doors when Thailand hosted the last big CITES meeting,' Bill commented, 'but now it's out in the open again.'

Upstairs, in an art gallery, two giant, gleaming, polished tusks, which had stickers on them suggesting they were certified, cost the equivalent of $14,000. At the entrance to one shop, an enormous carved wood elephant that was about my height had real ivory tusks. The saleswoman objected to me taking a picture, but since none of the other ivory sellers had seemed bothered about photos, I guessed that her objection might have been more about me stealing the design.

You had to be very wealthy to afford the ivory artwork we saw at this place, leading to jokes about the three of us clearly being in the wrong line of work. Either that, or in the right line of work, but on the wrong side of it.

I had seen a lot of ivory in just two marketplaces in Bangkok, but it was the next morning, in Thailand's largest weekend market, Chatuchuk, that we hit the jackpot. The irony of it was that the market was also filled with elephants. There were elephant towel holders, elephant tissue boxes, elephant neck ties for men, elephants on fridge magnets, scarves, purses, wine buckets with elephant handles. Thailand was obsessed with elephants, and yet it was one of the countries contributing most directly to the trade chain causing Africa's elephants to be slaughtered.

At this market there was even a CITES stall which had free postcards and leaflets to raise awareness of the wildlife trade. The postcards had pictures and cartoons of elephants on them and the slogan underneath said: 'No export of elephant ivory and other elephant product from Thailand . . . DO NOT PURCHASE'. But if the CITES team were trying to deter buyers, they were a long way from where we would later find the bulk of the ivory for sale, and in the gentle, peaceful way of the Thais, they certainly weren't forcing people to take notice of what they were advertising. Unlike in other parts of Asia that I had visited – Indonesia, for example – market sellers in Thailand didn't hassle you to buy their wares. But this was one issue that could have done with a little more hassling of the public. It was great that the local CITES team had a stall at the market, but I had my doubts they were stopping people buying ivory. It was a gut feeling that would turn out to be all too true a short time later.

After a couple of hours of finding dribs and drabs of ivory jewellery and small carvings at various stalls, we hit what Tom described afterwards as an 'ivory bonanza'. There were three specialist ivory stalls near each other in the same area. They shone with the pearly white substance, literally metres of it spread out like gourmet treats on a banquet platter. My eyes hurt at the sheer extent of it, but I forced myself to act like a normal tourist interested in buying a new necklace.

Tom was an old hand at acting casual in places like this. He smiled and spoke in a friendly way to the sellers, saying he was looking for something special for his wife. I quickly took some footage with my Canon SLR camera. Again, no one seemed bothered by me taking photos.

While I filmed, the seller was negotiating with two young Asian women who looked to be in their mid-twenties, either Chinese or Thai. The elder of the two was trying on an ivory necklace with a large round centrepiece. After money changed hands, the two women walked off, the one with the new necklace stroking the circular ivory locket as if it was a precious new pet.

I wanted to run after her and ask her if she knew that the necklace she had bought was probably from illegally killed

African elephants. I wanted to know if she cared. If she wasn't from here, did she know that she couldn't legally take that ivory out of Thailand? Did she know the true cost of what was strung around her neck? That the short-term pleasure of it for her meant immeasurable pain for another?

I had seen enough now to know that what I was reading about the ivory trade in Asia was true. The woman who bought the ivory necklace that day was too young to have experienced the worldwide anti-ivory campaign that led to the ivory ban in 1989. Now Africa's white gold was for sale in the open again, as if the worldwide ban had never occurred and was no longer in effect, as if history was simply repeating itself. There was no question in my mind that the world needed a reminder that buying ivory was not on.

As I squeezed through the crowds, heading for a cab to the airport, Tom's words from the day before were fresh in my mind: 'It's as if they are carving the epitaphs of elephants,' he had said. How right he was, I thought to myself. Whether they knew it or not, these gentle people of Thailand who loved elephants and worshipped them were, along with China, now the architects of their demise.

CHAPTER 11

HORNS FOR HANGOVERS IN VIETNAM

Hanoi, Vietnam, January 2013

It was the smell that captured me first on Hanoi's Lan Ong Street, an intoxicating mixture of sweetness and spice that I inhaled greedily. The aroma seemed to dispel the acrid fumes of motorbikes, which people rode with fabric masks over their noses and mouths, and the rotting contents of rubbish bins that we had passed on other streets. Before me lay an open invitation to the world of Vietnamese traditional medicines, for which this street was known. Here, nothing was too strange a thing to ask for. Need a little dried seahorse for your impotence? Welcome to the Viagra of the sea! Maybe you need a few grams of ground pangolin scales for your rheumatism or stomach or liver problems? Well this is the place for you! Probably the only thing that these sellers weren't going to have on display in the open was the substance that I was here to investigate: rhino horn.

Each of the dozens of stalls along the street had a façade showcasing products and paraphernalia ranging from bags of dried, ground leaves and gnarled roots that resembled ginger to boxes of mushrooms labelled 'Longevity mushrooms'. Suspended from the ceiling of a couple were plastic bags containing dead geckos the size of large rats. Several sold bags of whitened starfish skeletons. Inside bottles of what looked like white wine were giant scorpions and tiny cobras. There were boxes with bold tigers and lions on them, pictures of the big cats used to attract the buyer's attention to the qualities of the animals. Whether they actually contained the body parts of tigers and lions was anyone's guess, but the idea was that if you took what was contained inside you would be instantly imbued with the strength and power of the advertised animal. There were powders of every colour, curled bark that smelt like cinnamon, hard, spherical fruits and gigantic mushrooms – all manner of plant and animal products used to treat illnesses in Asian traditional medicine.

As I walked along Lan Ong Street, my white face stood out like a penguin in Fiji. I knew that even if I had been able to speak Vietnamese, it was highly unlikely that I was going to get many answers from the sellers on this street about rhino horn's availability and who was buying it. The sellers were wary, and there was probably a good reason for that. It was two months before the next official CITES meetings were to be held in nearby Bangkok, and with the growing international recognition of Vietnam's role in the illegal wildlife trade, especially in the trade of rhino horn, journalists had been asking a lot of questions on the ground on which I now stood. The word on the street was that some organisations were encouraging CITES to call for sanctions on Vietnam for not taking adequate steps to stop the illegal rhino horn trade.

So lucrative was the trade that it had seen Vietnam lose its own single remaining Javan rhino to poachers a few years earlier, the carcass found with its horn hacked off in Cat Tien National

Park, the last of its kind exterminated by a bullet. The species had only been rediscovered in Vietnam twenty years earlier, yet it seemed that few even noticed it was gone. Now, the criminal syndicates behind the illegal trade had descended on South Africa and Zimbabwe, the last strongholds for Africa's rhinos, where hundreds of white and black rhinos were being killed to supply Vietnamese markets. Southern Africa was the African rhino's last hope for survival as populations of both black and white rhinos in the north had been decimated. The last western black rhino, endemic to west Africa, had been declared extinct in 2011, and there were well under a thousand of the critically endangered eastern subspecies in Kenya and Tanzania. The northern white rhino was a heartbeat away from extinction as well, with only four potential breeding animals left at a single game ranch in Kenya, and requiring constant surveillance.

Things were bleak now, but this wasn't the first devastating wave of rhino poaching to happen this century. From an estimated 100,000 rhinos in Africa in 1960, a catastrophic wave of poaching to provide for traditional medicine in Asia and dagger handles in Yemen saw most rhino populations decimated. Since the mid-1990s, however, effective management in South Africa had brought white rhinos back from the brink of extinction to a population numbering 18,800, about a quarter of which lived on private ranches. Black rhino populations had edged slowly upwards following the catastrophic poaching of the 1970s and 1980s, doubling to 4,880 animals, but remained listed as critically endangered. Now, just as there were signs of recovery through the good management of governments, NGOs, local communities and private ranchers, all of that work was being undone by renewed demand from a different part of the world. History was repeating itself, and this time, rhino populations were starting from a lower baseline.

I wanted answers and I knew that the best way to find them was to hit the ground and listen. So I travelled to Hanoi in northern Vietnam to find out what was happening. I wanted to know who was buying rhino horn and why, and what it would take to stop them. Rhino horn had become one of the world's most expensive substances and those involved at the top were criminals of the worst kind. This wasn't a mission I undertook lightly. I knew that those behind the illegal rhino horn trade would think nothing of teaching someone like me a lesson for asking too many questions. I was a woman alone in a communist country that had been invaded by foreigners three times in the last century and I was fishing around in the shadows. In this sinister underworld, those growing fat on the trade had a lot to lose if people like me got their way and the authorities really clamped down and stopped them selling their wares. Thankfully, I had company.

Over a strong, sweet Vietnamese coffee and sweet and sour chicken at a café in Hanoi's Old Quarter, American Brett Tolman of TRAFFIC gave me the lowdown on what I could expect to see over the next few days. The answer was – not much rhino horn. It wasn't that it wasn't here – and plenty of it – but there was pretty much no chance of me actually seeing any. As Brett put it, 'It's more valuable than gold, so people don't just have it lying around.'

Rhino horn was illegal according to Vietnamese law, with possible jail time of up to seven years and a fine of around $23,000, though rarely imposed, for those caught dealing in it. This was an illicit substance, just like cocaine, and no one was going to want to show it to me or even talk about it.

'What about you?' I asked Brett. 'Have you seen it yourself?'

'Yeah . . . I was at a party of a friend of a friend and a girl offered me some. I asked her what it would do and she said it would help my hangover. When I asked where she got it from, she told me that her father worked in government.'

The involvement of corrupt government officials, such as the Vietnamese embassy staff caught red-handed with rhino horn on film in South Africa, adds a whole other level of complexity to this problem, Brett explained.

The next morning, the coordinator of TRAFFIC's Greater Mekong Program, Bendigo-born Australian Naomi Doak, explained further: 'The illegal rhino horn trade is high profit and low risk. This isn't going to change until you have strong penalties and enforcement – and high-profile coverage of those penalties. Right now the chance of getting caught is ridiculously low.Vietnamese authorities say they check every flight from Africa, but there are no direct flights from Africa. They all come from other parts of Asia and these flights are hardly ever checked for illegal wildlife products.'

I thought back to the day before when I had flown in from Singapore. I realised that my bag hadn't been checked. If I had had a bag full of rhino horn I would have walked through and got away with it scot-free.

'It's scary,' Naomi went on, her Australian accent still strong despite having lived in Asia for many years. 'Those who can afford to use it are [using it]. Those who can't afford it would be if they could.'

What was it about this cursed growth on a rhino's face that had made it so much more attractive to people recently? Rhino horn had been a part of Traditional Chinese Medicine for a very long time, used to treat a range of illnesses from delirium and headaches to epilepsy and measles. Rhino horn has cooling properties, according to the pharmacopoeia, which is believed to make it effective in reducing the temperature of the blood and purging toxins. Contrary to popular belief, there is nothing in the books of traditional medicine about rhino horn acting as an aphrodisiac. That was a myth promoted by the western media, that, ironically, has now led to the false belief among some Vietnamese men that it may enhance sexual prowess.

But something had changed recently, something that was leading to a much greater demand for horn. Over a hundred rhino horns had been stolen in the last few years from government stocks, private game farms and lodges, museums and educational institutions in Africa and Europe. Then there was the recent practice of Vietnamese 'pseudo hunts', in which Thai sex-workers were recruited to undertake legal white rhino trophy hunts in South Africa for criminals who wanted to obtain the horn to sell in Vietnam. It seemed like some people would do anything to get rhino horn now. What was driving the renewed demand?

Traditional Chinese Medicine had been around for thousands of years, much longer than western medicine. Personally I had nothing against it and remained open-minded about natural herbal remedies and alternative treatments such as acupuncture and massage to assist with healing processes. A friend in Sydney had given me acupuncture to help bring on labour when I was overdue with Solo, and it wasn't long after the second treatment that my contractions started. Traditional medicine is becoming increasingly popular in the West as a complement to modern medicine.

The two systems work very differently. Traditional Chinese Medicine focuses on the body in a holistic sense, while western medicine looks at the structure and function of the individual parts of the body. Western medicine manages disease and is based on science whereas traditional medicine works to maintain health and is considered a healing art. The goal of Traditional Chinese Medicine is to harmonise yin and yang by regulating *qi* (vital energy) in the organ networks, opening congested channels, dispersing excess, cooling heat, warming coolness, and so forth.

One of the most valuable things that Traditional Chinese Medicine has done in recent times is help prevent and rapidly treat malaria with the Chinese herb artemisinim, which comes from the sweet wormwood plant. Artemisinim has been used in traditional medicine for two thousand years, but only recently has it become widely used in malaria-prone countries following a report in the *Chinese Medical Journal* in 1979.

Personally, I would use modern medicine if I was sick, but that's because I'm an Australian and that's what we do. If I was Vietnamese, I would probably consult a traditional medicine doctor as well as a modern medicine doctor. Vietnam's hospitals have both modern and traditional medicine departments, often in the one building. Both types of medicine are actively promoted by the government.

There was no scientific evidence that rhino horn was any more effective in reducing fever than cheaper modern treatments available, but in contrast, there also wasn't any showing that it didn't work. That left a mystery, and a void like that can lead to mythology.

However, the use of rhino horn and other traditional remedies that came from *endangered* plant and animal products was not sustainable. It was destroying the species that provided it. Nothing from nature should be used in quantities beyond which it can be replaced. And so even if rhino horn did reduce fever, we had to stop killing so many rhinos to get it or soon all the rhinos would be gone. I was all for taking the edge off a hangover, but not if it wiped out a species. The question was how to convince Vietnamese users of rhino horn of that. Most people in Vietnam had never seen a rhino in the wild, and even if they had seen one in their own country before the last one died in 2008, what did it matter to them whether or not a species on the other side of the world was becoming extinct?

I had to ask Brett the obvious question: 'Does it actually work? Does it reduce fever?'

'It's mostly keratin – hair,' he replied. 'So you'd be much better off taking a Panadol. But it's not about what it does or doesn't do. It's about social status. People are trying to "keep up with the Joneses".'

A recent report by TRAFFIC's Tom Milliken and Jo Shaw identified four main user groups for rhino horn in Vietnam. The first were terminally ill patients who used it because of what they believed to be its ability to cure cancer, a rumour probably spread by rhino horn dealers to increase its value. The second, and probably largest group, were habitual users on the social circuit, like those in the situation that Brett had described to me when he had been offered it at a party. These wealthy, urban-dwelling individuals believed that rhino horn mixed with water or added to wine could detoxify the body after excessive drinking. Due to its high value, there was a strong element of status and 'face' associated with using rhino horn in these settings. The third group of users were affluent, middle to high income young mothers who used rhino horn to treat high fever in children. The fourth were elite gift givers who presented it to important political officials and elites to gain influence. Gift giving to maintain relationships is an important part of Vietnamese culture, and rhino horn is an expensive gift that can be very powerful in this regard.

But I got the sense from talking to the team at TRAFFIC that there was still a long way to go in terms of understanding the dynamics of this growing market. They had just commissioned a consumer survey to try to work out the percentage of the population using rhino horn within the middle to high income bracket, the demographics of those users (sex, age etc) and the reasons they were using it. Armed with that information, and with the right public awareness campaign, perhaps they would be able to target the users and change their behaviour.

A major contributing factor to the surge in demand for horn was Vietnam's growing wealth and, concomitantly, an increasing appetite for luxury products. The country is predicted to be one of the fastest developing economies by 2025. To get a sense of this side of modern Vietnamese life, I made my way to the expensive, historic Metropol Hotel in Hanoi's Old Quarter at sunset, found a table out on the footpath and ordered a Hanoi lager. A little earlier I had taken a walk through the hotel's luxury boutique stores – Louis Vuitton, Chopard, Cartier, to name a few. If I had had a million bucks I would have been at home there. Leather bags, watches, diamond jewellery and men's wallets lined the shelves, with nothing under $500, most things in the thousands, and price tags in both US dollars and Vietnamese dong.

I asked a young saleswoman the price of a particular diamond necklace on display. US$8,000, she told me. I swallowed, trying to pretend I was a serious contender for it. When I casually asked her whether it was mostly tourists buying in the store, she told me there were some, but also Vietnamese.

Now, as I sat slowly drinking my beer, I watched tourists being pedalled past by local men riding bicycle carts with red fabric roofs and orange tassels. There was a production chain of wedding photography happening right in front of the hotel, where at least eight local brides and grooms were taking turns to pose romantically the week before their wedding ceremony. I watched people entering the hotel and others ordering drinks at tables near mine. One thing was apparent: the clientele of this up-market hotel consisted not only of western tourists. Young Vietnamese walked past me in expensive designer clothes, having parked out the front in their flash new modern cars. There was money in this town. New money. A lot of it. And those who had it wanted everyone to know about it.

So rhino horn was just like any trend or fad among the elite of any country. You used it to show off your wealth, to make sure your friends knew that you were part of the 'in' crowd, to be seen to be cool. But one thing baffled me about this. Surely a newer generation would see rhino horn as belonging to an older world, something that parents and grandparents might use but not the cool set? When I broached the question with Brett he told me something surprising: in Vietnam, higher levels of education were not correlated with lower use of traditional medicines like rhino horn. It was the opposite. If you were well educated, you were *more* likely to use it. It wasn't about the effect at all, because unlike rhino horn, modern medicine was scientifically proven to be effective and cost a lot less money. It was about being *seen* to be using something that was worth a lot of money. If you could pull out a little rhino horn at a drinking party, it showed your friends you had the disposable income to buy it. It really didn't matter whether it worked or not.

To change the behaviour of this consumer group, which was thought to be the largest, we had to find a way to make the use of rhino horn 'uncool'. An advertising campaign targeted at users along the lines of Australia's successful 'If you drink and drive, you're a bloody idiot' campaign might be the answer, with influential celebrities pushing the message home to the public. Until consumers started to say no to rhino horn, the criminals and government officials involved in the trade would keep lining their pockets.

Yet another facet of the ugly illegal rhino horn trade in this part of the world was that not only the rhinos were being taken advantage of – people were too, in particular those dying of cancer who had nothing to lose and everything to gain. Cancer rates in Vietnam had surged in the last decade (for example, from 142 per 100,000 men in 2000 to 181 per 100,000 men in 2010), and this perhaps accounted for some of the more recent increased demand for horn. The traditional medical literature does not promote rhino horn as a cure for cancer, but this has not stopped the popular belief that it might work, particularly as several prominent celebrities and government officials have claimed to have been miraculously cured of cancer after taking it. I decided to join Brett and Minh Nguyen from TRAFFIC in a survey at a state government hospital for children, the National Hospital of Pediatrics, asking parents questions about the methods they had employed in the treatment regime of their children. Specifically, they wanted to know whether they had tried rhino horn. If they had, what had happened, and if they hadn't, would they consider it if modern medicine failed?

I'm not good at hospital visits at the best of times. Something about them makes me light-headed as soon as I walk in the door. As we entered the ground floor of the hospital and squeezed into the lift with a dozen others to go up to the eighth floor, I took a few deep breaths and tried to prepare myself for what we were going to see. I felt palpably nervous already and knew that this was always the way I felt before I passed out. It wasn't lost on me how far I had come from the wild savannahs of Africa that had first inspired me to become a wildlife conservationist. The front line for Africa's wildlife was now being fought in places like this, a world away from the campfires I loved.

In the first room we entered, about eight hospital beds were lined up around the walls with a table in the centre. Children ranging from about three to twelve years old were attached to drips via plastic tubing which fed through the backs of their hands. As a result of the chemicals used in their treatment, most had no hair on their heads. Their mothers and also some fathers were with them. Some were playing with the kids, sitting on small blue plastic chairs by their child's bed. Others were trying to sleep on the bed beside them. The white sheets on the beds looked clean, but the light green walls were filthy. The hospital had tried to liven up the room with a painted mural of elves leaping from trees on one side and, on the other, one with mice and rabbits and lions. There was a television turned off at one end of the room and next to it a door that led to a small balcony. The dark wooden window shutters were closed. Before I even heard their stories my heart broke for these people. I couldn't imagine what it must have been like to have your child diagnosed with cancer and then to have to go through the harrowing treatment regime of chemotherapy alongside them. There was no laughter in the room and very few smiles. They were living in a version of hell.

Brett and Minh set to work on the interviews, starting with a woman in a pink tracksuit near the entrance, who was sitting on the side of her little boy's bed. Her name, she said, was Thom, and her little boy was Quing. He was three years old, the same age as my own son, and her first child. She had been in the hospital with him for over seven months. She had known something was wrong when Quing suffered a fever for two weeks. He also had red spots on one leg and hand, so she took him to a doctor – a modern medicine doctor – to find out what was wrong. Quing was sent for a blood test and the results showed that he had leukemia. She told us that his doctor prescribed a three and a half year chemical treatment regime.

Thom had begun by speaking in Vietnamese, translated by Minh, but now switched to English. She said she wasn't using traditional medicine and was sticking to the regime that the doctor had given her. But when Brett asked her whether she had heard about other people using rhino horn in the hospital she confirmed that she had. Other patients had told her that if the chemotherapy treatment didn't work, she should try it. Would she consider it? Brett asked. Yes, she would, but not yet. Brett asked her where she would obtain the rhino horn if she decided to use it. Not here, she told him through Minh's translation, not in the hospital. She would buy it from outside. We thanked her for her time and asked her if she thought there were signs of improvement in her son's condition yet. She shook her head. It's too early to say, she told Minh. She just had to follow the treatment regime.

The eyes of another woman, mother of an eight year old boy who also had leukemia, welled up as she told Minh in a quiet voice how worried she was about her son. While I couldn't understand her words, her face told a story of unbelievable pain. Other mothers did talk about using rhino horn, she said, but it was also said that it could have adverse effects. She also said that it was very expensive.

Another woman had sought to buy rhino horn for her four year old son, Giing, but had been unable to find any. She said she would try anything if there was a chance it might work. As his mother spoke to us the boy, wearing a yellow Adidas jumper, stared into the distance as if he was on another planet. I felt my own eyes filling with tears as I tried not to stare at this sick little boy with his far-off gaze. For the last two months that he had been receiving treatment there they had barely left the hospital.

When we departed the ward a bit later in search of a doctor to talk to, Thom, the first woman we had spoken with, touched Brett's arm and asked him in clear English, 'Does it work . . . rhino horn?'

The hope I saw in her eyes was heartbreaking. As Brett explained that rhino horn was just like eating hair, that it didn't work, I realised that our mere presence there asking questions about the substance could create false hope about its healing properties. And we weren't even supporting its use – quite the opposite, in fact.

'Why do you ask me these questions,' she went on, clearly disappointed and I sensed a little angry, 'if it doesn't work?'

Brett explained that the animal that produced horn was becoming extinct and that the organisation he worked for was trying to understand why people were buying it so that the practice could be reduced. Brett's mature and compassionate response was impressive, but we were in a hospital where kids were fighting for their lives and to anyone in that situation, conserving Africa's rhinos was a long way down the list of priorities.

How easy it would have been to promote a make-believe cure for cancer among these desperate mums and dads. What a catch they were for the fraudsters seeking to sell the horn. By spreading rumours of its so-called miraculous properties they stood to gain more buyers and higher prices. It made me sick. I knew that if I was in this mother's position I would have done anything to save my child's life. And that level of desperation was ripe for abuse.

Brett's explanation seemed to appease Thom because a second later she suggested that we go to another room up the corridor where patients had private insurance. The implication was that they might have been able to afford the expense of rhino horn, whereas those in her child's ward could not afford insurance, let alone rhino horn.

In the private room we met Vinh, a little boy of four and a half years, and his father, who had been working on his laptop computer when we entered. He agreed to talk to us. Vinh was wearing sunglasses and playing with a toy gun, shooting plastic bullets with suction rubbers on the end. I smiled when I saw that half a dozen plastic bullets were already stuck up on the ceiling. These kids were sick but they must also have been incredibly bored. I couldn't imagine trying to entertain Solo inside a little room for a day, let alone for months of his life.

Like the other patients, this man's child was following a modern medicine treatment plan that included chemotherapy. When Brett asked his father if he had heard of rhino horn being used to treat cancer he said he had because he himself had used it. He'd heard about it from friends who were drinking it with wine one night. They told him it would be good for his health and help his hangover. He laughed as he told us that he had seen no benefit from it at all so he wouldn't bother using it again. He joked that perhaps it was fake horn and that was why it didn't do anything. But he said the only way he would use it to treat his son's cancer was if the doctor recommended it, reflecting the sentiments of other parents we interviewed, and the integral role of the medical profession (both modern and traditional doctors) in preventing its use.

This man told us he was a labourer in the seafood business, but the standard of his attire, the laptop and private room suggested that he was in a more lucrative line of work than that. He didn't believe in rhino horn's supposed healing abilities and said that he knew of friends who had sick parents who had tried it but it had failed to help. He believed that people were using it more for appearances than for genuine healing.

The doctors in this hospital were incredibly busy and in the two hours we spent interviewing patients' parents Minh hadn't been able to find one who was willing to talk to us for five minutes. Finally, just as we were about to leave, Dr Dieu Duong agreed to have a quick chat. People did ask her for traditional medicines, the young doctor said, her arms crossed, and she knew that patients were using rhino horn, although she hadn't seen it herself. If people asked her whether it worked, she told them that she couldn't give them an answer because there was no scientific evidence to prove it did.

Brett asked her if she would suggest it as a last resort if modern medicine had failed to make a difference to a patient's health. She told us she would always be honest with patients' parents and told us that there was a separate department for traditional medicine and that we should talk to doctors there. Our time was up and she had patients to treat. It was clear that as far as she was concerned, rhino horn was not a serious medication for someone dying of cancer.

I decided I needed to talk to a traditional medicine doctor to find out more about what they were recommending. The next morning, after numerous attempts to contact nearby traditional medicine hospitals failed to get me a meeting with a doctor, I gave up and sat in the foyer of the hotel where I was staying. Then Ruby, one of the hotel staff members who I had been asking about the use of traditional medicine the day before, came over and sat beside me.

'I have an idea,' she said kindly. 'Why don't you pay for a regular appointment at the doctor? I think then they will give you a meeting.'

Ruby jumped in a cab with me and we barged through the throng of motorbikes to the National Hospital of Traditional Medicine, which, as it turned out, was only about ten minutes away. I paid 500,000 dong (about $23) to the receptionist and a few minutes later we were ushered into the office of a doctor who Ruby said was the hospital manager.

The doctor was probably in his sixties and wore the white coat of doctors all around the world. His office was clean and tidy. He told us that he was an associate professor at the University of Hanoi as well as the manager of the institute. I explained that I wanted to ask him about the use of wildlife products in Traditional Chinese Medicine, specifically whether he recommended the use of rhino horn. His English wasn't brilliant and at first he didn't know what animal I was talking about. I drew a very rough picture of a pig-like creature with a horn on its nose. Immediately he crossed his arms as he realised which animal I was referring to.

'This is against Vietnamese laws to use this. They can punish you,' the doctor said vehemently. 'We follow the World Health Organisation. If animal in red book [presumably the IUCN Red Data book which lists endangered species] Vietnam don't use for treatment.'

'But what about cancer?' I asked him. 'Do you recommend for cancer?'

'Cancer is very difficult for treatment,' the doctor said. 'Modern medicine make operation and chemical treatment. After that we can use traditional medicine to take fever from patient. Might affect them better.'

He paused for a moment as I took rapid-fire notes, then went on in an authoritarian tone: 'Very seldom you see this animal in forest in Vietnam. Receive now from Africa. But Vietnam government punish if you use. Need to protect that animal.'

I nodded, then asked him to explain how it would be used if it was not illegal to do so.

'For long time Vietnam and China have not modern medicine. Then we use for high fever. Now can use modern medicine for cure. Not used in treatment for patient now.'

'So if a person asks you for rhino horn, what do you tell them?'

'If ask, I say do not use it. There are penalties.'

This was one doctor who was not going to say anything other than the party line. Undercover TRAFFIC surveys in Vietnam indicated that some traditional medicine doctors regularly suggest that patients use rhino horn if they can afford it, usually only after modern medicine has failed to produce a result, but clearly this doctor was not going to tell me anything that might get him into trouble.

If what I was hearing from the staff at TRAFFIC was correct, Traditional Chinese Medicine was part of the problem but not all of it. The main contributor was the same thing that was causing the extinction of most threatened species across the world: excess and consumerism. Vietnam was far from the only country in which profit came before people and planet. This was something of which countries in the west, like Australia, were just as guilty. Even if it did take the edge off a hangover, which I still had serious doubts about, the social use of rhino horn in Vietnam was directly linked to people's hedonistic desire to look wealthy in the eyes of others. While a small few profited enormously from the trade, hundreds of rhinos were dying, along with the rangers employed to protect them.

Who was to blame? The parents of the children who were dying of cancer certainly weren't, although they probably accounted for some of the demand. The people at wine-drinking parties buying horn to offer to their friends were definitely a big part of the problem, but they weren't evil. Chances were these folks had never even seen a rhino in the wild and Africa was another universe away. Did they even know that the species was becoming extinct as a result of their practices? Would they care?

In my view, the government officials and criminal syndicates who were cashing in on the prize definitely needed to be brought before the authorities and punished appropriately. But the likelihood of that happening depended on the government's commitment to strengthening existing laws and enforcing them. At the very least, much more thorough checks needed to be done of baggage coming into Vietnam from other Asian countries. If Vietnam ever wanted to be a part of a legal rhino horn trade, as some parties in South Africa were suggesting was a way forward to save the species, then it had to prove that it could regulate it, and stop the system being corrupted. As I boarded the plane back to Singapore, I knew that scenario wouldn't eventuate any time soon.

The only way to stop Africa's rhinos being killed was to make sure everyone in Vietnam knew what was happening and for powerful, influential Asian voices to start saying 'no' in a public way that set a trend. It was the same for Africa's elephants and the buyers of ivory in Thailand and China. The government had a role to play, but people needed to know about the problem in order to be convinced to stop buying it. It was time to start thinking outside the box to make a difference, and I was beginning to have an idea about what to do.

CHAPTER 12

THE GOOD, THE BAD AND THE UGLY IN KENYA

December 2012

Every so often in life an opportunity presents itself that allows a vision to take shape. First you must have the presence of mind to recognise it for what it is, and second, you need the courage to dare to seize the moment. If you're lucky – and determined – a dream that sprang from an idea in your head can turn into reality.

I met Asian television host Nadya Hutagalung on a rare night out on the town just before Christmas in 2012. While not particularly well known in the land of her birth, Australia, Nadya was a prominent celebrity across Asia, known for her acting, modelling and MTV VJ roles. Andy knew her because she was a global ambassador for Earth Hour, and he introduced us at an MTV reunion party at Robinson Quay on the Singapore River. In a short space of time, somehow our conversation led to African elephants, and I quickly realised that Nadya was genuinely interested in what I was saying. I was surprised by her keenness, to be honest, as one doesn't really expect a high-profile television star and model in a bustling Asian city to be concerned about the plight of elephants on the other side of the world. She asked a lot of questions and when I spoke about the way elephants lived in the wild I could see her eyes light up. She had never been to Africa.

'You should come with me to Africa,' I suggested, in the off-hand way that one does after several whiskey and ginger ales, never expecting in a million years that this striking woman might take me up on the offer.

It wasn't until the next day that I realised the opportunity that had just presented itself. Andy explained that Nadya had hundreds of thousands of Twitter followers across Asia, that *Asia's Next Top Model,* the TV show she hosted on the Fox network, was currently the highest rating in the Asian region, and that while she had a mainstream following in several of the ivory and rhino horn buying countries, she also had won awards for her environmental work.

When we met again, this time sober over a coffee and with her delightful mum, Dianne, I learned that Nadya was serious about coming to Africa and seeing for herself what was going on behind the scenes. We started discussing how we could make it happen, and in particular how we could use the trip to raise awareness of the plight of African elephants and rhinos and the threat of poaching caused by the demand in Asia for ivory and rhino horn.

That day I also learned that Nadya was the daughter of an Indonesian father and an Australian mother, and had been raised in country Tamworth until the age of eight, before moving to Sydney. Then, in an extraordinary act of bravery at the tender age of twelve, she had dropped out of school and moved to Tokyo by herself to pursue a modelling career. Raised by a single mum herself, Nadya later became one as well after becoming pregnant to a violent and abusive boyfriend before she was even out of her teens. She eventually managed to disentangle herself and her toddler son from this unhappy relationship and used the hard knocks life had thrown her to make herself stronger. Soon her face was well known across Asia and in the United States as one of MTV's foremost television presenters and her career was flying.

It went without saying that Nadya had lived the wild life of the celebrity music scene in her twenties, a world I associated with drugs and sex and rock 'n' roll, and I didn't ask her for details. The truth was, it was hard to visualise her in that context, so stark was the contrast with the elegant, gentle mother of three sitting opposite me in a suburban café just down the road from her house in Singapore. Approaching forty (although she didn't look a day over twenty-six), this former party-girl was now a practising Buddhist who appeared to care deeply about the planet she was bequeathing to her children. After that meeting, I was left with the indelible impression that this was one celebrity who wanted to use her voice to make the world a better place for elephants. I was delighted and we agreed to work together to try and reduce demand for ivory and rhino horn in Asia.

In the months to come, I coordinated the most inspiring safari I could think of that would allow Nadya to see the grandeur and beauty of Africa, its species and people, but also the ugly side of what was happening to elephants and rhinos. Nadya's audience included hundreds of thousands of people across the region, including potential buyers of ivory in Thailand and rhino horn in Vietnam. If we could show them what was happening to Africa's elephants and rhinos through Nadya's eyes and make the connection to Asia, perhaps we could help reduce the demand that was causing the killing in Africa.

I decided on Kenya, because it was famous for its elephants and also because some of the most prominent voices in elephant conservation were based there. Although poaching had significantly increased in Kenya since 2007, it wasn't where the worst poaching was occurring in Africa – that dishonour belonged to central and western Africa, where the forest elephants were being decimated – but unlike other safaris I had organised for tourists, I had to consider the security situation for a celebrity who could become a hostage target, and I felt that these places were just too risky. I had never been to Kenya, having focused on southern Africa for so long, but the south wasn't the place to see elephant poaching; it was the place to see how effective conservation programs led to booming elephant populations. I needed Nadya to see the other side of the story, the bad as well as the good, and there was plenty of both in Kenya.

Nadya organised for the producer of *Asia's Next Top Model*, Serena Lau, to join us on the shoot, and Serena managed to convince their cameraman, Yves Simard, a French Canadian based in Auckland, to join us on the trip and film the whole thing. All of us were completely self-funded. Our goal was to produce several short videos for YouTube that would be shared extensively on social media across Asia. Nadya also enticed the Fox network to let us produce a public service announcement aimed at deterring people from buying ivory that Fox would air across multiple mainstream channels in Asia on our return.

Our trip to Kenya was planned for late April, just a few months after Nadya and I had first met, and only a few weeks after the CITES meeting was due to be held in Bangkok, Thailand. In the lead-up to the international conference, WWF together with AVAAZ had been pushing hard in the media and mobilising public voices through an online petition to influence Thai Prime Minister Yingluck Shinawatra to commit to banning the ivory trade in Thailand. In particular they wanted her to close the legal loopholes that allowed illegal ivory from poached African elephants to be sold in Thai marketplaces. Even Hollywood star Leonardo DiCaprio stepped in to help spread the word.

On the first day of CITES, after WWF representatives presented her with 1.6 million signatures urging Thailand to ban the ivory trade, the Prime Minister made a public statement in which she stressed the national importance of elephants to the Thai people and committed to amending the legislation that allowed the illegal ivory trade to thrive. It was a step in the right direction. WWF praised the Prime Minister's statement in international media, seeing it as a huge win for the conservation movement.

However, some conservationists, including myself, were much more hesitant to crack the champagne just yet. There was no timeline attached to the legislative changes, and my colleagues at TRAFFIC had told me that the Thai government had been saying for years that they were going to amend the legislation, so other than the high-level public statement, I wasn't convinced that much would change at all. Would this actually mean anything on the ground in Africa where elephants were facing the bullets and spears of poachers on a daily basis? Had the Thai Prime Minister just made this statement to get the international media off her back or did she really intend to follow through? I hoped it was the latter, but I felt strongly that a positive follow-up campaign would be necessary to provide some gentle encouragement for real action beyond words. That was where Nadya and I came in. If we could start our own targeted awareness campaign across Asia using her local voice to spread the word, perhaps we could also go one step further and keep the pressure up on the Prime Minister in Thailand to help her keep her promise.

Chyulu Hills, Kenya, April 2013

The first thing that struck me about Kenya compared to the southern African countries that I had worked in (with the exception of South Africa) was that it was much more heavily populated. And the wildlife was prolific – only two minutes after leaving the international airport we saw a family of giraffes just off the main road into town. The capital city, Nairobi, has about one and a half times the entire national populations of Namibia or Botswana, and around 43 million people country-wide. In spite of all those people, it also had a national park right on the edge of the city.

The next morning, we were all up before dawn and boarding a Safari Link light aircraft for a forty-minute flight to Ol Donyo Wuas, a bush airstrip near the exclusive Ol Donyo Lodge, where we would be staying for the next week. Ol Donyo was also the headquarters of the Big Life Foundation, the anti-poaching operation that would be our host in south-eastern Kenya. Wedged between two areas made famous for their elephants by conservation greats like Daphne and David Sheldrick and Dr Cynthia Moss, the lodge was in the Chyulu Hills between Tsavo West National Park to the east and Amboseli National Park to the west. I had read that this was the home of the traditional Maasai people and that this vast wilderness was so close to the border of Tanzania that snow-capped Mount Kilimanjaro was often clearly visible.

From the air our excitement mounted as agricultural fields gave way to jaw-dropping, expansive vistas of wild, green, seemingly endless open plains in which elephants and giraffes resembled miniature toys upon a gigantic picnic blanket. The Chyulu Hills rose up from this primitive landscape just east of the Great Rift Valley, forming relics of the shoals of extinct volcanoes, although it was only recently, apparently, in the mid-nineteenth century, that the last ones erupted. It felt like the landscape was alive, living and breathing, a creature with a will of its own and not an inanimate landscape of ancient larval flows, frozen in time. With the hill slopes carpeted in lush grass after the early April rains, I felt like I was in a scene from the film *Out of Africa*. It was breathtaking and we hadn't even hit the ground yet.

The pilot executed a bumpy though safe landing on a thin, short stretch of dirt that apparently doubled as an airstrip among the grassy plains. I stepped out into the savannah. A few seconds later, when the plane's engine stilled, my ears filled with the peaceful trill of millions of insects and birds. I took in the endless, undulating sea of knee-high grasses, their seed heads waving gently in the slight breeze. The grassy plains stretched as far as the eye could see, beyond the Kenyan border to where, today, Mount Kilimanjaro was largely obscured by its own low cloud weather system. The deep sense of space and peace at that moment forced us all to simply stop and breathe it in, as if we had just stepped into a sacred cathedral and come across the tomb of an ancient prophet. We all just stood there in silence. I couldn't take my eyes off the dozens of colourful butterflies flitting between vibrant wildflowers. Perhaps the moment was more sublime because we had come from Singapore, where space is in short supply, but for me it was a moment I will never forget. And I could see from the tears in Nadya's eyes that she felt it too. This was a special place and it was an incredible start to what was going to be a magical journey. Even if I didn't know Kenya, I did know Africa, and to those who are open to its magic, it always provides.

On the short drive across the plains and up into the hills where the lodge was situated, our guide Jeremiah pointed out several species that were unique to East Africa, like the statuesque Maasai giraffes, darker in colour than their southern cousins, the delicate Grants gazelles that reminded me of southern Africa's springboks, and the larger, fawn-coloured Cokes hartebeests or kongonis. As this was Nadya's first time in Africa, every species was a revelation and she was taking everything in with fresh delight, but for me, too, this was a new experience as many of the East African species are not found in the south, or are different subspecies.

Jeremiah pointed out a thorny bush known as the whistling thorn acacia, which had thick thorns up to three inches long protruding out of not only the limbs but also the pods themselves. He explained that the shrubs existed in a kind of symbiosis with the large, stinging cocktail ants that I could see crawling all over it, which helped protect it from species like giraffes, while providing the ants with food. Edible trees like this had to have serious self-defence mechanisms to survive the sheer number of browsing creatures that lived on vegetation in this part of Africa.

After settling in to our rooms at Ol Donyo Lodge, we met Richard Bonham, the Director of Operations for Big Life in Africa, and his dog, a blonde bitzer called Genghis, under an ostrich-egg chandelier in the open lounge area. Prior to leaving Singapore I had read that the organisation had been co-founded by Richard and Nick Brandt, the famous photographer, in 2010, in response to the escalating poaching crisis. The son of a game warden, Richard was a third-generation Kenyan who had been raised on a farm north of Nairobi. He had been working closely with the Maasai community in the Chyulu Hills since 1986 when he started the Maasailand Preservation Trust and built an earlier version of Ol Donyo Lodge (now rebuilt) that would enable funds from tourists to support local communities and conservation efforts.

The first things I noticed about Richard were his striking light blue eyes and his humble manner. This was a man who managed a huge force of 280 anti-poaching rangers across Kenya and Tanzania, a wilderness of over two million acres, who got up every day before dawn and steeled himself to face a war against poaching that carried an enormous responsibility. He held the lives of men and wildlife in his hands, yet he was down to earth and accommodating, eager to show us Big Life's work and to help us spread the word in Asia to reduce the demand for ivory and rhino horn.

'Look!' Nadya exclaimed.

Two bull elephants had appeared at the waterhole in front of the lodge for a drink.

'Shall we take a closer look?' Richard said, his eyes twinkling, 'There's a hide down there.'

The four of us followed Richard's khaki-clad figure down the side of the hill through the thornbush along a dirt path that led to an open cement hide surrounded by logs. The logs might have kept the elephants a little way back from the people in the hide, I thought to myself, but lions would be inside in a heartbeat. The two bulls were well aware of our presence, but they didn't seem bothered by us.

The older of the two bulls was known locally as 'One Tonne', Richard explained, because of his enormous tusks, one of which was slightly longer than the other. The longer of his two tusks extended almost to the ground. He was the most impressive tusker I had ever seen – and it crossed my mind that, with all that ivory, he would have been a poacher's dream. The other bull was smaller, younger and had much shorter tusks. It was clear from their behaviour that they were good mates. The younger bull leaned in to the big bull while he sucked water up through his trunk, rubbing the side of his face against the larger one's, their trunks intertwining with each other just like humans hold hands. One Tonne seemed to be enjoying the younger bull's company and didn't push him away, even though he was focused on having a drink.

It was a special moment of intimate elephant camaraderie. I had seen mutually friendly interactions between bulls like this in other places before, especially between an older and younger one. Male elephants leave their mother's herd in their early teens and set out on their own or join all-male 'bachelor' herds, so such friendships between males are important. Females, on the other hand, stay with their mothers and aunties for their entire lives. The only way these bonds are broken is when one dies. It's not uncommon for an old bull and a young bull to hang out with each other over a period of time, with the younger bull providing better eyesight and hearing for the old bull, while the younger bull learns the tricks of the trade from the old bull. We stayed with the bulls for about half an hour before they wandered off into the lush woodland and we headed back up to the lodge for lunch, sweating but excited from our first wild elephant sighting on the ground.

Over a decadent meal of fresh green salads with mint, feta and roasted pumpkin, deli ham and salami, home-baked bread rolls and a cheese platter prepared by the lodge staff, Richard explained that the main focus of Big Life's work was to protect elephants and rhinos from poaching because they were now the species most at risk. However, they also ran a predator compensation fund to help protect lions and other carnivores from illegal hunters by financially compensating local pastoralists when a lion killed one of their cattle. Their whole approach to conservation centred on community engagement, working closely with the local Maasai.

'One of the most powerful weapons we have is that we employ solely from within the community,' he explained. 'When a guy becomes a game ranger he gets status in the community. They're relatively well paid. Give him a uniform, training . . . you get morale. And they're protecting animals on their land. Plus they grew up in villages, these guys. They've got engrained bush knowledge. We have quite a few ex-poachers. They're very valuable because they know the ways of the bush.'

Big Life also used donations and their share of tourism profits from the lodge to fund local Maasai schools, reforestation projects and to supply water to villages. In 2012 a very successful project, initiated by an idea that came from local village elders, was the first Maasai Olympics, enabling young men to compete (for women!) by participating in sport rather than killing lions to demonstrate their manhood. The winner of the Maasai Olympics was taken under the wing of a famous Kenyan Olympic gold medal winner for training. Richard was clearly someone who understood the true value of community-based conservation.

'So the rangers get status from their jobs,' Nadya said, 'but surely it's very dangerous?'

Richard nodded gravely, 'Yes. Being a game ranger *is* a dangerous job. They're up at first light, bumping into all sorts of dangerous game. Buffaloes, elephants, lions . . . We've had guys injured. When they have contact with poachers, they'll [the poachers] do anything not to get caught.'

'And how is it going? I mean, overall? Are you winning?' I asked.

'What we're doing here is a little band-aid on a huge war,' Richard responded. 'We haven't lost an elephant since December. Locally we're containing them, but overall in Kenya, in Africa . . . we're losing. You can stem the tide, but you can't stop it. The future of these animals depends on people not buying [ivory and rhino horn]. Maybe we'll be able to save this population in the shadow of Kilimanjaro, but across Africa I see a dismal future.'

It was a grave way to end lunch, to hear someone with so many years of experience expressing despair, even though they were making progress locally.

'Let me show you what I'm talking about,' Richard said, 'and I'm afraid what I'm going to show you this afternoon isn't a pretty sight.'

After collecting our camera gear, we all piled into Richard's dark green, double cab LandCruiser and headed out across the plains, passing more gazelles and Cokes hartebeests on the way.

'Over there . . .' Richard indicated to our right. 'That's where our black rhinos live, in that thick bush.'

He was pointing out a long stretch of densely vegetated hills alongside the plains on which we were driving. As black rhinos are solitary creatures and browse on leaves, bark and twigs, it looked to me like perfect habitat for them, dense and with lots of food.

Over the preceding month, Nadya and I had been following a story on Big Life's website about a rhino that had been caught by the neck in a poacher's cable-wire snare. In desperation, he must have pulled the wire away from where it was fixed and got away, but in doing so, caused the wire to tighten around his neck like a noose, and so had been unable to remove it. A camera trap had captured a photo of it one night, showing the severity of the wound and alerting the Big Life team to the problem. Immediately the team sprang into action. Dozens of men scoured the area where the rhino had last been seen. Tens of thousands of dollars were spent on an extensive ground and air search involving not only Big Life but other organisations too, trying to find this poor animal so they could remove the snare and give it a chance at survival before the poachers found it and removed the horn. On the flight to Kenya we had been hopeful that they might find the rhino while we were there, but we were too late.

As we drove, Richard explained the final days of the mission to find the rhino.

'When we finally got to him, he was in bad shape. He still had the energy to charge us and knock one of our guys over, but once we immobilised him we could see how bad it was. The snare was down to the bone and it was an open wound.'

I tried to imagine what this animal had gone through in the preceding five weeks as the rangers had scoured the thick terrain, tracking him in every waking hour. The rhino wouldn't have known that the rangers were trying to help him. For all he knew, the humans tracking him were poachers, and, in any case, wild black rhinos are shy and tend to avoid humans of any description. This is particularly the case where they are persecuted and live in fear of people. The thick wire would have been strangling him slowly, and extremely painfully, as the deep wound became inflamed and infected by bacteria and parasites.

'The rangers refused to take leave during this time,' Richard said. 'No one would stop searching. Every day, up at dawn, searching all day.'

Their hopes must have soared when, after so many weeks of looking, the team finally managed to get to and immobilise the rhino with a tranquilliser. Now at last, they thought, they could remove the snare that was choking him, treat the septic wound with antibiotics and give him a chance at life.

I could only imagine how devastating the blow must have been to those involved in the rescue when the rhino could not be revived. He was so weakened from his dreadful physical condition, he simply didn't wake up.

By the time we reached the remote ranger base, consisting of a couple of tin-roofed, prefab rondavels next to a campfire in the middle of the bush, Richard had finished telling us the story and we were all feeling nauseous. The rhino had died the week before and now he wanted to show us the carcass.

'We'll walk from here,' he announced, lighting up a cigarette. 'It's about twenty minutes in.'

The rangers were using their hands to eat a late lunch of rice and some kind of stew when we arrived. There were about a dozen men in tidy dark green Big Life uniforms and shiny boots, both old and young, almost all of them Maasai. I noticed that some of the older men had traditional pierced and stretched ear lobes that they looped over the top of their ears. After an initial shaking of hands, one of the better English speakers among the men pointed at one of the older men and told me that he had four wives! They all laughed, clearly at his expense. While the Maasai have clung on to their traditional lifestyle more than many ethnic groups in Africa, resisting the influence of the missionaries and colonialists, some traditional practices like body piercing, multiple wife taking and the traditional raw meat, milk and blood diet were becoming less common among the new generation. These men were Maasai warriors who knew the land intimately, the perfect wildlife protectors, the kind of men who made you feel safe in the bush.

Richard led the way into the thicket, followed by some of his men, with Nadya, myself and the crew behind them and the rest of the rangers bringing up the rear. The bush really was as dense as it looked. The ground underfoot consisted of loose volcanic lava rocks that moved underfoot. It was prime ankle-twisting country. Thorny 'wait-a-bit' acacia bushes scratched and dug into skin and snagged any clothing not made of thick materials as we ploughed through. It must have been incredibly demanding work for the rangers patrolling this area every day.

There were only between seven and ten black rhinos left in this area, Richard had told us, but there were also Cape buffaloes and sometimes elephants, not to mention poachers, so one had to stay on guard at all times. He pointed out an old rhino midden that had probably belonged to the dead rhino. Middens are dung piles that rhinos repeatedly return to to mark their territory.

At one point, some of the rangers in front of us stopped dead in their tracks and I heard one say, 'Elephant.'

Nadya froze in front of me. This was not the sort of place you wanted to run into an elephant at close range. It was impossible to get out of there in a hurry and there were no climbable trees without sinister thorns. The threat seemed to pass a minute later as the rangers moved on again.

Much more comfortable walking through the dense vegetation in their thick, thorn-proof clothing, the long-legged Maasai rangers took some keeping up with. I was sweating when we finally came upon the head of the rhino in a small clearing. Predators had separated it from the rest of the body and dragged it away.

In fact, it was the smell that reached us first, that unmistakable stench of rotting meat that makes your stomach lurch involuntarily. The head was oozing maggots and the rotten skin had been pulled back, revealing yellowing bones beneath. It was barely recognisable.

But just around the corner was something much worse. It was the rest of the body, decapitated and heaving with moving walls of maggots, the small larvae crawling over each other and falling into the stomach cavity below hundreds at a time. It was such a putrid sight as to be mesmerising. Sickening though it was, I couldn't take my eyes off it. The lions and hyenas had devoured what was edible, leaving the skeleton complete with skin. The feet were still intact, the three-toed soles of them one of the few things that made it clear that this mound of rotting meat had once been a wild rhino.

The stench was so overwhelming, it took a little while for what I was looking at to sink in. As I listened to Richard explaining again how hard it had been to find this rhino, the human and financial toll of the search, and how much the animal had suffered because of poachers, I thought back on my own journey to Vietnam in pursuit of information on the rhino horn trade just a few months earlier. I thought about those poor mothers I had met with children suffering from cancer who would try anything to save them, their desperation making them easy targets for rhino-horn touts to take advantage of. I thought about the government officials and rich businessmen who were growing fat on dead rhinos like this, Africa's natural heritage, people a world away who didn't see themselves as responsible for this. And I thought about how it was poverty in Africa that was driving the illegal wildlife trade, while in Asia it was driven by rising wealth. And I just felt sick with the emotion of it all.

The producer, Serena, suddenly interrupted my thoughts: 'Tammie, how do you feel about this?'

It took all I could muster to stop the tears rolling freely down my face as I tried to find my inner hardened scientist and a professional answer. But the truth was, I was struggling. I had seen rhino carcasses before, but for some reason this time it felt different. When you are faced with the hard reality of the price that Africa's wildlife is paying for the wealth of a small few, raw emotions bubble to the surface. It's in the stench of death, the gore of the maggots, the eyes of the men who are fighting for these species. And it was all the more powerful for me on this occasion because for the first time in my life, I was connecting the dots across two continents through my own personal experience. This rhino had suffered immeasurably for five weeks, and he was one of hundreds being slain annually. This rhino represented the loss of so much more than one animal.

As the camera moved off me back to Nadya, I could see that she was also visibly affected. As it began to rain lightly, I turned away from the group and let the tears come.

The next day Richard served up another platter of carcasses, this time elephants. Both of them were bulls killed by poisoned spears, the first in a poaching scenario, the second due to human-elephant conflict. All that was left of both carcasses was bones and dead skin as they had been killed several months earlier. Richard explained how the poached bull had been in his prime. He had been speared to the kidney and so didn't take long to die (we were told that sometimes it can take months for the effects of the poison to kill an elephant). The mortally wounded bull had lain down, resting his head on a termite mound like a pillow, and breathed his last. In the days and weeks that followed, the rangers told us, the bull's dead body was visited by multiple elephants, their dinner-plate footprints fresh in the mud straight afterwards, grieving and paying their respects to a giant they had probably known personally. Even as recently as two days ago, several months after his death, the rangers said elephants had been there.

I thought of One Tonne and the young bull we had watched at the waterhole at Ol Donyo. Had this bull been teaching a younger one the ways of the wild? Had he been old enough to pass on his genes to a younger generation? Although he was just one elephant, I knew that he was part of an interconnected family of elephants to whom he mattered greatly. And as a conservationist, I knew that losses like this bull were increasingly significant as tens of thousands of elephants were being slain annually across Africa for their ivory. Reinforcing the point, that night we returned to the lodge to the devastating news that a new report just released by the Wildlife Conservation Society had revealed that almost two-thirds of central Africa's endangered forest elephants had been illegally killed for their ivory between 2002 and 2011. It was almost too much to comprehend.

In the days that followed, we focused on seeing live elephants, not dead ones. We visited Dr Cynthia Moss, now in her early seventies, who had worked on elephants in Amboseli National Park for forty-five years, and spent time watching elephant families with Amboseli Trust for Elephants researcher Katito Sayailel. Both women had a wealth of knowledge about elephant social behaviour and knew every elephant in the park individually. Over a lunch of vegetable samosas and oriental noodles, Cynthia spoke fondly about the elephants, as if they really were her family.

'Elephants are such incredibly sensitive, intelligent, loving, caring animals that you can't help but get wrapped up in their lives,' she said, with genuine warmth, laughing as she spoke.

And it was easy to understand why both women were so involved in the intricate social lives of the elephants as we watched the babies playing with each other and suckling from their enormous yet incredibly gentle mothers, so close to Katito's Land Rover. In this world of smartphones and constant overstimulation, elephants still provided compulsive viewing, especially when you got to know them personally.

But one of the happiest moments of this trip arose in Nairobi a few days later at the David Sheldrick Wildlife Trust, where we had the privilege of meeting the founder of Kenya's famous elephant and rhino orphanage, Dame Daphne Sheldrick, and her baby elephants. Like the wild elephants in Amboseli, these elephants appeared to be genuinely happy and calm, accustomed to the presence of people. Raised on a special milk formula that Daphne discovered only through trial and error, we watched the young elephants rolling and frolicking in the mud as if they had no cares in the world. With saggy bums in the air, unruly trunks swinging and the occasional head shove into another's rump, it was like watching a disorderly bunch of toddlers in a crèche. Every so often the keepers had to intervene to stop a little one being pushed around too much. But it was such a joy to watch them because these elephants were really having *fun*! It was tempting to get into the mud and join them for a roll. They were completely in the moment, and they pulled you in there with them.

But of course, there was another side to their story, because they wouldn't be there at all if their mothers hadn't been killed for their ivory.

We joined Daphne on the front verandah of her house, which also seemed to be a refuge for other animals, including a rock hyrax and a family of swifts that had nests in the ceiling. The verandah overlooked a muddy wallow where the baby elephants came for a bottle of milk followed by a mud bath in the afternoons.

'These orphans come in and they just want to die. They've lost their mother, their family, everything . . . and it's very intensive and difficult to actually turn that around,' Daphne explained. 'The secret is the other orphans in the nursery that are established. When one comes in we bring the other orphans in and feed them in front of the new one, because all elephants that come in here, having seen their elephant family killed, know that humans are the enemy, and they just want to take revenge for the loss they've suffered. But when you bring the other orphans around and they see the rapport they have with the keepers . . . You can actually turn around a completely wild orphan overnight.'

Listening to Daphne speak with so much love and passion for the elephants, we were all drawn in to her world.

'It's very important to take care of the mind as well as the body because when it comes to the rehabilitation of an orphan it has to be psychologically stable, because otherwise the wild elephants won't accept it, and that can only come with tender loving care to try and replace what an orphaned elephant would have in a wild situation . . . a family.'

She explained how important the keepers in their green uniforms were. They were with the elephants twenty-four hours a day, even sleeping with them in special bunks off the ground inside the wooden stables where the babies slept on hay. They fed them through the night, on demand initially, and continued with regular milk feeds until they were three years old.

'It's not just the milk, it's the care,' she went on. 'It's very important that the keepers love the elephants and that the elephants love the keepers. It's got to be a two-way thing, because elephants can read your heart. They know exactly what you're thinking.'

This seemed like a magical thing to me, the idea that an elephant could read my heart and know how I felt about it.

'At any age an elephant duplicates a human at the same age,' Daphne explained. 'Most of the elephants you see here are just two or three years old.'

My mind swung back to my own family then, and my own three year old son. How unimaginably awful would it be for him to witness the death of his mother, as these baby elephants had at the same age?

'Elephants are just like us emotionally, and in my fifty years of working with the orphans I know that for a fact. They're in some ways much smarter than us, such as the ability to communicate with infrasound, to detect seismic energy through the feet, to be telepathic, to be able to read what a person feels for them. They have very mysterious perceptions that we'll never be able to understand. Every time we move elephants from here to Tsavo where they go back to the wild, the ones that are already there are there to greet them ahead of time. Now they don't know these elephants and the new ones don't know them, so how do they know that? They are really amazing animals and so worth our protection and care.

'You know the saying "elephants never forget" is actually true, because one of our ex-orphans who is an elephant nearly fifty years old living wild in Tsavo, she recognised a man she hadn't seen in thirty-five years. Our keepers didn't know her, but this man approached from a long way off and she saw him and rushed towards him and embraced him with her trunk and then walked back with him to the stockade. The man had been her keeper when she was five years old. Imagine that . . . I can't even remember someone I met only yesterday!' She laughed good-naturedly.

If elephants could read our hearts, as Daphne believed, was it not also possible that in some latent way we had the capacity to read theirs too? If so, what would they say to us, I wonder? Would they give us a gentle reminder, perhaps, that we're not the only ones on this planet, and that until very recently, there was plenty of room for all of us?

I couldn't help thinking that in this fast-paced, money-driven world where human populations and wealth were rising and greed and excess consumption overruled the most basic of all human understandings, we had forgotten that, since the beginning of time, we have been part of the environment, and not apart from it, that without nature, without species like elephants, we too will no longer exist. When we start to see the demise of the great mammals like elephants and rhinos – and make no mistake, this is happening on our watch, right now – we are losing much more than these animals. We are losing an essential part of our very own nature – our capacity to coexist in harmony with others.

My journey with elephants and rhinos will never end, but over the past few years, as I crossed continents and time zones in my journey with them, I have witnessed the destruction of their habitats, the killings for profit, the efforts of extraordinary people fighting for their survival and, most wonderfully, the privilege of seeing these great creatures in the flesh, living wild and free in Africa and Asia. Elephants and rhinos have been incredible teachers and I owe them a lifetime of gratitude for letting me share their story.

As I boarded the plane back to Asia with Nadya and the crew at the beginning of May 2013, all of us had been deeply touched by what we had seen in Kenya and were inspired to do all we could to reduce the demand for ivory and rhino horn in Asia. But one word kept filtering persistently into my head – connections. We can no longer ignore the interconnectedness of our own worlds to others, the links between Asia and Africa that are decimating species, the connections between tourists who buy ivory souvenirs in places like Thailand or shoppers in supermarkets in Australia inadvertently choosing products containing palm oil and the species paying the real price for our cheap purchases – extinction. This is one planet, a planet of elephants, of rhinos and many other species in addition to us – and we are all connected.

EPILOGUE

Today the wildlife trade is the fourth largest illegal trade in the world after narcotics, counterfeiting of products and currency, and human trafficking, and is worth an estimated US$18 billion, according to WWF. In her address to the US State Department in November 2012, United States Secretary of State Hillary Clinton called for action, highlighting in her speech that wildlife trafficking has become so widespread, lucrative and dangerous that it has serious implications for the security, health and prosperity of many nations.

'We need governments, civil society, businesses, scientists, and activists to come together to educate people about the harms of wildlife trafficking,' she said. 'We need law enforcement personnel to prevent poachers from preying on wildlife. We need trade experts to track the movement of goods and help enforce existing trade laws. We need finance experts to study and help undermine the black markets that deal in wildlife. And most importantly, perhaps, we need to reach individuals, to convince them to make the right choices about the goods they purchase.'

Clinton's words have come at a time when the world's elephants and rhinos are sliding perilously close to extinction, and the worst thing is, we should know better because we have been here before. In the 1970s and 1980s, as African elephants were being slaughtered across the continent, it was to provide ivory for different markets – largely American, European and Japanese. As for rhinos, the same applies. There were half a million rhinos in the world at the start of the twentieth century. In 1970, there were 70,000 and today there are fewer than 29,000. In the 1970s and 1980s, 96 per cent of Africa's black rhinos were wiped out by poaching, in large part to provide ornamental dagger handles in the Yemen. Since the early 1990s until 2007, both white and black rhino populations increased (by 9.5 per cent and 6 per cent per year respectively), but now there are new markets fuelling a new wave of poaching.

African elephant guru Dr Iain Douglas-Hamilton of Save The Elephants has seen it all before, having worked with elephants since the 1960s. At his home in Nairobi at the end of our Kenyan expedition, he told Nadya and me: 'What is happening now is as bad or worse than what happened in the seventies and eighties because there are fewer elephants around. Demand for ivory is higher than ever before and there's no sign of let up yet.'

The worldwide ivory ban effected in 1989 gave Africa's giants a small reprieve for a time, but now there are new markets for their teeth in Asia and the players have changed. The increase in the number of very large seizures of ivory suggests that organised criminal networks are doing the damage this time around, and the high price tag of rhino horn has attracted the worst, and best resourced, kind of criminals in the game.

'I think we're on the verge of a global crisis,' Iain told us. 'You look at what's happening with global warming. You look at the collapse of key species and whole ecosystems. It's terrifying. If elephants are bad, fisheries are even worse, and there are other animals in even worse trouble, like the rhinos. If the rhinos survive this next century it's going to be a miracle. We're losing things because of our uncontrollable exploitation of this world. It's insane what we're doing to this planet. And economists have not woken up to this. They think that unending growth is possible all of the time. It's not. We have to limit what we take, our own populations. We have to start thinking about living in balance with nature. If we take nature for granted we'll be the ones becoming extinct along with everybody else.'

Daphne Sheldrick shared Iain's view: 'I think the rhinos could be extinct in my lifetime. And I think it's absolutely cata-strophic that humans have done this to the planet. Wildlife is essential to the environment. Everything's interlinked. We only have one home and it's this.'

It's not too late to stop the poaching in Africa. Solutions exist. The demand for ivory and rhino horn must end, legislation must be strengthened to prevent illegal trading and the punishments handed out to the criminals profiting from the trade must fit the crime. Africa's poaching is not just an African problem; it is a global one. Elephants and rhinos don't just belong to Africa. They belong to the whole world.

Most of the conservationists I spoke to in Kenya felt that the CITES meeting in Bangkok had failed Africa's elephants. Many felt that China's dominant role in the illegal trade of ivory was not dealt with at all, and that the Thai Prime Minister's commitment to amend relevant legislation to stop the ille-gal ivory trade in her country was little more than rhetoric without action.

Iain was more optimistic than some. 'The demand for ivory in Japan has completely collapsed, just as it did in the west, in America and Europe. So my great hope is that the demand for ivory will collapse when people know that they're killing off elephants by buying it. We have to live with hope. We're not going to give up. We've beaten this ivory crisis once before. We've got to do it again. And we can do it if we all work together.'

There is good reason to hope. As this book went to print, I received word that the Thai Prime Minister had given the directive to consolidate Thailand's laws to realise an end to the ivory trade in this country, a huge process that will take two to three years. This is heartening, but two to three years is a long time in politics, and we can only hope that Yingluck Shinawatra stays in power long enough to see it through.

I also take heart from recent awareness-raising efforts by Chinese celebrities like basketballer Yao Ming and actress Li Bingbing, who are using their influence in China to spread greater understanding of what's at stake. My hope is that Nadya Hutagalung will be the first of many high-profile south-east Asians to fly the flag for the world's endangered species in other Asian countries. She has come back from Africa deeply touched by its magic and inspired to do all she can to help. While in Kenya she tweeted, 'Dr Tammie Matson told me before the trip to Africa "get ready to have your mind blown". She was so right.' As we move forward with our own awareness-raising campaign, I think that elephants are just the beginning, and that our joint project to shine a light on what is happening to the natural world, and what everyone can do to help, will expand in the future to include other species, like rhinos.

So what about rhinos? A Memorandum of Understanding to address rhino poaching in South Africa was signed by South African and Vietnamese government ministers in December 2012.

While not legally binding, it is an encouraging sign that the two countries have said they will work together to combat the illegal rhino horn trade. In May 2013, a United States judge who had personally seen the effects of poaching in Africa sentenced a father and son to four years in jail for trafficking rhino horns. Most of the horn was old, but in the words of the judge, according to the *LA Times*, 'There are parts of Africa where rhinos are completely gone. Lord knows if they'll ever come back.'

The punishment should have been even stiffer in my view, and many more examples of strong deterrents dished out to the criminals involved in the rhino horn trade are needed across the world, and especially in Vietnam, the end point for most of the horn from poached African rhinos. Unfortunately, to date the much more common result from the legislative processes in Asia and Africa is one of gross under-punishment for wildlife trafficking crimes, making it a high-profit, low-risk game for the world's worst criminals.

A major part of the rhino horn trade problem is the primary involvement of wealthy businessmen and high-level government officials in Vietnam. The latest consumer research conducted on behalf of TRAFFIC Southeast Asia suggests that rhino horn is mainly used in Vietnam to reduce the effects of a hangover, but another key factor is that the possession of rhino horn, which is considered to be precious, expensive and rare, has become a fashionable way to show oneself to be equal to or better than others in society. It's a case of wanting to 'keep up with the Joneses'. These users don't see themselves as connected in any way to the killing of rhinos in Africa, nor do they feel responsible for it.

The use of both ivory and rhino horn has been a part of some Asian cultures for a long time, and now their association with status and wealth is, above all, what is driving the demand. I strongly believe that this can be changed by making both substances 'uncool' and stigmatised, focusing on the younger generation to spearhead the movement. This has to happen today, because the poaching continues to escalate unabated as human populations expand and wealth and consumption rise in these countries. In Africa, the illegal wildlife trade is driven largely by the desire to escape poverty, but it is Africa that is losing its most precious natural resources as a result of this demand by increasingly wealthy people many oceans away. Asia has already lost many of its own elephants and rhinos. To me, that is the most heartbreaking thing, and the reason why *all* of us must do *all* we can to halt and reverse this trend.

In my other home, Zimbabwe's Save Valley Conservancy, the land holders have not been issued with official trophy hunting quotas for the second year running. That might sound like a good thing to some, but if you go a little below the surface, what that actually means on the ground is that it's the second year in a row that the ranchers have had no income. That means there are fewer financial resources to pay the rangers to do anti-poaching across the conservancy, opening up opportunities for criminals to take advantage of their weakness by targeting the rhinos.

On the upside, since Bryce and Lara Clemence started their rhino anti-poaching work in the conservancy with their hardworking scouts, only four rhinos have been lost, one of which was a calf that died as a result of its mother being poached. That's a marked improvement on the fourteen killed the previous year, and fourteen the year before that. In November 2012, Bryce's men captured a notorious poaching gang and gleaned vital information that will help them capture others. They soldier on.

On another positive note, in India, Dr Bhaskar Choudhary from the Wildlife Trust of India recently told me that although one of the elephant calves that was released into Manas National Park has not been seen for a long time, Hamren, the young bull who was the first to escape, has been sighted and is doing well. Tinku and Tikla continue to hang out together in their own little herd and are in good health, and, in the best news of all, Soni, the young female, has been accepted by a wild herd!

Soumen's chilli crop, for all his good intentions, didn't survive the Assamese floods, but I visited another organisation's work over there, the Assam Haathi Project, and they had experienced some early success using chillies as a deterrent to elephants and a cash crop in northern Assam. So there may be hope for that idea to take off in India yet.

Tragically, in January 2013 in Sabah, Borneo, just a few months after we spent those glorious hours watching the rare pygmy elephants from a boat, fourteen elephants were poisoned in a reserve next to a palm plantation. A very young and distressed calf, found by its dead mother's side, was rescued and is now being raised in the Kota Kinabalu zoo along with other rescued elephants. This is a devastating loss to what is already a relatively small population on the island of Borneo.

Things may be looking up a little for the critically endangered Sumatran rhinos of Malaysia and Indonesia, following an emergency crisis summit held in April in Singapore. Scientists at this summit agreed that the species was in even worse shape than they had thought, with fewer than a hundred animals remaining. But on the positive side, for the first time, the two governments agreed to work together to try and bring the species back from the brink. Only time will tell whether this cooperation has come along too late, or whether this species can be revived in the same way that South Africa's white rhinos were from similar low levels in the 1990s and early 2000s.

From Sri Lanka, shortly after we visited in January 2013, I received word that the confiscated African ivory that the President had allocated to Buddhist temples had instead been given to a private company. Local conservationists were deeply concerned that the ivory would swiftly disappear into the black market. However, as this book goes to print I understand that the seized ivory is still being held in storage by customs. Time will tell if the government of Sri Lanka has the foresight to conduct a ceremonial burning of it as a symbol of their commitment to the fight against the illegal ivory trade.

Botswana continues to be a model country for conservation and wildlife-based tourism. But, interestingly, while it is the country with the greatest number of elephants in the world, that population is now thought to have remained fairly stable – at around 130,000 animals – since the early 2000s. Conservationist Dr Mike Chase of Elephants Without Borders suggests this lack of growth in numbers could be a result of reduced birth rates or increased mortalities, but it could also reflect the movement of elephants out of Botswana and into neighbouring countries, such as across Namibia's Caprivi to Angola.

With 56 per cent of Africa's elephants, southern Africa has for some time been the world's stronghold for the species. The most severe elephant poaching in Africa is currently in central and western Africa, in internally conflicted nations like the Central African Republic, but, disturbingly, the latest data from the IUCN's African Elephant Specialist Group suggests that elephant poaching is now also on the rise in southern and eastern Africa. As populations of elephants are exterminated in western and central African countries, the poaching will simply move to other places unless the demand for ivory stops.

Unfortunately, the documentary that I worked on with producer Steve Van Mil, 'Elephant Wars', never made it to the big screen due to lack of funds on the production side. The footage of human-elephant conflict in Africa and India taken during that period remains in storage.

Earth Hour has gone from strength to strength since Andy moved the global team to Singapore. This year, for the first time, just six years after the first Earth Hour in Sydney, it expanded from the symbolic 'lights off' initiative that it started as, going beyond the hour by producing multiple, impressive conservation outcomes across the world. In Russia, the Earth Hour team used its digital community to get 120,000 signatures on a petition asking the government to protect a particular marine area from oil spills. This led to new legislation being debated in parliament, and the protection of these seas. In Uganda, half a million trees were planted by businesses and local community members for Earth Hour. In Argentina, the movement is being used to mobilise the public to encourage the government to pass a bill that would see this country's marine protected area increased from one to four per cent. Earth Hour is a model for what can be achieved when many work together and we raise our collective voices.

As for me, I'm still working out, day by day, how best to juggle being a good mum to Solo and a caring wife and fulfil my own dreams to conserve Africa's wildlife. I'm fortunate to have such an understanding son, who thinks it's cool that his mum gets to drive a Land Rover in the African bush every so often, and a wonderful husband, who treasures the 'boy time' with Solo and who does an amazing job of holding the fort while I'm away. And later this year, we'll welcome an addition to the family, a brother or sister for Solo, who will add just a little more magic and mayhem into the mix.

Moving forward now, I'm focusing on doing all I can to reduce the demand for ivory and rhino horn in Asian countries. I ask you to join us in spreading the word about this terrible crisis and to use your voice to help conserve Africa's precious wildlife.

For more information about how you can get involved and what you can do to help, please head to my website www.tammiematson.com. There you'll also find a list of projects and/or organisations that I recommend donating to or supporting in other ways, such as by volunteering, going on a safari that benefits local communities and conservation, or by being a thoughtful and conscious consumer.

ACKNOWLEDGEMENTS

The process of writing this book was very different to that of my previous two. *Elephant Dance* and *Dry Water* each took less than four months to write the first draft, a level of efficiency I could only dream of since having a family; this one has been a work in progress for almost eighteen months. Part of the reason for this was the result of having a fun-loving toddler in the house. The other reason was the rich learning curve I've been on since moving to Asia and discovering the intrinsic links between my current home in Singapore and the land where my heart lies, Africa. What you've read in these pages is the result of that wild ride across continents, because this book has been written literally 'on the run' from one wildlife adventure to the next.

With every month that passed since moving to Asia I found new material that I simply couldn't leave out of the book, and it was with great tolerance and patience that my wonderful

271

publisher and friend, Alex Craig, allowed me to postpone my deadline not once, but twice, in order to be able to tell this story fully. Thanks Alex for having faith in my ability to pull this off (finally!) and for believing that this was a story that needed to be told, both for the elephants and for the people who share their world. Special thanks also my tireless editor, Samantha Sainsbury, for her invaluable advice on pulling it all together and for forcing me, in the kindest way possible, to focus on what I really wanted to say. My copy editor, Jo Jarrah, took the book to another level with her attention to detail and insightful improvements. Special thanks to my literary agent, Charlie Viney, for helping me get book number three on the shelves. The kind of conservation work that I do rarely pays the bills as it usually doesn't fit into a mainstream job, so the advance I received for this book literally paid for the travels and conservation work that led to the chapters.

I am a wildlife conservationist first and a writer second. I use the stories of what I see in the field of conservation to try and get more people on board the causes that are close to my heart. Having said that, working in conservation can be a lonely and insular task at times, frequently disheartening and overwhelming, and the opportunity to write books has connected me to an audience that has given me enormous inspiration and hope for the future of the planet. I am so grateful to my readers, subscribers and social media followers for providing me with daily doses of encouragement and support. Few things make me happier than hearing about when someone tells me they have taken a leap of faith to make a difference in the world around them, no matter how small. Everyone can do something to help Africa's elephants and rhinos, whether it's donating to a cause, signing a petition, sharing information on facebook or twitter, or going on safari (or volunteering) in Africa. All those drops in the ocean do add up, so make yours count!

This book became much bigger in scope than I originally planned it to be and now covers ten countries with elephant and/ or rhino populations. There are lots of people to thank for making the journey possible.

Dave van Smeerdijk and the wonderful team at Wilderness Safaris, the Classic Safari Company (especially Sarah Hoyland and Julia Salnicki) and Epic Private Journeys (Richard Field, Brad Horn and Kirstie Walia). If you are booking a safari from Australia, these are the guys to contact for a guaranteed mind-blowing African adventure.

In the Save Valley Conservancy, Zimbabwe, Roger and Anne Whittall and my dear mate Sarah Whittall, Adrienne Pienaar, long-time friends Karen and Jean Paolillo of the Turgwe Hippo Trust, Dr Peter Lindsay, Bryce and Lara Clemence and the rhino anti-poaching team, Fungai Chimsa and all the wonderful teachers at Humani Primary School, Dr Rosemary Groom of the African Wildlife Conservation Fund, and the fantastic Turgwe Camp staff, especially Lucia and Fungai who took such good care of Solo.

In Namibia, to IRDNC's Richard Diggle and my friends Dries Alberts and Stacey Main for support during the filming of *Elephant Wars*.

In Botswana, to Dr Mike Chase and Kelly Landon – for the window into your amazing part of the world and all that Elephants Without Borders is doing to better understand their ecology for the conservation of Africa's largest elephant population.

In Zambia, to Malvern Karidozo, Michael Gravina and Dr. Loki Osborn from the Elephant Pepper Development Trust for showing me the value of chili to deter elephants and improve livelihoods.

In India, thanks to the Wildlife Trust of India's Dr Vivek Menon, Dr Bhaskar Choudhury and Devna Arora for exceptional field support while looking for the CWRC's rehabilitated elephants in Manas National Park, Assam.

In Borneo, to Sulaiman Ismael for showing me a pygmy elephant for the first time and for saving my life shortly thereafter, and to Megan English for providing exceptional advice on every last detail of both the trip to Sabah and this rare subspecies.

In Sri Lanka, special thanks to Dr Manori Gunawardena, Dr Missaka Wijayagunawardane and Dr Thusith Samakone for their insights into the elephant situation in this beautiful country.

In Kenya, I met all my elephant heroes! Huge thanks to the indefatigable Richard Bonham of the Big Life Foundation and his outstanding anti-poaching rangers who went out of their way to show me, Asian TV host Nadya Hutagalung and our film crew the good, the bad and the ugly on the ground. Also special thanks to the fantastic team at Ol Donyo Lodge (one of the most divine lodges on the continent), Angela and Daphne Sheldrick, head keeper Edwin and all the team at the David Sheldrick Wildlife Trust, Dr Cynthia Moss and Katito Sayialel of the Amboseli Trust for Elephants, and Dr Iain Douglas-Hamilton of Save The Elephants for helping us share the message about what's happening to Africa's elephants and rhinos due to the illegal trade in Asia.

In Singapore, thanks to Nadya Hutagalung for being a true wildlife crusader with a big heart - working with you to raise awareness in Asia about elephant conservation has been a blast! Thanks also to Serena Lau, Yves Simard and everyone who helped out on a pro-bono basis to turn the idea of an awareness campaign into a reality.

To the team at TRAFFIC, especially Dr Bill Schaedla, Tom Milliken, Brett Tolman, Minh Nguyen, Dr Naomi Doak and Dr Chris Shepherd, for letting me into your world and providing me with a view of the wildlife trade that I never could have imagined.

In Australia, big thanks to authors Tony Park, Sally Henderson, Peter Allison, Frank Coates and Ace Bourke for donating their time and books to fund raising events for the Save Valley Conservancy, Zimbabwe's rhino anti-poaching efforts. Thanks to all the volunteers and participants who made those nights at Ripples on Sydney Harbour happen. Thanks to those who donated laptops for Humani Primary School and to everyone involved in making the expedition to Zimbabwe a reality in 2012. Even though I am no longer involved with Animal Works, I appreciate the support you provided for this worthy cause and I am immensely proud to know that it made a real difference where it counted.

Special new-mama friends Michelle McKemey (formerly Higgins), Hester Gat, Melissa Maclean, Heather Welch – without your support of these particular wonder mums in the last few years there is no question I would never have even attempted to write this book. Thanks for being there with daily feedback, advice and down-to-earth reality checks about combining motherhood with career!

Certain people made it possible for me to write this book by taking Solo to the beach, playgrounds and all sorts of other adventures. Huge thanks to Alina Duncan, my wonderful mother-in-law Lizzie (Elizabeth Ridley-Thomas), my dear mum (Rhonda Matson) and in Singapore, Julie Reyno.

It's only when you become a parent that you appreciate what your parents actually did for you all those years ago. Thanks Dad for fostering my African dream from such a young age. Thanks Mum for helping us raise all the pets and for cleaning up after all those epic outback camping trips, both things that gave us such a love and respect for animals. My younger sister Kek deserves a mention for being such a calming, rational voice during my pregnancy, and my brother Davo for all the inside knowledge on making the most of traveling in Asia.

Finally, to Andy, for always reminding me who I am, for making sure I take the mickey out of myself, and for providing endless inspiration through his fine example and long pub chats. And to my darling Solo, now approaching four years old, who has provided me with even more motivation to ensure that the wild places of the world survive this human-induced mass extinction that is now underway. And to both of you, for understanding when I need to go away to spend time with the elephants.

Tammie Matson
Elephant Dance

It's the middle of the night in the Namibian desert when Tammie
Matson wakes to find two bull elephants standing just inches from
her head. Totally vulnerable in her tiny tent, she promises the
night: 'If you just let me survive tonight I will give up Africa. I'll give
it all up. Just don't let them stand on me.'

It's not a promise she will easily keep. At 29, Tammie has spent
half her life in Africa working as a conservationist. Africa – with its
big skies and extraordinary wildlife – is her first love, and Tammie
has just landed her dream gig researching human-elephant
conflict.

But as her thirties approach, Tammie is conscious that Africa has
left little room for pursuit of dreams that are becoming increasingly
important: a partner, kids, a house . . . With her visa running out
and close to broke, it seems like Africa may just force Tammie to
give it up after all.

On returning to Australia, Tammie unexpectedly lands a job at the
World Wide Fund for Nature in Sydney. There she meets Andy,
a charismatic Brit, and Africa suddenly has a rival. But she's not
ready to give up on the elephants yet . . .

From the magic of Bushmanland in Namibia to the civil strife of
Assam, India, *Elephant Dance* takes us to the heart of a quest for
elephants to live peacefully in a world with too many people and
too little space.

Passionate, funny, and wise, *Elephant Dance* is also a young
woman's story of self-discovery, love and the courage it takes to
follow a calling, especially when life has other plans.

Sara Henderson
From Strength to Strength

Sara Henderson's bestselling autobiography has touched the hearts of thousands of people all over Australia. As tough, spirited, warm and funny as the woman herself, *From Strength to Strength* is the inspirational story of one woman's extraordinary courage and determination.

In 1959 Sara met American war hero and shipping magnate, Charles Henderson III, and so began what she calls the world's most demanding, humiliating and challenging obstacle course any human could be expected to endure.

Three years after their marriage, Charles presented Sara with her new home – a tin shack in a million acres of red dust. Bullo River. After twenty years of back-breaking work on this remote Northern Australian cattle station, Charlie's death revealed that Sara had not only been left with a floundering property, but also with a heart-breaking mountain of debt.

With very little to lose, Sara and her daughters Marlee and Danielle, took up the challenge of rebuilding Bullo River . . . with such tremendous results that in 1991 Sara was named the Bulletin/Qantas Businesswoman of the Year.

'Everyone has a book in them, they say, but not everyone has the kind of story Sara Henderson tells, and tells well'
THE BULLETIN

Fiona Higgins
Love in the Age of Drought

When Fiona meets Stuart at a conference in Melbourne she isn't looking for a relationship, let alone the upheaval of falling for a cotton farmer from South-East Queensland. But then life never quite goes according to plan . . .

When Stuart sends Fiona a pair of crusty old boots and a declaration of his feelings sixteen days into their relationship, it's the start of a love story that endures – in spite of distance, the strain of Stuart's farm entering its fourth year of drought, and Fiona's issues with commitment.

Something's got to give, and eventually Fiona puts everything on the line – her career, her Sydney life, her future – and moves to Stuart's farm. Nearest township? Jandowae, population 750.

Here, Fiona encounters an Australia she's never really known, replete with snakes on the doorstep, frogs in the toilet and the perils of the bush telegraph. Gradually, she begins to fall in love with rural life, but as Stuart struggles to balance environmental and commercial realities she realises that farming isn't quite as simple as she'd imagined. Ultimately, Fiona has to learn to cope with the devastating impact of the drought that grips the countryside, and what it means for Stuart, the farm and their future together.

Love in the Age of Drought is a delightful fish-out-of-water story about the city–country culture clash overcome by the course of true love. Written with heart and humour, it's also a moving portrait of country Australia's capacity for survival and renewal amid a drought that won't be broken.

Sheryl McCorry
Diamonds and Dust

Sheryl McCorry grew up in Arnhem Land carrying crocodiles to school for show and tell. When she was 18, Broome beckoned, and it was there that – only hours after being railroaded into marriage by a fast-talking Yank – she locked eyes with Bob McCorry, a drover and buffalo shooter. When her marriage ended after only a few months, they began a romance that would last a lifetime and take them to the Kimberley's harshest frontiers.

As the only woman in a team of stockmen, Sheryl soon learned how to run rogue bulls and to outsmart the neighbours in the toughest game of all – mustering cattle. The playing field was a million acres of unfenced, unmarked boundaries, but Sheryl soon saw that to survive in the outback a woman needed goals. Hers was to become the first woman in the Kimberley to run two million-acre cattle stations. But it was to come at an unimaginable cost.

Inspiring and unforgettable, *Diamonds and Dust* is a classic story of a woman finding her destiny in the further reaches of the outback.